*Loving the World as Our Body*

# Loving the World
## as
# Our Body

*The Nondual Path in a Dangerous Time*

## David R. Loy

Wisdom Publications
132 Perry Street
New York, NY 10014 USA
wisdom.org

*Library of Congress Cataloging-in-Publication Data is available.*
Names: Loy, David, 1947– author
Title: Loving the world as our body: the nondual path in a dangerous time /
    David R. Loy.
Description: New York, NY, USA: Wisdom, [2026] | Includes index.
Identifiers: LCCN 2025040238 (print) | LCCN 2025040239 (ebook) |
    ISBN 9781614297451 paperback | ISBN 9781614297604 ebook
Subjects: LCSH: Monism | Human evolution | Human evolution—Religious
    aspects | Love—Religious aspects
Classification: LCC B105.M6 L688 2026 (print) | LCC B105.M6 (ebook)
LC record available at https://lccn.loc.gov/2025040238
LC ebook record available at https://lccn.loc.gov/2025040239

ISBN 978-1-61429-745-1      ebook ISBN 978-1-61429-760-4

30  29  28  27  26
5  4  3  2  1

Cover design by Marc Whitaker. Interior design by Tim Holtz.

Printed on acid-free paper that meets the guidelines for permanence and durability
of the Production Guidelines for Book Longevity of the Council on Library
Resources.

Printed in the United States of America.

Please visit fscus.org.

Those who love the world as their own body
Can be entrusted with the world

*—Daodejing*

The entire earth is the true human body.

*—Dogen*

# Contents

# Introduction

*A Path on the Precipice*

Is this the most dangerous time in human history? That's the opinion of Noam Chomsky in a September 2020 interview. It's such an extraordinary claim that I tried to think of a counterexample. World War II? Chomsky is old enough to remember the 1930s, when there was a real possibility that Nazism could take over much of Eurasia, "but even that, horrible enough, was not like the end of organized human life on earth, which is what we're facing."[1]

When he gave the interview, the COVID-19 pandemic was near its peak, but Chomsky didn't mention it. Instead, he focused on three issues: the climate crisis, the growing threat of nuclear war, and the decline of democracy—that is, rising authoritarianism—around the world. Unfortunately, each of these problems has become markedly worse since his interview.

Urgent though it is, accelerating global heating is only part of a much larger ecological catastrophe, which includes many other threats, most obviously loss of biodiversity. Back in 1900 (when world population was only 1.6 billion), humans plus our domesticated livestock, such as cattle and pigs, constituted about 83 percent of the total biomass of all mammals that live on land. By 2000, it had increased to 96 percent: 36 percent human, 60 percent other mammals. The biomass of our poultry is about three times that of all the wild birds on earth.

We have also reduced the world's biomass of plant matter by half.[2] For every five wild mammals living in 1970, there were two in 2017, and less than that now. Species are disappearing at rates variously estimated to be one thousand or even ten thousand times as quickly as they would without human impact.

In addition to this ongoing extinction event—the sixth in the earth's 4.5-billion-year history—deforestation (250 trees cut down every *second*) and desertification (8 acres per *minute*) are increasing. Every year, 24 *billion* tons of topsoil are lost due to erosion.[3] There are now more than 500 dead zones in the ocean, their total area being larger than Europe, and they are growing. Toxic industrial chemicals are present in the breast milk of every mother, on top of Mount Everest, in the deepest ocean trenches, and at the North Pole. Micro- and nanoplastics can also be found everywhere, even in our brains.[4]

We could go on, but the point is made. Reducing greenhouse gases is certainly necessary but cannot be a sufficient response, because the deeper ecological challenge is humanity's dysfunctional relationship with the rest of the natural world.

Long before the war in Ukraine, Chomsky emphasized the persistent risk of nuclear war. There are also ongoing problems with nuclear reactors, including accidents such as those at Chernobyl and Fukushima, as well as thousands of tons of radioactive waste that will remain dangerous for hundreds of thousands of years because no one knows how to store it safely for such a long period.

Chomsky also warned about rising authoritarianism. More than a few of the world's democracies look increasingly fragile because autocratic regimes, having attained power, are subverting their own democratic institutions. The January 6 attack on the Capitol building in Washington, DC, along with an increasingly polarized and acrimonious political climate culminating in Donald Trump's reelection in 2024, shows that the United States is not invulnerable to such a development. His actions since then have reinforced such apprehensions.

One perhaps should add to this some other serious concerns that Chomsky did not mention, including social justice issues. Economic problems often contribute to political strife, especially the enormous and still-growing disparity almost everywhere between a small group of obscenely wealthy individuals and the precarious situation of most people—a gap the COVID-19 pandemic aggravated. "Nearly 40% of all Americans say they have skipped meals in order to meet their housing payments, and more than 70% admit to living with economic anxiety."[5]

Finally—one must stop somewhere!—is the growing impact of all the above on mental health worldwide, especially that of young people, who face a dismal future burdened with the challenge of cleaning up the messes their elders have created. Although aging is no fun, I would not want to be a teenager today.

We can describe all this as a *polycrisis*, but even that term may be inadequate. It's not simply that many problems are occurring at the same time. Nor is it enough to emphasize that they are interacting with and often reinforcing each other. Is it more accurate to say we have a *metacrisis*? No, this is not a reference to the corporation formerly known as Facebook. The Greek root *meta-* (literally "beyond") is an adjective that can be translated as "more comprehensive" or "transcending"—the point being that the various crises facing us may in fact be different facets of a deeper problem. What might that problem be?

The tragic irony is that, just when humanity has achieved a truly global civilization, our civilization has lost its way and seems to be self-destructing: "The day of reckoning has come," according to the ecotheologian Thomas Berry. "In this disintegrating phase of our industrial society, we now see ourselves not as the splendor of creation, but as the most pernicious mode of earthly being."[6] Why so pernicious? For John Gray, "The destruction of the natural world is not the result of global capitalism, industrialization, 'Western civilization' or any flaw in human institutions. It is a consequence of the evolutionary success of an exceptionally rapacious primate."[7] Although I wouldn't give a free pass to what Joanna Macy calls industrial growth society, the important point is that Gray roots the ecological crisis in an all-too-human character trait that all-too-often interacts with other problematic tendencies, such as tribalism (including national-ism, racism, and religious fundamentalism) and aggression (including militarism and terrorism).

E. O. Wilson sums up our quandary: "The real problem of human-ity is that we have Paleolithic emotions, medieval institutions, and god-like technology."[8] Despite the unexpected adverse effects of some escalating technologies—for example, the internet—the problems fac-ing us today may be grounded in something much older and more fundamental: the way our minds have been sculpted by evolution. Are human rapacity, tribalism, and violence just bad habits we can blame on regrettable (but correctable) social conditioning? Or have they been built into the DNA of our species over many millennia by the competition to survive and reproduce?

That the dysfunction might be at least partially innate is a pos-sibility that may be dangerous to ignore. Can an understanding of evolutionary psychology—how human emotions and behavior have evolved—grant us some insight into its genesis, and might that insight help us respond more appropriately? If our predicament today is a consequence of prehistoric as well as more recent developments, we need to consider how and why we evolved the ways that we have. Might that help us understand why the efforts we have been making are not working well enough?

There is another dysfunction that needs to be addressed. Humans are not only products of biological evolution. Both individually and collectively, we are also artifacts of cultural evolution. When we con-sider basic existential questions about the meaning of life (beyond mere survival and reproduction) and how to live (the moral codes to follow), nothing has been more important historically than our reli-gious traditions. I am not sure that is still true: one could argue that consumerism has now become, in effect, the most popular religion. In either case, the mainstream religious traditions are failing us today. In fact, their failure is one of the main motivations for this book.

The theologian Paul Tillich developed what he called a theology of correlation: the answers that religions have to offer should correspond to the questions that a culture is asking. If they fail at doing this, then those religions become irrelevant. By that standard, our spiritual traditions are no longer fit for our purposes. Their premodern mythologies and doctrines are increasingly incompatible with contemporary worldviews, scientific and otherwise, and so it is not surprising that their traditional ethical codes do not help enough when we try to address the problems mentioned above. Their dualistic theologies not only draw our attention away from what is happening here and now, but their emphasis on an otherworldly salvation has also contributed significantly to the ecological crisis, because this world is devalued in comparison to whatever postmortem bliss that we can enjoy somewhere else. Why be so concerned about what is happening here when we will soon go to a much better place?

In short, the spiritual paths that our religions offer are outdated and need to be revised. My hope is that this book will contribute in some small way to their reformation.

This book is divided into three chapters. Chapter 1 offers an overview of evolutionary psychology, which reveals the deep source of the crises that confront us today. Chapter 2 shifts the focus to cultural evolution, especially the historical role of religion as our main collective effort to deal with the tensions created by our biological evolution. Chapter 3 critiques those attempts, which have largely failed, and offers a more "this-worldly" version of the spiritual path. What we need to transcend is not this reality but our usual ways of experiencing and understanding it. If this world is different from what we have thought, might salvation also be quite different from what we have been taught?

## *What We Can Learn from Our Evolution: The Bipolar Ape*

Darwinian evolution is essential for understanding how our species has developed, but its implications for how our minds work has received little attention until the last few decades. Chapter 1 summarizes many of the important (and controversial) claims of evolutionary psychology. One widespread cultural fiction is the belief that we are mostly "blank slates" until conditioned by our social environment. In fact, psychological research has discovered that heredity plays a major role—often *the* major role—in many behavioral traits, predisposing us to problems such as anxiety, depression, schizophrenia, bipolar disorder, autism, attention deficit disorder, compulsive gambling, smoking, alcoholism, drug abuse, suicidal behavior, psychopathy, and even a predilection for marital infidelity.

Nonetheless, the implication is not nature over nurture, but nature *via* nurture—how they interact. Genetic predispositions do not predetermine what we will do: we are born as unfinished animals and become human as we are socialized. Culture is another form of trait-transmission, social and learned rather than hereditary. Most of our brain development occurs after birth, during the many years that we are dependent on adult caregivers and influenced by them.

Perhaps the most intriguing aspect of our behavioral tendencies is that they can work against each other and pull us in different directions. Like Rousseau, we want to believe we are born free and benevolent, and only later become corrupted by society. Hobbes's view, that we are basically self-centered and need to be tamed by culture, is less flattering. The never-resolved argument between the two is suggestive: Can both be true? Do both propensities co-exist within us, inclining us to be both selfish and selfless? And is it possible that, due to our complicated genetic legacy, human nature is both inclined to egalitarianism and susceptible to authoritarianism?

The most controversial topic in evolutionary psychology is whether there is *multilevel* selection. In the struggle to get one's genes into the next generation, is each individual competing only with other individuals, or does competition for genetic survival also occur between groups? This issue may seem abstract, but it provides an important insight into the origins of morality—especially if the conflict within us between "good" and "evil" is hardwired into our psychology. Most vice—murder, theft, rape, fraud, and so on—originates from self-ishness, while virtue—cooperation, altruism, generosity, sympathy, kindness—benefits the group because it expresses concern for others' welfare.[9] Individual selfishness can provide a competitive advantage within a group but works against group cohesiveness; being coopera-tive and altruistic reduces one's individual advantage but contributes to the survival and competitive success of the group. But it can also replace murder with genocide. As Matt Ridley puts it, "It is a rule of evolution to which we are far from immune that the more cooperative societies are, the more violent the battles between them."[10]

Agriculture and pastoralism led to the greatest transformation in human history. Our relationship with the earth changed radically, and our relationships with each other changed just as radically, as animis-tic hunter-gatherer cultures developed into (or were displaced by) theocratic agrarian states. Civilization shifted the focus from nature to nation. Farming could support much larger populations, settled in dense communities with more anonymous interaction. Nature deities were superseded by "big gods," aware of everything you do, and who were now needed to prescribe ethical principles and punish transgres-sions. By no coincidence, hierarchical pantheons of gods also stabilized the new class system by legitimating its earthly political hierarchy.

Whether individual or collective, acquisitiveness, aggression, and selfishness seem to correspond to what Buddhism identifies as *the three poisons* (or three fires): greed, ill will, and delusion. Buddhist teachings have usually viewed these three as personal problems, but today they have been institutionalized as our economic system (corporate con-sumer capitalism focused on indefinite growth), militarism (now over a trillion dollars per year for "defense"), and sophisticated fake news (including advertising and propaganda).

Do the three poisons, both individualized and institutionalized, point to the source of the crises that confront us today? Although the scale of our metacrisis is unique, the problems bequeathed to us by our evolutionary psychology are not new.

## *What We Could Have Learned from Our Religions: How to Transform*

In early agrarian civilizations there was no significant distinction between religious authority and secular political power. Theocratic kings served as the crucial link between human society and the cosmic order. For everyone else too, social roles were not distinguished from religious obligations, both of which maintained the sacralized social order.

Archaic empires reinforced tribalistic identity on an ever-larger scale, increasingly aggressive and imperialistic. But they proved to be unstable. The Bronze Age collapse (c. 1200 BCE) in the Mediterranean, the Middle East, India, and China was violent and disastrous. In its aftermath, however, an extraordinary cultural development occurred in all these places.

Historically, the most important attempt to control and channel our conflicting predispositions was provided by Axial Age religions. The Axial Age can be viewed as cultural evolution's way of compensating for the problematic propensities, both individual and tribal, that originally enabled our species to survive and reproduce in competitive and often-threatening environments. Today, however, those tendencies threaten our very existence. When the push of a button can launch thousands of nuclear weapons, nationalistic and ethnic tribalism are more dangerous than ever. An economic system that must keep growing in order to avoid collapse is irreconcilable with a biosphere that does not, and neoliberalism's penchant for producing billionaires while billions of other people struggle to get by is incompatible with a just or harmonious global civilization.

The *Axial Age* is a term coined by Karl Jaspers to describe a pivotal period that began in the middle of the first millennium BCE, when "the spiritual foundations of humanity were laid simultaneously and independently in China, India, Persia, Judea, and Greece."[11] Religious revolutionaries such as Lao-tzu, Gautama Buddha, the Hebrew prophets, Jesus, and Muhammad were not official priests but marginal figures, responding to a widespread sense of social and moral failure by offering innovative conceptions of cosmic order that juxtaposed this mundane (and unsatisfactory) world with an idealized transcendent realm (heaven, nirvana). This was accompanied by a new emphasis on one's own relationship with that higher reality, shifting the focus from temple rituals to personal morality. Salvation became radically individualized: no longer a destiny restricted to elites but a possibility for each of us, according to how we live. The basic religious teachings we usually take for granted today—*individual* morality and salvation, with compassion for *everyone*—were Axial Age developments.

These ideals are so important to our spiritual traditions today—which does not mean we actually follow them, of course—that it is difficult to appreciate how radical they were when first proclaimed. Nonetheless, most Axial Age teachings have two serious flaws that limit their relevance to our difficult situation today: *cosmological dualism* and *individual salvation*.[12]

Belief in another and better postmortem reality was important for liberating the individual from what had become tight embeddedness in a hierarchical social structure, but *cosmological dualism* tends to devalue *this* world. In Christian terms, the earth is merely a backdrop to the human drama of sin and salvation. Why worry about what's happening here and now if our eternal bliss is elsewhere? This implied another dualism that has become especially problematic for us today, between humanity and the rest of the biosphere. Lynn White Jr. has (controversially) traced the ecological crisis back to "the Christian axiom that nature has no reason for existence save to serve man. . . . Despite Darwin, we are *not*, in our hearts, part of the natural process. We are superior to nature, contemptuous of it, willing to use it for our slightest whim."[13]

*Individual salvation* means that my well-being is ultimately separate from yours. Sure, I hope you will make it to heaven too, or attain nirvana, but in either case my own spiritual destiny will be unaffected. Replacing self-centered evolutionary selection—preoccupied with reproducing one's own genes—with self-centered afterlife selection—preoccupied with personally qualifying for heaven and so on—was not necessarily a big improvement.

Historically, the Axial Age failed. The revolutionary personal and social transformations implied by its teachings—attempting to address the tensions inherent in our evolutionary psychology—were aborted as the new religions became reappropriated by despotic rulers and institutionalized into their empires. With the Roman Emperor Constantine's conversion, Christianity became Christendom. Later European kings ruled by divine right, and their Asian equivalents (who must have extraordinarily good karma from past lifetimes!) sometimes declared themselves to be bodhisattvas or buddhas. A good example is the way that Christian teachings have been used to rationalize the forceful conversion of pagans, the persecution of Jews and heretics, the subordination of women, crusades against Muslims, and the establishment of brutal empires. What is now known as Christian nationalism, in particular, is an oxymoron—it has almost nothing to do with the teachings of Jesus—but it is not new. More generally, nationalism has been described by Arnold Toynbee as "ninety percent of the religion of ninety percent of the people of the Western world and of the rest of the world as well."[14] A sacralized social order continues to sanctify our overgrown tribalism.

The good news is that the Axial Age *teachings* have survived, and they have served an important role in the development of democracy and human rights. Nonetheless, it is increasingly difficult to take their hallowed mythologies and theologies literally, especially belief in a transcendent salvation that supersedes whatever happens here. In order to revive their revolutionary potential, we need to interrogate and recuperate the insights of their founders. The spiritual path needs to be updated, which is the focus of the last chapter.

## *What We Need Today:*
## *A Spirituality That Loves This World*

Although most people still identify with one of the Axial religions, their emphasis on postmortem salvation in another reality has made those traditions incapable of responding adequately to the problems we face in *this* reality. Today we need a spirituality that focuses on realizing the true nature of this world, which by no coincidence also happens to be our own true nature. We too are manifestations of this earth, not exiled spirits that should be preoccupied with qualifying for eternal bliss somewhere else. Nor do we need such an otherworldly reward. The challenge is not to transcend the world but to transcend our usual ways of experiencing it. It turns out that this world is quite different from what we thought. And so are we.

In contrast to Axial dualism, what we have understood as the sacred is not something "higher" that occasionally interjects itself into this world, but is its ever-present ground. The impermanent phenomena we experience every day are the manifold ways that the sacred assumes form and expresses itself here and now.

We usually perceive the world as a collection of separate, self-existing things that interact in objective space and time—one of those things being *me*. We learn to see it this way as we grow up, socialized into relating to it in the same way that everyone else does. Living this way has served the evolutionary process by contributing to our survival and success: once we identify things and their functions, we can utilize them for doing and getting what we want. So this way of perceiving serves an important role in our lives and our collective development. But it is not the only way to experience and understand the world, or ourselves.

Preoccupied with *using* things to achieve certain goals (such as satisfying desires), we overlook something important: the world as normally experienced is a psychological and social construct. That is why *de*constructive practices such as meditation can lead to a different and more nondual experience, in which supposedly separate beings are actually *hierophanies* revealing the sacred. To use theistic terms, "God" is not an invisible, super-powerful transcendent being who created everything, but is better characterized as a formless nothing (or *no-thing*) that manifests as all the phenomena we encounter—including ourselves.

Although *mysticism* is a broad term that refers to a variety of spiritual experiences, the most insightful ones involve unmediated awareness of an ultimate reality right here. In such encounters, the usual duality between a self *inside* and an objective world *outside* dissolves when I *let go* of myself. That is possible because the sense of being separable from the rest of the world is part of that psychological and social conditioning. Letting go of the habitual thought patterns that sustain the illusion of an autonomous self can lead to the most important realization of all: that we are not separate from each other, or from the earth on which and with which we have evolved, but are part of a biosphere that continues to nurture us.

It is no coincidence that the principal mystical traditions— Abrahamic theistic as well as Asian nondualist—agree that the fundamental obstacle to God-realization or enlightenment is the ego-self, the subjective pole of the self-object duality. Many of the great mystics have emphasized this when they talk about *how to experience* God or Brahman or the Dao. It is surely no coincidence that in every shamanic culture, too, candidates must endure a difficult trial that involves regression to an undifferentiated condition: dissolution of self, ego-death, and rebirth. "There is always a point where the potential shaman remains for a time on the threshold, experiencing the primal void—a state of unbeing—and its greatest mysteries. Only when he has surrendered himself utterly can he be reborn."[15]

According to the Jewish Kabbalah, when we empty ourselves of selfhood, we reach true reality, which is divine nothingness. In his letter to the Philippians, Paul exhorts us to follow the example of Jesus, who humbled himself and "made himself nothing." Meister Eckhart encouraged the same self-emptying (*kenosis*): "If you could naught yourself for an instant, indeed I say less than an instant, you would possess all." And Sufism? According to Rumi, "If you could get rid of yourself just once, the secret of secrets would open to you. The face of the unknown, hidden beyond the universe, would appear on the mirror of your perception."

Asian nondualist traditions such as Vedanta, Buddhism, and Daoism describe the absolute in more impersonal terms, but their spiritual paths involve the same transformation: ego-death and rebirth into a transfigured world. According to Vedanta, we perceive the everyday world as real due to our ignorance (*avidya*), but when true knowledge dawns we are freed from the delusion of individuality and wake up to our true nature: we have always been one with Brahman. For Buddhism, according to Dogen, "to study the way of enlightenment is to study the self. To study the self is to forget the self. To forget the self is to be actualized by myriad things."[16]

For Daoism, the Dao ("the Way") is the inexhaustible womb of all life here and now, "an empty vessel that yet may be drawn from without ever needing to be filled." Becoming no-thing is how we return to the source from which all things including us originate. By "mind fasting" (*wang xin*) we can forget our usual dualistic sense of self, and the *Daodejing* tells us that the world may be entrusted to those who know and love the world as their true self.

To let go and "forget oneself" is not to rise above this world but to become one with it—or rather, to realize that we have always been nondual with it. Is this the spiritual awakening that we seek? The salvation that the world too needs us to realize?

Joseph Campbell liked to say that all religions are true, one way or another, when understood metaphorically; the problems arise when their metaphors are taken literally. Perhaps it was inevitable that a different and unexpected way of experiencing this world would sometimes be (mis)understood as the temporary irruption of a "higher" reality into this one. And how much the better if such transcendence seems to offer an escape from our persistent dissatisfaction with this "lower reality"! But then what are we overlooking about our undervalued world?

When we are not so fixated on transcending it, we will be able to appreciate that the earth is not only our home, it's our mother—and we never cut the umbilical cord. Our interdependence with other species and ecosystems means that their well-being is not separable from our own. Despite the fantasies of some wealthy survivalists, who hope to ride out the apocalypse in well-stocked bunkers, worldwide ecological degradation makes it clearer than ever that human and nonhuman destinies are inextricably tied to each other in a biosphere that encompasses us all.

In sum, our problematic spiritual traditions will not be able to help us address the various crises we face today without questioning and reforming themselves to recover their essential spiritual message about *here and now*. Until that happens, our religions, with their many billions of adherents, remain more a part of the metacrisis than contributors to its solution.

A century ago, H. G. Wells said that "history is a race between education and catastrophe"—and today both are accelerating. It remains to be seen: what role will our spiritual traditions play in that race?

Just as we can gain a better understanding of ourselves from knowledge of our parents and their lives, so we can draw solace and a sense of orientation from knowledge of the genetic and cultural evolutionary processes that created our human natures and shaped humanity's long history and much longer prehistory.

   —**Paul Ehrlich**

We human beings are what we have been for millions of years—colossally greedy, envious, aggressive, jealous, anxious and despairing, with occasional flashes of joy and affection. We are a strange mixture of hate, fear and gentleness; we are both violence and peace. There has been outward progress from the bullock cart to the jet plane but psychologically the individual has not changed at all, and the structure of society throughout the world has been created by individuals. The outward social structure is the result of the inward psychological structure of our human relationships, for the individual is the result of the total experience, knowledge and conduct of man. Each one of us is the storehouse of all the past. The individual is the human who is all mankind.

   —**Jiddu Krishnamurti**

*Homo sapiens* is an innately dysfunctional species. We are hampered by the Paleolithic Curse: genetic adaptations that worked very well for millions of years of hunter-gatherer existence but are increasingly a hindrance in a globally urban and technoscientific society. We seem unable to stabilize either economic policies or the means of governance higher than the level of a village. Further, the great majority of people worldwide remain in the thrall of tribal organized religions, led by men who claim supernatural power in order to compete for the obedience and resources of the faithful. We are addicted to tribal conflict, which is harmless and entertaining when sublimated into team sports, but deadly when expressed as real-world ethnic, religious, and ideological struggles. There are other hereditary biases. Too paralyzed with self-absorption to protect the rest of life, we continue to tear down the natural environment, our species' irreplaceable and most precious heritage.

  **—Edward O. Wilson**


The destruction of the natural world is not the result of global capitalism, industrialization, "Western civilization" or any flaw in human institutions. It is a consequence of the evolutionary success of an exceptionally rapacious primate.

  **—John Gray**

The human race's prospects of survival were considerably better when we were defenseless against tigers than they are today, when we have become defenseless against ourselves.

 —Arnold Toynbee

The greatest achievement of humanity is not its works of art, science, or technology, but the recognition of its own dysfunction, its own madness.

 —Eckhart Tolle

When I was a young scientist, I genuinely believed that if we understood the science behind environmental problems, conservation would naturally follow. Forty years later, my life experience intrudes and says that it might not be so. It may indeed be the case that effective responses to obvious problems are being delayed by human behaviors that are deeply rooted in the past. Some of these behaviors were diagnosed by Gautama Buddha two and a half millennia ago.

 —Paul A. Keddy

We are among the first generations to understand not only that we have evolved, but also the mechanisms by which we have evolved and how this evolutionary heritage influences our behavior.

In the story of evolution we are automatically forgiven for all our supposed sins and mistakes because we see that we are just a baby species. There were about 10 million generations of dinosaurs, and 10 to 20 million generations of mammals before humans came along. We've only had about ten or twenty *thousand* generations of modern *homo sapiens*. We just got these big brains and don't know how to use them very well yet. They didn't come with a good instruction manual. In the story of evolution we see that humans are just a baby species, and therefore should not be tried as adults. Indeed, the most profound spiritual message of evolution is this: *You are not your fault!* . . .

Friends, if you believe you have sinned, or that you are seriously flawed as a human being, I am happy to tell you that salvation has arrived. It is the story of evolution, revealing that we were all created out of the shape-shifting stream of life as it danced with ever-changing Earth conditions and natural phenomena. You did not choose to have your brain and nervous system or your instincts for bonding and self-preservation any more than you choose to have thumbs. We can take no credit or blame for who we are. In the eyes of Mother Nature we are all forgiven. Accept it! *You are not your fault.*

—Wes Nisker

# 1

# What We Can Learn
# from Our Evolution

## *The Bipolar Ape*

DARWIN'S THEORY is sometimes called the greatest scientific discovery ever, and its implications for our self-understanding remain incomparable. Darwin did not discover biological evolution—the idea that species evolved was already "in the air" and widely discussed in his time. What Darwin (and Alfred Russel Wallace independently) provided was a scientific explanation for how it happened: *natural selection*. *Natural* because there is no one *selecting*, which was the shocking point—evolution is a self-organizing process that precludes any need for a creator god.

Although there are complications (epigenetics, horizontal gene transfer, genetic drift, and so on), the basic mechanism of that process is simple. Reproduction usually results in more offspring than can survive. Genetic mutations—which occur for various reasons but are common—can result in differing physical and psychological traits. Some of those traits are more beneficial than others in helping the organism cope with its living conditions, so offspring with those features are more likely to survive and reproduce. The genes that cause these beneficial traits are thereby reproduced and become more common, and compounding this development can eventually produce new species.

Gradual evolution by natural selection refuted one of the traditional proofs of God: that a supernatural intelligence was necessary to design the millions of incredibly complex species that compose life on earth. But this is not necessarily a deathblow for religion. If we do not presuppose a reductive materialism, there may be a more "spiritual" way to understand the process. Might evolution be how the self-organizing cosmos is becoming self-aware, as Thomas Berry and Brian Swimme have argued in books such as *The Universe Story*? "The mind that searches for contact with the Milky Way is the very mind of the Milky Way galaxy in search of its own depths."[17] Such a perspective is still a big stretch for most religious traditions, insofar as they continue to be rooted in premodern worldviews. In any case, the implications of evolutionary psychology remain largely unaddressed even by those who promote such new cosmologies.

Evolution explains why our bodies are so vulnerable to back and knee problems. Humans evolved from four-legged mammals, and shifting to an upright posture resulted in different skeletal stresses, as well as a more difficult birthing process. Likewise, our cravings for high-caloric sweet and fatty foods, which cause so many health problems today, were beneficial for nomadic hunter-gatherers (98 percent of our species history) who had no experience of refined sugar, ultra-processed food, or a sedentary lifestyle.

But what about the evolution of our minds?

The basic structure of the human brain is similar to that of other primates, although our brains are much larger than those of our nearest extant relatives, chimpanzees and bonobos. While the relationship between brain and consciousness remains controversial, we cannot ignore the obvious implication that our minds have also been molded by the nature of the evolutionary process, insofar as "the brain evolved as a prediction system to enhance its owner's survival—the more we interact with the world, the better our predictive capability."[18]

If our long evolutionary prehistory helps to explain present physiological problems, can it also help us to understand some of our present psychological and sociological problems? From infancy, humans seem to be instinctively afraid of spiders, the dark, heights, and thunder. Infants are not instinctively afraid of electric sockets, guns, or cars, which, although more dangerous today, have developed too recently to affect our genome.[19]

A more emotionally charged issue is reproduction. We don't like to think of a mother's selfless devotion—our primary example of genuine love—from that perspective, but of course maternal care serves an important evolutionary function. Although the relationship can go wrong, mothers are genetically programmed to love their offspring, motivated by an instinct that, by no coincidence, helps their children—and hence their own genes—to survive. Does knowing that make a mother's love any less wonderful?

And that focus on genetic survival brings us to the heart of the matter.

## An Inevitable Certainty

> Given that genes are the replicating currency of natural selection, it is an inevitable, algorithmic certainty that genes which cause behavior that enhances the survival of such genes must thrive at the expense of genes that do not.[20]
>
> **—Richard Dawkins**

In *The Selfish Gene*, Dawkins goes further to argue that "we are survival machines—robot vehicles blindly programmed to preserve the selfish molecules known as genes." For genes, the world is a place of "savage competition, ruthless exploitation, and deceit" and "this gene selfishness will usually give rise to selfishness in individual behavior." But is that claim a metaphor too far? Genes are neither selfish nor selfless, because they are not conscious and have no intentions of their own. As we shall see, his conclusion is also one-sided: emphasizing the ruthless selfishness of genes downplays the role of human culture—especially the way that the coevolution of genes and culture has built sociality into our chromosomes. The insights that evolutionary psychology, or evopsych, is discovering are much more complex and interesting than any genetic reductionism or determinism, and also more open-ended in the future possibilities they reveal.

Yet Dawkins' basic point about algorithmic certainty remains true: some genes are more adaptive than others, in that they tend to produce traits that tend to cause behavior that tends to lead to more successful reproduction. And for biological evolution, the only factors that ultimately matter are those that help to get your DNA into successive generations. If you don't reproduce, it doesn't matter how special your unique genetic variations might be, because they will disappear with you. This raises the crucial question: What psychological predispositions are associated with the genes that tend to proliferate? Do they sometimes include—and thereby perpetuate—what Buddhism calls the three poisons: greed (acquisitiveness), ill will (aggression, war), and delusion (egoism, tribalism)? But before diving into that, let's take a moment to reflect more generally on the implications of this algorithmic inevitability. Although some of them are not obvious, all are consequential.

Contrary to what was once believed, evolutionary success does not require veridical perception that accurately reflects reality. We see only what we need to see to guide our adaptive behavior—that is, to survive and reproduce. For example, the photoreceptor cells in our eyes respond to only about one ten-trillionth of the electromagnetic spectrum, while other species have found it beneficial to perceive other wavelengths. Reindeer and salmon, along with some butterflies, bees, birds, and rodents, can see ultraviolet light; some snakes, frogs, mosquitoes, fish, and bats can detect infrared light; curiously, goldfish see both. Humans perceive neither ultraviolet nor infrared radiation, apparently because those wavelengths confer no significant advantage in responding to our environment.

The point about perception can be expanded to include our general understanding of the world. According to E. O. Wilson, "Natural selection built the brain to survive in the world and only incidentally to understand it."[21] According to modern physics, even our normal experience of space-time—three spatial dimensions plus linear time as a fourth dimension—does not correspond to the way the world really is; it is a construct that works for us, because (to say it again) it helps us survive and reproduce. Einstein said that time and space are modes by which we think, not conditions in which we live. What can we actually know about objective reality? Donald Hoffman compares what we experience with the desktop icons on a computer screen. Such an interface hides what's going on inside the computer, because when we are using the computer there is no advantage to knowing about that. As the polymath scientist J. B. S. Haldane put it: "The world is not only queerer than we imagine, it is queerer than we *can* imagine."[22]

We may revere truth and its servant, reason, but for evolutionary success truth is not what we really need, and therefore not what we usually get. According to Steven Pinker, "Our minds evolved by natural selection to solve problems that were life and death matters to our ancestors, not to commune with correctness."[23] And the problems involved are not only life and death matters, but all the challenges involved in mating and reproducing, tasks that prioritize our sociality. David Hume's famous claim—that reason is, and ought to be, the slave of the passions—is consistent with an evolutionary perspective, although I prefer the way Wes Nisker puts it: We are not so much rational animals as rationalizing animals.[24]

Despite our alleged pursuit of objective truth, psychological experiments have confirmed the universality of *confirmation bias*: we are adept at detecting the flaws in someone else's argument but not in our own. That bias is not itself a flaw, but an important aspect of how reasoning functions. "Reason developed not to enable us to solve abstract, logical problems or even to help us draw conclusions from unfamiliar data; rather, it developed to resolve the problems posed by living in collaborative groups." Some type of reasoning became inevitable once we acquired language, as "an adaptation to the hypersocial niche humans have evolved for themselves."[25] That ability developed in order to justify our own beliefs to others and to persuade them to do what we want—in other words, it evolved for better communication and social coordination, which supported reproductive evolutionary success.

> In short, reasons are for social consumption. "To alienate your peers by stubbornly contesting their heartfelt beliefs would have lowered your chance of genetic proliferation."[26]

And according to Todd Rose,

> Just as fish have an instinct to swim toward the center of their schools to avoid being picked off by predators, we stick close to the majority in order to hedge our bets on survival. Indeed, being out of step with what we think is the crowd . . . makes us feel incredibly vulnerable. This bias towards the majority manifests itself in humans at a very early age. Indeed, studies with infants demonstrate that as early as nineteen months, babies who have no experience with certain toys look to the numerical majority of adults to learn which ones they should like the best. Even in the absence of intentional pressure or incentives, we like to go along with what we think is the consensus because, quite simply, we're biologically wired to do so.[27]

Today the increasing polarization of American politics makes it more obvious that what we believe tends to be more about belonging—what group we identify with—than about what is objectively true. Or, more precisely, the group we belong to largely determines what for us is true. This is the origin of many of the problems we struggle with today, especially when social media offers many contradictory "facts" that we can pursue down different rabbit holes, where we meet others who have taken refuge in—or been sucked into—the same cognitive black hole. People can end up living in a co-constructed fantasy world. Recent prominent examples are QAnon, the "stolen" 2020 presidential election, and the overblown dangers of COVID-19 vaccines.[28] We are gullible because our evolutionary inheritance leads us not to search for truth but to bond and cooperate with our own group.

This point can be extended to describe consciousness generally. "Consciousness, having evolved over millions of years of life-and-death struggle, and moreover because of that struggle, was not designed for self-examination. It was designed for survival and reproduction."[29] No wonder it is so difficult to think clearly and objectively. To "know thyself"—the ancient Delphic maxim inscribed at the Temple of Apollo—has always been a radical and challenging project.

But what about *fair play*? Same point. Natural selection is not opposed to morality, just oblivious to it except insofar as moral behavior affects reproduction—which it does, especially through *group selection*. (More on that later.) "Our moral brains evolved to help us spread our genes, not to maximize our collective happiness."[30]

The evolutionary process is also indifferent to whether we are personally happy—although unhappiness can affect the process by stressing our immune systems or making us less attractive to others. It uses pleasure (a proximate goal) to motivate us for reproductive success (the ultimate goal). This raises a crucial question for us today: How might our understanding of the process affect the process? In a world of over eight billion people, where you and I are not personally needed to perpetuate our species, what *is* our responsibility? Biologists agree that evolution has no goal, but whether or not it makes sense to talk about progress (a controversial issue), increasing complexity and consciousness have generated not only *Homo sapiens* but human society—and now, a global civilization. Cultural evolution opens up new possibilities: individually and collectively, we can set other goals and strive to achieve them. In that sense we are not bound by our genetic inheritance.

One general implication of the above is that the intentions we are conscious of, which apparently induce us to do what we do (the manifest function) are often quite different from what actually motivates us (the latent function, which may be unconscious but serves an adaptive purpose). The big appetites of children serve their need to grow, but that's not why they eat. They want to eat because they are hungry.

This distinction between manifest and latent intentions sometimes applies to cultural evolution as well. In order to maximize its nutritional value, lime must be added when maize is prepared, and that is what many South American cultures have traditionally done. Until recently, however, they did not know about the chemistry supporting that custom, even though they reaped the nutritional benefits.

To make all this more confusing, not only are we normally unaware of the difference between manifest and latent functions, but apparently there is no selection advantage in knowing that we don't know. According to Robert Wright, "The basic evolutionary logic common to people everywhere is opaque to introspection. Natural selection appears to have hidden our true selves from our conscious selves."[31] This is where things get especially interesting. How much of that basic evolutionary logic can be discovered, and how important might it be for us to do so? If our dangerous situation today is a result of the way that evolution has shaped our minds, perhaps nothing could be more important than understanding those minds—revealing our true nature. As the German poet Friedrich Hebbel remarked: "It would be a good thing if man concerned himself more with the history of his nature than with the history of his deeds."

The opacity of our latent motivations means that, in general, we have a better understanding of social evolution than we do of psychological evolution. Societal and technological developments are more obvious because they have accelerated in the last few thousand years, and especially in the last five hundred. The world we take for granted today, dominated by nation-states and corporate capitalism, with instantaneous communication and almost-as-fast transportation, is a thin epidermis over humanity's thick evolutionary history. Agriculture originated about 11,500 years ago, and pastoralism a thousand years or so after that, but it was only about five thousand years ago that half of us had shifted from hunting and gathering to farming. Although that may seem like a slow development, those and subsequent changes have happened too quickly for the evolution of neurological circuits adapted to what are now postindustrial lifestyles. Human genetic evolution still continues, of course—in fact more rapidly now that cultural developments have become the main driver of genetic change. During the past ten thousand years our genomes have been evolving ten to a hundred times faster than ever before,[32] but these new physiological and psychological developments remain dwarfed by the formative social changes that apparently occurred during the many millennia that we lived in small nomadic bands in Africa. According to Leda Cosmides and John Tooby,

> Generation after generation, for ten million years, natural selection slowly sculpted the human brain, favoring circuitry that was good at solving the day-to-day problems of our hunter-gatherer ancestors—problems like finding mates, hunting animals, gathering plant foods, negotiating with friends, defending ourselves against aggression, raising children, choosing a good habitat, and so on. Those whose circuits were better designed for solving these problems left more children, and we are descended from them.[33]

Cosmides and Tooby conclude that "our modern skulls house a stone age mind." Their main claim—that human psychology was molded on the African savanna during the Ice Ages of the Pleistocene era, which ended about 11,700 years ago—remains controversial largely because it is difficult to confirm. How do we know if such hypotheses are anything more than just-so stories—speculations no less fanciful than Kipling's fables about the long trunks of elephants and tall necks of giraffes? Another contentious issue is the modularity of such traits: if the predispositions that evopsych highlights correspond to localized brain networks, those specific neurological modules have not yet been identified.

Such challenges bolster resistance to explanations that prioritize heredity, which is understandable since genetics has had a problematic history. It has been used to justify racism and eugenic programs that sometimes involved horrific abuses. After a 1927 U.S. Supreme Court decision approved of forced sterilization in mental institutions, at least sixty thousand people were sterilized in thirty-two states, mostly women of color. Hitler admired American eugenics in his *Mein Kampf*, and in Nazi Germany hundreds of thousands of people with "undesirable characteristics" were sterilized. While Jews and Romany (gypsies) were murdered en masse, others were selectively mated to produce the desirable traits of the "Aryan master race."

If the eugenics movement overvalued heredity, some other approaches have undervalued it. Social scientists are sometimes inclined to dismiss evolutionary psychology because it challenges what is often the fundamental premise of their methodologies: the paramount importance of social conditioning. The radical behaviorism of John Watson and B. F. Skinner, which focused on stimulus-response habituation, is the classical example of this other extreme, presupposing that our basic human nature is a malleable blank slate. Grounding our psychological propensities in heritable genes seems to imply a determinism similar to the instincts that regulate most animal behavior.

This longstanding polarity between nature and nurture—between heredity and socialization—continues to thrive in politics. On one end of the spectrum, Neo-Nazis and white supremacists distinguish superior races from inferior ones. On the other side, liberals and political progressives are generally resistant to any explanations that involve genetics, out of concern that they can be used to justify social discrimination.

Today, however, any sharp duality between nature (genetics) and culture (social conditioning) is no longer tenable. "Nature provides a first draft, which experience then revises. . . . 'Built-in' does not mean unmalleable; it means 'organized in advance of experience.'"[34] Your heredity does not by itself shape your character traits, because inheritance actually refers to an interactive process rather than a deterministic unfolding.

The human genome is a code, but it does not encode a person. It encodes a developmental program, similar in some ways to a complex architectural blueprint, that can create a human being when the appropriate conditions arise. In both cases, intricate sequences of events are essential. In the womb, a successful pregnancy involves a long series of precisely coordinated processes. The program does not code for everything, which is why even identical twins are not completely identical. (But note the discussion of twins later in this chapter.) Because we are a relatively new species, however, there is actually little variation among the billions of us. Although each of our genomes typically carries 100 to 200 major individual mutations and thousands of minor genetic variants, 99 percent of your genome is nonetheless identical to mine and the genome of every other human. There is more genetic diversity in a single group of West African chimps.[35]

As William James put it, humans have instincts (nature) to learn things (nurture). As we evolved, natural selection favored genes that could build big brains with the ability to learn from others. This ability does not make us completely unique: cultural transmission is also found in dolphins and monkeys, for example, as well as some bird species. In the case of humans, however, this capability became augmented by language and led to complex culture-gene coevolution, each influencing the other. Evolutionary biologists have a term for such interaction: the *Baldwin effect* is when a behavior that had been learned and shared with others eventually becomes genetically encoded.

A classic example of culture-gene coevolution resulted from taming fire. The ability to control fire led to major physiological changes: our mouths, teeth, jaws, stomachs, and colon all became smaller, because cooked food is easier to eat and digest. Their reduction also created more space for the brain cavity to expand. In effect, cooking simplified the digestive process, more efficiently providing more calories to help our evolving neocortex grow. It also gave us more time and energy to focus on other things—such as other cultural developments and Baldwin effects.

Several important examples of coevolution derived from adopting an upright posture. As our heads rose above the earth, smell became less important and vision became the dominant sense. Walking on two legs also freed our hands to grasp tools, which enabled us to become builders as well as better hunters. Humans are by far the best species at throwing hard and accurately. Animal husbandry, especially the domestication of cattle, eventually led to a genetic variant that today enables many adults to continue digesting cow's milk.

I'm not in a position to evaluate arguments about Pleistocene origins or brain modularity. What is fascinating to me, and partly motivates this book, is the extraordinary correlation between some deep-rooted propensities of our human nature—which are therefore found in all cultures to some degree—and what Darwinian principles imply about their origins and functions. So many of our psychological predilections accord with what the evolutionary process rewards. And perhaps the best example is how well natural selection can help us understand the peculiarities of human sexuality.

## Sexuality

If the only thing that ultimately matters for biological evolution is what perpetuates one's genes by getting them into the next generation, how might that affect our sexual behavior?

To begin with the obvious, we can understand why sex is so enjoyable and such a strong drive—the most intensely pleasurable activity for most people. Note again the difference between that proximate goal and the ultimate goal. The whole process does not depend on any desire for children, and indeed we know all too well that pregnancy often occurs despite the intention to avoid it. In fact, even understanding the relationship between cause and effect is not necessary. We don't need to want lots of kids, just lots of sex, for our species to survive and natural selection to continue.

Nonetheless, unwanted newborns have sometimes been killed or allowed to die, but now effective forms of birth control and abortion can preempt the process. This new development is important in a world that arguably has become overpopulated with humans. Death control—that is, modern medicine—without some means of birth control must sooner or later create a problem. Birth control is important for another reason too: it demonstrates that the tendencies built into our species by the evolutionary process are just that, *propensities* that can be consciously obstructed. Thanks to cultural evolution, our present evolutionary psychology is not necessarily our destiny. And that's all the more important insofar as our sexual predilections are not designed to make us personally happy or to promote the betterment of society.

Our gendered roles in reproduction explain much about other differences between male and female behavior, sexual and otherwise. As we know, the biological contribution of men is normally a few moments of pleasure culminating in orgasm. The biological role of women—which does not require their own orgasm, or even any pleasure at all—is nine months of pregnancy, much of it uncomfortable in one way or another, culminating in a painful birth, followed by the need to nurture the infant and take care of the helpless child for many years. This gender imbalance is not unique to humans, of course, and is consistent with another important difference: females in many species, including most mammals and birds, are choosier than males when it comes to mating, usually preferring to copulate with those that can give their offspring a good start in life. For women, quality over quantity; for men, often vice-versa.

Does this help to explain why women often prefer men that are somewhat older, with wealth and higher social status? Men normally want younger and physically attractive women (beauty, including facial symmetry, is usually a sign of health). Cross-culturally, beauty standards appear to be much the same. There are (controversial) claims that the preferred female waist-to-hip ratio is about 0.7 everywhere, a ratio that indicates youthfulness and fertility and implies that the woman is not already pregnant. These facts suggest that, in human sexuality, the contribution of biology dwarfs that of cultural diversity.

Gender differences include the emotions that accompany our sexual behavior. Studies have shown that men are more concerned about chastity and sexual infidelity, women about emotional infidelity. That difference makes evolutionary sense: men want to avoid unwittingly raising children who do not have their own genes, while women are more concerned that their mate might become attached to someone else. All else being equal, a man who jealously controlled the activities of his partner(s) was likely to have more offspring than another male who was not so concerned—tendencies which encouraged patriarchy.

The difference in reproductive investment continues to have enormous implications, although social norms and legal obligations (such as court-ordered child support by divorced fathers) have tempered some of them. It is uncommon for a woman to bear more than a dozen children, but it can be easy for a man to father many more—historically, a strong motivation to become powerful and wealthy. Genghis Khan had so many wives and concubines that a substantial percentage of Mongolians today are said to inherit his genes. Ismail ibn Sharif, a seventeenth-century king of Morocco, is believed to have fathered 1,171 offspring.

More than 90 percent of bird species are socially monogamous and mate for life. Humans are one of over 500 primate species, and only about 29 percent of them are monogamous. That does not include chimps and bonobos, our two closest genetic relatives, who are quite promiscuous. In fact, we are the only species of great apes that is monogamous . . . well, sometimes. Until the spread of modern Western ways, more than 70 percent of human societies were polygynous. Another source claims that 85 percent of them were "preferentially polygamous" (when a man was able to support multiple wives), with less than 0.1 percent polyandrous (a woman having multiple husbands).

With polygynous species, males are naturally selected to be bigger than females, because larger males have a significant advantage. There is a striking correlation: the larger the harem, the fiercer the competition and the bigger the evolved difference in size between males and females. Elephant seals are an extreme example, with bulls up to ten times larger than females, and having harems of up to a hundred cows. On average, males of our species are about 10 percent taller than females and 20 percent heavier—a disparity greater than usually found in monogamous species, but less than many polygamous species. (Although male brains also tend to be 10 percent bigger, there is no detectable difference in intelligence.) According to Steven Pinker, "The larger size, strength, and upper-body mass of men is a zoological giveaway of an evolutionary history of violent male-on-male competition. Other signs include the effects of testosterone on dominance and violence."[36] From an evolutionary perspective, then, it's not coincidental that adolescent boys sexually mature later than girls: their greater size and strength has been selected for, because human males too needed to be ready to fight for access to mates. With other species, this often involves lethal weapons such as fangs, antlers, and tusks, as well as an aggressive temperament. Among humans today, such competition is more commonly sublimated into social status, and into the risky behavior common with adolescent boys (less so with girls) after they hit puberty. "[M]ale stupidity is actually an adaptation to female choosiness, as male risk taking and conflict seeking are products of sexual selection."[37] They are ways to attract attention, like the peacock's extravagant tail.

The incest taboo, which is virtually universal in human societies (although sometimes violated, of course) is another example of the difference between manifest and latent functions. The extent of this taboo varies across cultures, but with very few exceptions (such as ancient Egyptian royalty) sexual relations with first-degree relatives (parent, sibling, children) are forbidden everywhere. This makes evolutionary sense, of course: inbreeding can cause congenital disorders and developmental disabilities when offspring receive two recessive versions of the same gene from parents who are closely related. Many other animals, such as capuchin monkeys, elephants, some seals, and even cockroaches, also avoid interbreeding. Even unrelated children who grow up together during their first five or six years usually experience a "reverse sexual imprinting," being unattracted to each other (this is known as the Westermarck effect). Unrelated mice raised together also avoid sexual relations.

Finally, there is an especially consequential difference between humans and other mammals. Almost all social mammals organize themselves into groups of females (usually related) with their immature offspring. Males are normally absent except when the females are ovulating and sexually receptive. The physical changes at that time are usually obvious, yet human ovulation is distinctive because concealed, and women can become sexually receptive throughout the month. This has created pair-bonding, with the effect of keeping men around and creating families and society as we know it. Nonetheless, there is no mammal species in which males do as much parenting as females, including ours, even today—which will not surprise many mothers who read this.

Pair-bonding created a deeper, long-term relationship but did not thereby replace another predilection, the desire for sexual variety—especially among men, whose genes could benefit from spreading their seed more widely. That men are more interested in one-night stands or short-term relationships, while women seek deeper psychological commitment, is a stereotype with many exceptions, yet nevertheless might be rooted in the implications of our evolutionary psychology. This difference is reflected in sexual fantasies. Male fantasies tend to be more visual, physical, and promiscuous than female fantasies, which are usually more contextual and emotionally intimate. The stereotype is amusing because so often true: men watch pornography, women read romance novels.[38]

The result is that we are not "naturally" monogamous, polygamous, or promiscuous, but all the above. Evolutionary selection "has bequeathed us a diverse palette of evolved desires and drives, and these are compatible with a variety of socially molded mating systems." Our species history reflects this: apparently early humans were polygynous until about 300,000 years ago. Then, hunting-gathering societies, which tend to be fiercely egalitarian, became monogamous; the agricultural revolution, about 11,500 years ago, fostered the creation of empires with hierarchies and polygynous elites; during the last 2,000 years, however, monogamy has become much more common than any other arrangement.[39]

That there are these various possibilities is intriguing, but they come at a considerable cost. "This is the irritating reality of the human condition: Whatever we do, we're left with unfulfilled desires. Human beings are chronically conflicted animals. And that's because that's what [natural] selection made us."[40]

This perspective is quite helpful for understanding the uncomfortable situation we sometimes find ourselves in, with incompatible longings. The occasional sexual attraction to someone other than one's partner is something that natural selection has built into us, especially (but certainly not only) men. It is helpful to know that such a temptation, in itself, is not a personal character defect. It is a legacy of our evolution. That does not mean such a proclivity is destiny, something that therefore justifies whatever we want to do. We can still choose how to respond to internal conflicts. Does it help if we know what is motivating us?

Such tensions between discordant psychological drives are not restricted to our sexual behavior.

## Beyond Freedom and Determinism

As the above evopsych perspective on human sexuality reveals, human minds are not blank slates. John Locke's conception of the mind as a "white paper, void of all characters, without any ideas," might apply to some temporary states of mindfulness, or mindlessness, but there is much more to our minds than what we are normally aware of—an insight that is perhaps the most important discovery of modern psychology. Karl Marx believed that human nature is simply the ensemble of one's social relations, and the influential anthropologist Franz Boas likewise emphasized our social environment over any biological factors. For the Spanish philosopher Ortega y Gasset we don't have an essence, we have a *history*, which largely accords with existentialists such as Sartre, for whom our existence precedes any essence we may have.

We can now see how one-sided such perspectives are, because longitudinal psychological research has determined that heredity plays a major role—often *the* major role—in many behavioral traits such as intelligence (both verbal and spatial ability), language facility, motor skills, sexual orientation, musicality, sleep patterns, appetite, and even how religious we are. Our genes can also predispose us to problems such as anxiety, depression, schizophrenia, bipolar disorder, autism, attention-deficit disorder, compulsive gambling, smoking, alcoholism, drug abuse, suicidal behavior, and even marital infidelity and the likelihood of divorce. Psychopathy (along with criminal behavior) also seems to be substantially heritable, and, on the other side, perhaps altruism as well.[41] "One of the most striking revelations from recent discoveries is that the clinical effects of high-risk mutations do not respect the boundaries of psychiatric categories. Without exception, all of them increase risk across a range of disorders, including autism, ADHD, epilepsy, intellectual disability, schizophrenia, and bipolar disorder." In other words, if your parent or sibling experiences one of these conditions, the chance that you will also suffer from any of them is much higher than average.[42]

The mutations that put us at risk for such disorders apparently arise regularly—schizophrenia and autism each afflict about 1 percent of the population—but tend to be removed by natural selection, because people with neuropsychiatric disorders normally have fewer children. Why is our species so vulnerable to these mutations? According to Kevin Mitchell,

> [I]t seems likely that the runaway process that led to our increased brain size, complexity, and intelligence carried a price of increased vulnerability to mutations. Like any piece of machinery, the more sophisticated it gets, the more ways there are for it to break down. Evolution can't future-proof things. . . . We are, in effect, early adopters of a new operating system, but the downside is that we are constantly beta-testing it.[43]

More generally, one's underlying temperament and talents are mostly heritable, including where we are located on the five major personality spectra: introverted or extroverted, neurotic or stable, incurious or open to experience, agreeable or antagonistic, and conscientious or undependable.

Heritability is so potent that the influence of being raised in the same family is much less than the effect of one's genes. An extreme example is provided by accounts of identical twins separated soon after birth and raised in very different families, who nonetheless turn out to be similar in what they like and believe—for example, sexual attraction and political views, respectively. Such stories are common because they are substantially true: identical twins tend to end up very similar whether they grow up together or not. When environmental influences are also similar, the results can sometimes be extraordinary—even uncanny.

> Behaviors as diverse as smoking, insomnia, marriage and divorce, choice of careers and hobbies, use of contraceptives, consumption of coffee (but not, oddly enough, of tea), menstrual symptoms, and suicide have all been found to have far higher rates of concordance for identical than for fraternal twins—a finding that suggests these traits to be more influenced by genes than was previously suspected.
>
> A survey of Australian twins in the early nineteen-eighties also found a surprisingly significant genetic component for attitudes toward such wide-ranging political and social issues as apartheid, the death penalty, divorce, working mothers, and some forty other subjects.[44]

A notable instance is the Australian twins Judy and Cara, who were separated at birth and grew up unaware of each other until a case of mistaken identity connected them. At that time—the late 1980s and 1990s—Australia had only two department store chains, David Jones and Myer. Judy was a fashion buyer for David Jones and Cara was a fashion buyer for Myer, both in their Brisbane stores. They only became aware of each other because fashion representatives visiting each store noticed the similarity and asked them "Why are you two-timing, working for rival chains?" At their reunion, they discovered that they were similar in dress, hairstyle, and postures, wore the same type of jewelry, smoked the same brand of cigarettes, and had the same favorite color, pale pink.[45]

Perhaps the most extraordinary example involves the identical twins Jim Lewis and Jim Springer, who were separated at the age of three weeks and grew up in Ohio without knowing about each other.

> They reunited at 39 and found that they were each six feet tall and weighed 180 pounds; bit their nails and had tension headaches; owned a dog named Toy when they were kids; went on family vacations at the same beach in Florida; had worked part-time in law enforcement; and liked Miller Lite beer and Salem cigarettes. There was one notable difference: Jim Lewis named his firstborn James Alan, while Jim Springer named his James Allan.[46]

In school both enjoyed math and carpentry but not spelling. Both married women named Linda, later divorced and then married women named Betty. Both drove a Chevrolet and were chain smokers.[47]

A less eerie version of the same correlation applies to other genetic siblings who are not twins. Amazingly, there is little difference between siblings raised together and siblings who have been separated at birth. And it works the other way around too: unrelated children who are adopted into the same home become only a little more similar than unrelated children raised separately. Researchers have found that parenting has only minor effects on their children's health, life expectancy, education, and religiosity, although they have moderate influence on drug use, alcohol consumption, and sexual behavior.[48]

This does not mean there is a one-to-one correspondence between a gene and a trait. In most cases, behavior is much more complex, involving a variety of interacting genes, and geneticists are far from understanding the intricate processes involved. The relevant genes may not be strongly functioning ("expressed") and the associated traits will not always develop, but the disposition to do so is inherited and often robust. "When it comes to attitudes that are heritable, people react more quickly and emotionally, are less likely to change their minds, and are more attracted to like-minded people."[49]

Nonetheless, predispositions are not fate. Such hereditary regularities do not predetermine what we will do. Animal instincts normally function as fixed patterns of behavior that react predictively to particular stimuli, usually triggered by an external event. Perhaps because our brains continue to grow significantly after birth—when we become exposed to external stimuli—humans are not limited by innate conditioning. Most of us have a taste for sugar and fatty foods, but it is possible—although not always easy!—to curtail how much of them we eat. Instead of controlling what we become and what we do, our genes provide distinctive propensities, dispositions, predilections, behavioral tendencies—pick whatever term you prefer—that interact with the environment, including the conditioning provided by one's language and culture. According to Kathryn Paige Harden,

> The fact that income, educational attainment, subjective well-being, psychiatric disease, neighborhood advantage, cognitive test performance, executive function, grit, motivation, and curiosity are all heritable does not mean that these things cannot be improved by intervention or bolstered by environmental privilege. They can.[50]

To say it again, despite the above examples of identical twins raised apart, it's not nature versus nurture but rather how they work together. As Clifford Geertz put it, we are incomplete animals who complete ourselves through culture. "Nature bestows upon the newborn a considerably complex brain, but one that is best seen as *prewired*—flexible and subject to change—rather than *hardwired*, fixed, and immutable."[51]

Is this the answer to the age-old question about the nature of human nature? According to Loyal Rue,

> There is a human nature, a wide range of universally endowed defaults and dispositions shared across the species. These universal characteristics are fixed in neural systems that are in turn constructed from information stored in genetic material. But many of these systems are open to modulation by acquired information. Sometimes we override our default behaviors by repressing them or by designing alternative behaviors. And sometimes we reinforce them with learning.[52]

I suggest pausing a moment to reflect on these remarkable findings, which are so counterintuitive to our usual sense of free will and inconsistent with widespread beliefs about how much we are conditioned by our upbringing and other socialization. These discoveries about the impact of genetics on our behavioral tendencies, in combination with what evolutionary psychology is discovering, offer a serious challenge to our usual self-understanding of who we are and why we do what we do. They also imply a different way of understanding our collective predicament today, as we shall see.

## How to Be an Ape

Much of the resistance to evopsych insights is due to anthropocentrism: our species remains convinced of its superiority over all other animals and the rest of the natural world. Don't human history and culture reveal that we are special, exceptional, unique? As we learn more about our closest relatives, however, this collective version of narcissistic hubris is becoming more difficult to rationalize. Recent studies of chimpanzees and bonobos have discovered how similar they are to us in their emotional and social lives. This would have been no surprise to Darwin, who wrote *The Expression of the Emotions in Man and Animals*.

Primate evolution ramified quickly after the extinction event that killed off the dinosaurs 66 million years ago. As most of the new mammal species gave up nocturnal life for daylight and improved vision, important new psychological traits also developed, including

> facial muscles so moods could be communicated by expressions; a still more powerful bond between mother and child; a longer period of infantile dependence; and an improving ability of the newer, higher brain centers of the cerebral cortex to moderate aggression and other behavior patterns emanating from the older, lower layers. All this in turn led to major changes in primate society: The less aggression, the more a true communal life is possible; the longer the childhood, the more parents can teach their young. Alliances and support groups, reconciliation, reassurance, forgiveness, remembering the past behavior of specific individuals, and planning future actions swiftly evolved. Our ancestors were by now well along a path toward greater alertness, intelligence, communication skills, love.[53]

It is often presumed that only humans have a "theory of mind" enabling us to understand that others have mental states, which their expressions and actions reveal. But primate studies have revealed that apes can detect the mental states of others and even empathize with them—putting themselves in the shoes of another, so to speak. Moreover, apes are the only other primates who can recognize their own reflection in a mirror, implying a degree of self-awareness. Other cooperative mammals such as elephants and dolphins also exhibit a heightened sense of empathy, helping sick and distressed comrades.[54]

Empathy is an instinct that affects every mammal to some degree. It is an innate, automated, and ancient response: empathic feelings engage neural circuitry in the brain that originated over a hundred million years ago. We can suppress these feelings and decline to act on them, but except for psychopaths—estimated to be about 1 percent of the general population—none of us is emotionally immune to the situation of others. Nonetheless, we can discriminate by selecting what we react to and what we do not. The trigger is identification, which blurs the difference between oneself and another: we readily share the feelings of those in our own group, who are similar and familiar. That makes sense, since empathy apparently evolved to facilitate in-group cooperation and harmony. If harmony in small groups requires fairness in sharing resources, empathy would have encouraged early hunting-gathering groups to emphasize solidarity and egalitarianism—still fundamental characteristics of the hunting-gathering groups that have survived.[55]

Nonetheless, chimp society as observed today implies that empathy did not always predominate in our evolving socialization. According to Carl Sagan and Ann Druyan,

> From a human perspective chimpanzee social life has many nightmarish flourishes. And yet, despite its excesses, it's hauntingly familiar. Many spontaneous groupings of men are organized around hierarchy, combat, blood sports, and loveless sex. The combination of dominant males, submissive females, differential but scheming subordinates, a driving hunger for "respect" up and down the hierarchy, the exchange of current favors for future loyalty, barely submerged violence, protection rackets, and the systematic sexual exploitation of all available adult females, has some marked points of similarity with the lifestyles and ambiance of absolute monarchs, dictators, big-city bosses, bureaucrats of all nations, gangs, organized crime, and the actual lives of many of the figures in history adjudged "great."[56]

The uneasy status of chimp godfathers—alpha males—is quite differ-ent from the situation of female chimps:

Males engaged in power struggles sometimes have a permanently furrowed-brow expression suggesting internal turmoil, and they are known to have high levels of stress. A female ape, on the other hand, is mainly interested in her offspring and the duties that come with motherhood, such as taking time to nurse, find food, and deterring predators and aggressive members of her own species. She also works every day on her relationships, grooming her friends, consoling them after upheavals, and watching over their offspring if needed.[57]

Cross-cultural studies have confirmed that, among humans too, women are everywhere considered more empathic than men.[58]

Discussing the role of empathy in human evolution prompts us to consider its opposite: aggression. On the level of individual selection, violence is not some primitive, bloodthirsty urge to destroy, but a rational, adaptive behavior that can serve survival (hunting for food, defending against predators) and reproduction. We have already noted that violence against competitors within one's group could sometimes enhance reproductive success. There is, however, an interesting overlap with the incest taboo: like many other mammals, humans have a strong inhibition against aggression toward blood relatives.

But what about conflict with other groups? While the available historical evidence suggests that early hunting-gathering cultures were fiercely egalitarian, it's less clear how common organized collective violence against other groups was during our long prehistory. Before sedentism—settling in one place—there was much less to fight over.

Although chimpanzees are usually considered our closest living relative, chimps diverged from bonobos (once called "pygmy chimpanzees" but actually a different species) about two million years ago, whereas hominids split from our common lineage much earlier, perhaps five million years ago. This means humans are equally related to both, as genomic sequencing confirms. That is significant because bonobo behavior is very different from that of chimps. Bonobos are much less aggressive and warlike, instead preferring to diffuse interpersonal strife with (lots of) sex. Bonobos also share food more often than chimps do, and various groups mix easily, while chimps are much more likely to fight. In contrast to the constant tension between alpha males and subordinate male chimps, female bonobos dominate by cooperating with each other to keep the peace.

What does this difference between chimpanzees and bonobos imply about human nature? Which of them is more like us? Given the prevalence of war in human history, as well as the widespread propensity for society to be organized into oppressive and oppressed classes, our similarities to chimps (who have been studied more than bonobos) might seem more obvious. Yet, when the nightmarish flourishes of chimpanzee social life also predominate in a human group, we generally view such a society as deplorable, an attitude that presumes a preference for more prosocial alternatives. According to Matt Ridley,

> Our minds have been built by selfish genes, but they have been built to be social, trustworthy and cooperative.... Human beings have social instincts. They come into the world equipped with predispositions to learn how to cooperate, to discriminate the trustworthy from the treacherous, to commit themselves to be trustworthy, to earn good reputations, to exchange goods and information, and to divide labor. This instinctive cooperativeness is the very hallmark of humanity.[59]

But not the only hallmark. "Human beings are riven with both royalist and regicidal impulses; we're prone to erect hierarchies and prone to topple them. We can be deeply cruel and deeply caring."[60] As with our inconsistent sexual proclivities, might these incompatible tendencies coexist uneasily because different genes (or combinations of genes) push and pull us in different directions? Is it possible that, due to our complicated genetic legacy, human nature is both inclined to egalitarianism and susceptible to authoritarianism?

# Altruism and Tribalism

Altruism has been the greatest challenge for evolutionary psychology, because it seems incompatible with the competitive evolutionary process—or at least with the individualistic assumptions of some evolutionary psychologists. If our genes are selfish in the sense that we are preoccupied above all else with reproducing them, then it becomes difficult to understand why anyone would act altruistically, sometimes even risking one's own life to save someone else. Yet such things happen, so altruism needs to be explained—or cynically explained away: "Scratch an 'altruist,' and watch a 'hypocrite' bleed"[61]—and psychologists have duly come up with some clever accounts.

An obvious explanation is our relationship with relations. Normally we are grateful to parents and other caregivers, but we also feel affection for other kinfolk such as brothers and sisters (even if we quarrel), and to a lesser extent for aunts and uncles, nephews and nieces, and so on. Insofar as we are motivated to perpetuate our genes, altruism toward them makes sense: we share many genes with siblings, and some with more distant relatives. By helping them, we help to propagate those genes.

In addition to such *kin selection*, there is *reciprocal altruism*: it also makes sense to help others when they may be inclined to return the favor in the future. (As Hollywood gangsters like to say, "What have you done for me lately?") That does not require a rational evaluation of the situation, which would be too slow. "In everyday life, reciprocity is propped up not by abstract normative principles, but by emotions such as gratitude, guilt, sympathy, and anger. All neurologically normal human beings possess these emotions, and it seems highly unlikely that the emotions are inventions of culture."[62]

This encourages us to cooperate with others in our group but would not necessarily override the instinctive urge to pursue one's own personal advantage. Instead, we end up with the tensions naturally built into *multilevel selection*. When there are options, should I do what seems best for me as an individual, pursuing my own self-interest, or do I aid other family members? Shall I put myself out to help unrelated individuals? Should I risk myself (in battle, for example) for the well-being of the group?

Among other mammals, only a few social carnivores and some primates—notably chimpanzees—form aggressive coalitions that occasionally hunt and kill individuals in other groups of the same species.[63] Again, bonobos are more peaceful. That chimps and bonobos are our closest species relatives, and we are equally related to both, suggests another genetic discrepancy allowing divergent social options.

Cultural evolution rewarded the ability to collaborate to achieve common goals, which was especially important during times of intergroup conflict. Despite a predisposition for independence and egalitarianism, our long history as hunter-gatherers sometimes required strong group coordination, and even temporary "achievement-based inequality" (obeying skilled leaders). During the hunt, your own success (and in wartime perhaps your survival) does not rest solely on your own efforts. You may compete with others in your group, but you also depend upon them, and they on you. Darwin discussed the implications of this in *The Descent of Man*:

> It must not be forgotten that although a high standard of morality gives but a slight or no advantage to each individual man and his children over the other men of the same tribe, yet that an advancement in the standard and an increase in the number of well-endowed men will certainly give an immense advantage to one tribe over another.... [Such a tribe] would be victorious over other tribes; and this would be natural selection.[64]

In other words, *group selection* has been an inevitable dimension of human evolution, a component that has become more important as we have become more social and more interdependent. The ecosystem of early humans was not only biological but also social, and societies evolved in the same competitive way that individuals did: successful reproduction depended on group survival and the availability of contested resources.

Among our basic traits is the tendency to identify with others in one's group. And what holds *us* together is our opposition to *them*. "Humans are designed to be tribal. We are wired to organize ourselves socially into in-groups (our own group) and out-groups (others' groups), and to organize ourselves cognitively so that our reasoning processes and even our sensory perceptions support in-group solidarity."[65] This process can be observed even in young children. Starting around fourteen to sixteen months, infants are naturally altruistic. But by the age of four or so, children already group people according to race and gender, and have more negative views of "them." A study of Texas daycare centers found that the perceptions of kids aged three to five were "pervasively distorted by mere membership in a social group, a finding with disturbing implications." Those placed in a "blue group" quickly developed a dislike for those in the "red group" and vice-versa.[66] This polarization has biological correlates: oxytocin (the "love hormone") promotes trust, generosity, and cooperation—but usually only within one's own group, with nastier behavior toward those in other groups.

Many of the early evolutionary psychologists who were skeptical about altruism have also been dubious about the very concept of group selection. Surely the priority of individual selection—"looking out for number one"—would find a way to subvert any altruistic behavior? Well . . . sometimes, but other times that would be unwise. While individual competition within a group is about one's status, which affects opportunities to mate, competition between groups can be a matter of existential survival, which would provide a strong selection pressure for altruism. And another important aspect of our social life is relevant here: although generous people are sometimes exploited, they are everywhere more popular than people who are more self-centered and calculating, and popularity could be a big advantage in the mating game.

Altruism also has implications for social evolution, because virtuous people joining forces with other virtuous people leads to mutual benefit.[67] All this accords with one of the most distinctive aspects of human social life: the importance of friendship, which is obviously connected with reciprocity but cannot be reduced to it. Psychological research keeps confirming that what really makes us happy is not wealth or fame but the quality of our relationships with other people. In fact, close ties "are better predictors of long and happy lives than social class, IQ, or even genes."[68] For both longevity and reproductive success, relationships are key.

On the other extreme are the socially dysfunctional character traits of social Darwinists, who view the world as a competitive jungle where only the strongest thrive. This is based on a negative opinion of human nature, the belief that people are basically selfish and exploitation of others is the way to become successful. Psychological surveys have established that social Darwinists tend to admire power and want to dominate, pursue their goals regardless of the cost, and display hostility. Despite their preoccupation with strength and worship of power, they are also more likely to have a fragile self-image, with low self-esteem, poor self-sufficiency, and a fearful attachment style.[69] Social Darwinists may be good at manipulating others to get what they want, but they are less likely to be happy.

I wonder if this contrast between altruism and social Darwinism points to the origins of morality, and why the conflict between "good" and "evil" remains the central issue in our social relations. Most of the behavior we think of as bad (for example, murder, rape, theft, fraud) originates from selfishness, while virtuous acts (such as cooperation, generosity, kindness, altruism) benefit the group because they indicate concern for the welfare of others. Or as E. O. Wilson puts it,

> Selfish activity within the group provides competitive advantage but is commonly destructive to the group as a whole. Working in the opposite direction from individual-level selection is group selection—group versus group. When an

individual is cooperative and altruistic, this reduces his advantage in competition to a comparable degree with other members but increases the survival and reproduction rate of the group as a whole. In a nutshell, individual selection favors what we call sin and group selection favors virtue.[70]

Thus "an unavoidable and perpetual war exists between honor, virtue, and duty, the products of group selection, on the one side, and selfishness, cowardice, and hypocrisy, the products of individual selection, on the other side."[71] Do I look out for myself or attend to what the group needs? If the conflict between good and evil is hardwired into our psychology, it is expressed "as a complicated mix of closely calibrated altruism, cooperation, competition, domination, reciprocity, defection, and deceit. . . . Thus was born the human condition, selfish at one time, selfless at another, the two impulses often conflicted."[72]

This accords with a curious difference between individualistic and more prosocial cultures. In group-oriented societies, members accept their mutual dependence and support each other. In individualistic societies, people tend to be more competitive and less altruistic. Karl Marx believed in a historical progression whereby industrialized nations would eventually foster a communist revolution, but the two biggest examples of a successful revolution—Russia and China—were "backward" peasant societies where people in extended families and village communities were used to depending upon each other. In contrast, socialism has never been popular in the United States, which is likely the most individualistic society in human history. It also remains the only developed nation without a national health care system.

This tension between the individual and the group evokes an age-old issue. Is civilization a thin but necessary veneer of enforced civility over self-centered greed and aggression? Or does civilization exploit our empathy and interdependence, creating oppressive hierarchies of privilege that dominate our natural concern for the well-being of each other? Surely it is no coincidence that this debate corresponds in many ways to the divergence between conservative and progressive politics.

Could it be that the argument between them is endless because both views are valid?

According to Thomas Huxley ("Darwin's bulldog"), Malthus, Hobbes, Machiavelli, Augustine, Calvin, Freud, and many conservatives both religious and secular, human nature is essentially selfish and individualistic unless tamed by some social conditioning. This is the belief that underlies or rationalizes social Darwinism: It's a dog-eat-dog world, and if I don't want to play that game, I will be victimized by others who will. On the other side, Kropotkin, Godwin, Rousseau, Pelagius, and Plato, among many others, believed that we are born benevolent and later corrupted by society.

Curiously, Adam Smith, the great apologist for capitalism, came down on both sides. In his famous inquiry into *The Wealth of Nations*, he argued for the benevolent operation of "an invisible hand." By pursuing our own economic self-interest, we nonetheless promote something that we did not intend: the well-being of society as a whole. "It is not from the benevolence of the butcher, the brewer, or the baker, that we expect our dinner, but from their regard to their own interest."[73] But his earlier book *The Theory of Moral Sentiments* offered a more nuanced view of human motivation: "How selfish soever man may be supposed, there are evidently some principles in his nature, which interest him in the fortune of others, and render their happiness necessary to him, though he derives nothing from it except the pleasure of seeing it."[74]

Because this issue is so important, it is probably no coincidence that the same argument has been prominent in Chinese history, especially within Confucianism, its most influential social philosophy. The little that Confucius himself said on this topic was ambiguous, but two of his prominent followers offered contrary views. According to Mencius, our human nature (*xing*) is innately righteous and humane; poor social conditioning is responsible for bad moral character. For Xunzi, however, our *xing* is evil and ethical norms are necessary to rectify people.

Today that debate often appears as the difference between a social contract view and a sociological perspective. For the social contract tradition, society is composed of rational, self-interested individuals who agree to give up some of their autonomy for security; most economic theory presupposes something like this. For sociologists, however, individuals are better understood as members of a cohesive social organism. Darwin himself was influenced by Adam Smith and Thomas Malthus, both economists, which may be why he emphasized the adaptability of individuals more than the role of species or their ecosystems.

Neither view of human nature refutes the other. We tend to assume that our basic nature must be one or the other, but that is not the way evolution works. According to Lewis Dartnell,

> Evolution is restricted, in finding solutions to new conditions and survival problems, to tinkering with what is already at its disposal. It never gets the chance to go back to the drawing board and redesign from scratch. We have emerged from our evolutionary history as a palimpsest of overlaying designs, with each new adaptation modifying, or being built on top of, what already existed. To be human is to be the sum total of all our capabilities and constraints—our flaws and our faculties make us who we are. And the story of human history has played out in the balance between them.[75]

Because the tension between selfishness and altruism is crucial to social life, it's not surprising that humans have become so acutely sensitive at appraising the intentions of other people. The key to our species' success has been our ability to work together to achieve shared goals, but genuine cooperation is not something that can be taken for granted. We are experts at reading minds—and that includes detecting deception—because we need to know what motivates what others do. Are you speaking truthfully, or trying to manipulate me? Will you do your bit, or freeload off the rest of us? Spontaneous cooperation is our default reaction in situations where others need help, but we also react negatively when we believe that others are taking advantage of us. We are preoccupied with such concerns.

According to E. O. Wilson, "Selfishness beats altruism within groups. Altruistic groups beat selfish groups. Everything else is commentary."[76] Nevertheless, group selection does not preclude the problem with selfishness. In fact, it often amounts to a larger version of the same problem, because what normally holds groups together is their competition with other groups. "All human preliterate societies, and all modern ones as well, tend to have an 'enemy,' a concept of them and us [which means that] preferring the morality of group selection to the ruthlessness of individual struggle is to prefer genocide over murder. . . . It is a rule of evolution to which we are far from immune that the more cooperative societies are, the more violent the battles between them."[77] As Reinhold Niebuhr observed, "The group is more arrogant, hypocritical, self-centered and more ruthless in the pursuit of its ends than the individual."[78]

So what happens when the enemy—the other group—disappears? According to Joseph Henrich,

> Over time, history suggests that all prosocial institutions age and eventually collapse at the hands of self-interest, unless they are renewed by the dynamics of intergroup competition. That is, although it may take a long time, individuals and coalitions eventually figure out how to beat or manipulate the system to their own ends, and these techniques spread and slowly corrode any prosocial effects.[79]

Does Henrich's insight help us to understand why democracy (the archetypal prosocial institution) looks so fragile these days? It explains the "culture wars," including current political polarization, better than anything else I can think of. My father was part of the "Greatest Generation" that fought in World War II, in his case quitting high school to join the U.S. Navy. The life-or-death struggle against fascism brought out the best in many of them, who risked their lives and often paid the ultimate sacrifice. During that war different ethnic groups and economic classes mixed and worked together. People became more altruistic because they had to, in order to win. Immediately afterward, the Cold War began, a much longer struggle against "Godless communism."

In 1989, when the Soviet Union collapsed, a Soviet diplomat named Georgi Arbatov cautioned an American audience: "We are going to do a terrible thing to you. We are going to deprive you of an enemy."[80] His forewarning was prescient. Capitalism took off its velvet gloves and the divide between rich and poor in the United States began to grow dramatically, along with political tensions between Democrats and Republicans, left-wing and right-wing politics. World War II and its aftermath inspired Congress to pass the G.I. Bill, which provided a range of economic benefits for many (mostly white) returning veterans. In contrast, for a brief period after the Cold War ended there seemed to be no more foreign enemies to be afraid of, and by no coincidence that is when Newt Gingrich created his 1994 "Contract with America" and was able to shut down the federal government. His success heralded not only the end of bipartisanship but "*negative partisanship*—that is, hatred of the other team more than loyalty to one's own."[81] The loss of an external enemy led to identifying an internal enemy and becoming preoccupied with struggling against it. The War on Terror was not enough to revive bipartisanship, and so far the threat from China and even Russia's war in Ukraine don't seem to be doing that either.

## Self-Domestication

As part of our cultural evolution, we learned to domesticate plants into crops such as rice, corn, and wheat, as well as animals such as dogs and cats, sheep and pigs, cattle and horses. Unlike taming, which is behavioral modification—conditioning animals to accept the presence of humans—domestication involves inherited genetic changes that predispose animals to bond with humans. Most of the mammals that have been domesticated evolved from herd animals that had a dominance hierarchy, and in effect humans assumed the role of alpha male. The initial focus would have been breeding for docility to replace aggression, but a suite of other features usually develops along with that trait, including a more gracile (slender) body with smaller teeth and jaw, nonseasonal estrus (fertility) cycles for females, reduction in brain size, and especially *neoteny*: the retention of juvenile characteristics much longer than the original wild species did, even into adulthood.

All these modifications also happened to humans. "Man is a primate fetus that has become sexually mature."[82] As we became more sociable, we domesticated ourselves.

In the last twenty thousand years, the size of our brain has decreased from more than 1,500 cubic centimeters (for men) to less than 1,350—a substantial loss, about the volume of a tennis ball. At the same time, our bodies also became more gracile and *social* evolution increasingly important. As humans became more comfortable in controlling their physical environment, there was less preoccupation with day-to-day survival. Selection pressures shifted to focus more on one's relationships with other group members, favoring conformity and harmony. In a hunting-gathering community, ostracism is equivalent to a death sentence. We became more anxious about what other people think of us.

As this suggests, our emotional life can be understood as evolving to serve a social function. According to Robert Wright, "Our whole landscape of feelings—fear, lust, love, and many other feelings, salient and subtle, that inform our everyday thoughts and perceptions—are products of the particular evolutionary history of our species."[83] Emotions are far older than rational cognitive processes. They can be understood as shorthand guides for regulating social interactions, helping us to act appropriately in situations that require a prompt response. Despite its bad reputation, anger (not to be confused with hatred or persistent ill will) can serve an important function in small groups. Psychological studies have shown that expressing anger normally makes everyone involved more willing to listen closely and speak honestly, and more accommodating to others' complaints; those who vent their anger feel relieved afterward and more optimistic about the future. Moral outrage becomes more problematic in large groups, where personal relationships are not as deep, and especially when institutions are involved. "Corporatized outrage is fundamentally manipulative and tends to further the interests of the already rich and powerful. Rarely is it a force for social good."[84]

On an individual level, you are less likely to try to take advantage of me if you know that I'm prone to violence when aggravated. The urge for revenge can be self-destructive, but I might get angry enough that I don't care and do it anyway—another predilection that can serve as a social warning to others. Resentment of freeloaders means they'd better shape up and do their part, and soon. More generally, psychologists have identified four major families of social emotions that are closely linked with moral judgment. Other-condemning emotions such as anger and disgust provoke us to punish cheaters. Other-praising emotions such as gratitude and veneration inspire us to praise altruists. Other-suffering emotions such as empathy and compassion prompt us to help someone in need. Finally, self-conscious emotions such as shame and embarrassment motivate us to avoid cheating or to correct wrongdoing.[85] All of these social emotions can be viewed as adaptations promoting group identification and harmony. Religious support for them developed much later.

Despite the recent reduction in our brain size, the difference between us and our close relatives remains considerable. The human cortex has about sixteen billion neurons; orangutans and gorillas have about nine billion, chimps and elephants about six billion. Our genome is 98–99 percent the same as chimps and bonobos, but among the differences is a gene that keeps our cortex growing much longer, so that it becomes about three times as large as that of other same-size primates. Most of this brain growth occurs after we are born, making us more susceptible to social conditioning and cultural norms. In addition, one of the advantages of a larger cortex is better impulse inhibition, which allows delayed response and self-control. One can imagine different outcomes instead of immediately acting, enabling more conscious choice (rather than an instinctual reaction) and granting us a flexibility—a freedom—not available to other species.[86]

Dependence on parents and other caregivers during our exceptionally long childhood and adolescence conditions us to defer to authority figures. They provide models for much of our behavior, and our still-growing brains sop it up. Better than any other species, human infants learn to *share attention*, which makes us uniquely skilled at acquiring a variety of skills from others, preeminently language. We became a *symbolic species*: our oversized brains enable us to use—and sometimes become ensnared by—symbol systems.

Mimesis remains a distinctive trait of our species, both physically and cognitively. As Samuel Butler put it, "We think as we do mainly because other people think so."[87] For better and worse, we learn from others how to live: what to believe, what to value, and what to seek. Insofar as this is conditioned by socialization rather than genetics, however, there is the possibility of changing one's beliefs and lifestyle—a possibility that can be in tension with social expectations and group harmony.

This led to important genetic changes among those doing the conditioning. For biological evolution, parents are unnecessary once the offspring become independent, so there is little selection pressure to extend their lives. (A possible exception is postmenopausal grandmothers, who can assist inexperienced mothers.) With cultural evolution, however, there is more information to transmit, as well as an enhanced ability (language!) to help transmit it. Knowledge became heritable. Slower aging was selected for as elders became the repositories of experience and expertise, a role that became a little less crucial only when writing developed, and later print.

The most important social factor encouraging self-domestication was probably the fierce egalitarianism of hunting-gathering societies. Nomadic foragers were (and are) very concerned to maintain their freedom from the authority of would-be dominators. According to the anthropologist and primatologist Christopher Boehm, they do this by joining together to disobey, ridicule, shun, and if necessary kill aspiring alpha males.

By resisting the development of a privileged hierarchy, most males could have a mate. These ways of responding to bullies also made the bullies less attractive as partners, and tended to remove their belligerent traits from the gene pool. Social selection favored the genes of those who were generous, more even tempered, and less aggressive. One interesting consequence is the widespread tendency of hunting-gathering groups to share equally the meat of any large animal killed by any of its members; the successful hunter usually does not even supervise the distribution. The best hunters are not allowed to claim any special social status that would elevate them over others.

Among most primate groups, the main mechanism that bonds members is physical grooming, such as picking ticks and other small insects from the fur of others. There seems to be a direct correlation between the size of the group and the amount of time spent on mutual grooming. As groups become larger, however, this can become problematic. Was there another way for humans to achieve the same bonding? Robin Dunbar has argued that language may have evolved as a "cheap" form of "vocal grooming" that serves a similar function for us, enabling us to cultivate relationships—including gossip.[88]

Dunbar has also proposed that with primates and carnivores there is a strong correlation between the size of the brain and the average size of the social group: the larger the group, the larger the brain relative to the whole body, and the larger the neocortex in relation to the whole brain. Extrapolating for humans, our extra-large neocortex predicts a mean group size of about 150 people. Dunbar and others have contended that this is the upper limit of the number of stable relationships one can maintain—when everyone knows who each person is and their relationships with other people. Although there is considerable evidence for "Dunbar's number" among traditional human cultures, it remains controversial. Even if that number is imprecise, early groups of hunter-gatherers were obviously miniscule in size compared to human societies today. If our forebrain evolved to meet the challenge of living in such communities during our long history as hunters and foragers, we should not be surprised if evolutionary adaptations that developed during that period became problematic when we settled down and developed. . .

## Civilization

Agriculture (soon followed by pastoralism) involved the greatest transformation in human history. It was not only a technological but a cultural revolution that created endless new possibilities and unique social problems—some of which have never been solved. In contrast to the hundreds of thousands of years that we survived and often thrived as hunter-gatherers, settled agrarian civilizations apparently developed relatively quickly once they began to form. One of the main implications of evolutionary psychology is that, although our genome is evolving more quickly than ever today, agriculture and pastoralism have happened too recently to have had a significant effect on our genes. Is that why we struggle to cope with what is now an interdependent worldwide civilization of over eight billion people?

Agriculture increased the food supply, and thereby the population, but the price was high. Although it could provide up to five times as many calories as hunting-gathering, the variety and quality of foodstuffs worsened. Average height and overall health declined. According to James Neel, "The advent of civilization dealt a blow to man's health from which he is only now recovering."[89] Nomadic hunter-gatherers share food because it cannot be saved. They normally work only a few hours a day. Unnecessary possessions are a burden because everything must be portable. Sedentism enables food storage and property accumulation, but the opportunity to save is shadowed by the possibility of loss from fire, floods, vermin, spoilage, and other threats. And who controls that surplus? Oppressive social stratification develops, along with division of labor. A few end up with many more possessions than others. In place of the adventuresome independence and self-reliance of egalitarian hunter-gatherers, people become more compliant, defined and confined by their role as laborers—and there is a lot of work to be done, starting with the fields. Commoners are subject to taxation, conscription, and increasing bureaucracy. Authority is top-down: rulers now live in guarded palaces where they are protected from anyone who might become disgruntled. Centralized power has been called the great curse of history. War becomes more organized, more violent, and more profitable once there is more to plunder.

From the perspective of a global civilization now suffering from planetary degradation, the most important change is that agriculture and pastoralism led to a very different relationship with the rest of the natural world. For the first time in the history of the earth, cultural evolution enabled a species to restructure—and even destroy—its own local ecosystems. According to Paul Shepard,

> In the archaeological residue of the Mesopotamian states there is evidence of ox-drawn carts, trade, writing, slaves, wars, and theocratic kingships. During this same period there was debilitation of the total natural complex, pillaged ecosystems that never recovered. The signs of this were the local extinction of large wild mammals, deserts replacing forests, the degradation of grasslands and disappearance of soil, the instability of streams and drying up of springs, and the depletion of land fertility—all of which affected water supply, climate, and economy. The creeping dereliction was largely invisible then, as it seems to be extraneous now.[90]

Hunting-gathering relies on the gifts of nature: the wild animals available to be hunted, the fruit and nuts that miraculously ripen every year. With agriculture, nature as a generous parent was replaced by manipulation of the environment, leading to "a very different kind of spirituality characterized by a separation from and distrust of nature," which generated "the anxiety over cosmic disorder that seems to lie at the core of all the agrarian religions."[91] Indigenous forms of shamanism were replaced by more collective and hierarchical religion. Instead of being a part of something greater, and the humility associated with that, now humans are special because we are the apex dominator of all other species—of our whole ecosystem. Is the dissociation and alienation from the natural world that began then the root of our ecological predicament today?

> We master movers of the world, progressing by expanding our power, seem outside the choreographed order of things. Daily life is less ordered by customs associated with the sun or moon, the seasons are not celebrated, anniversaries are minimized, festival occasions are commercialized, and the holding strength of tradition is more tenuous. There are fewer confirmations of kinship in terms of either social or ecological ties. This discordance of personal life is highly stressful. Events do not memorialize or reanimate familiar patterns. In seeking change we perpetuate the problem in more change and more fragmentation. Modern culture not only magnifies this dislocation but perceives it as the human condition. The traditional role of participatory religion, making the cosmos whole, has eroded.[92]

Of course, agriculture and pastoralism have never really been independent of natural ecosystems, as has become more obvious today, to our chagrin. The exhausted soils of the Middle East and the Mediterranean (home to many of the earliest civilizations) bear mute witness to the hubris of short-term exploitation leading to long-term collapse.

This degradation may have influenced the way that religions—an essential part of cultural evolution—eventually developed. "All forms of escape from the earth—and the corollary of escape from the physical body—were probably unconsciously motivated by the desire to escape the degradation of the land, which began in Mesopotamia some eight thousand years ago."[93] In light of that degradation, and likely combined with something more existential, such as the fear of death—how wonderful to learn that we don't really die, that the soul can transcend the body and qualify for eternity in a better place.

## Religion

Today we usually associate religion with postmortem salvation: the liberated soul is released from this world and can attain immortality in a superior realm that may be vaguely described but is certainly better than here. Yet religions did not offer such a blissful escape from this vale of tears until relatively recently. For most of our history, they served a different function: preserving the status quo with rituals that focused on harmony and social stability, not salvation or enlightenment.

This difference highlights an important point: the role of religion in our cultural evolution has changed, which reminds us that it may do so again.

Although religions naturally claim that their belief systems are objectively true and their rituals necessary, doctrines and practices can also be viewed in terms of their evolutionary function. Religions became so important because they have adaptive value. They promote ways of thinking and acting that have been biologically and socially significant, helping us to survive and reproduce successfully. Today, however, that function prompts an unavoidable question. If our historical development has radically changed the circumstances of our collective life on earth, does that mean that the role of religion needs to change too? How might religion help us understand and respond to a world on the brink of ecological collapse and other forms of self-destruction?

The earliest agrarian religions were not like religions in our modern sense of the term: they were so tightly integrated into everyday life that they were not perceived as separable from other human affairs such as politics and economics. Our contemporary distinction between church and state, which continues to be so problematic today, would have made no sense to archaic societies. Modern religious teachings promote ethical behavior by grounding it in a transcendent reward-and-punishment judicial system, but that function was not necessary in hunting-gathering groups when everyone was more or less aware of what other members got up to, and where adaptive social emotions such as empathy, fairness, shame, anger, and revenge were already well developed. If you abused one of my children, you needn't worry about God's view of the situation; you had more immediate trouble with me and my family. (Outsiders were a different problem and not usually entitled to moral consideration.) In some ways, religion was more like a proto-science, attempting to explain the natural world in terms of supernatural forces and exert some control over it, using sacrifices and other rituals.

That usually worked well enough for small groups, which, again, were the fundamental unit of human society for well over 90 percent of our species' history. With agrarian civilizations, however, the social group expanded to the point where one might regularly encounter people one did not already know. How could social harmony be maintained? Societies with frequent anonymous interactions ended up outsourcing punishment to gods. The nature gods of hunter-gatherers were not usually concerned about the morality or fate of humans, and in fact were hardly good moral exemplars themselves, which is why they had to be bribed with sacrifices and other rituals. In contrast, the new agrarian "big gods"—who are aware of everything you do—prescribe ethical principles and punish transgressions. Varuna, for example, was originally an Indian sky god, but by the time of the Rg Veda his main role had become watching humans and punishing those who violated the sacred law. This supported a necessary psychological development. "Civilization is the detribalization of *blood* ties and the resocialization of distinct individuals based on *associational* ties. Empathic extension is the psychological mechanism that makes the conversion and the transition possible."[94] As Darwin put it in *The Descent of Man*:

> As man advances in civilization, and small tribes are united
> into larger communities, the simplest reason would tell each

individual that he ought to extend his social instincts and sympathies to all members of the same nation, though personally unknown to him. This point being once reached, there is only an artificial barrier to prevent his sympathies extending to the men of all nations and races.[95]

As an abolitionist against slavery, Darwin also saw the problem with this: "If, indeed, such men are separated from him by great differences in appearance or habits, experience unfortunately shows us how long it is, before we look at them as our fellow creatures."

Artificial or not, that last barrier has endured for quite a while, but in the meantime religion came to serve some other functions, including stabilizing the new class system by legitimating its hierarchy. According to Carlo Levi, "The farther the state is removed from each individual, . . . the more it breeds an all-pervasive sense of sacredness."[96] As the size of the social group grew, so did the role of ceremonies and ritualism. In addition to sacralizing the codes of conduct that were necessary for this new type of society to function, religion justified the differences between privileged classes and commoners. Elites were in control because they *should* be in control. "Investing arbitrary social conventions with sanctity made them seem natural— as if they were reflections of human nature—and this sanctification became a force justifying power relationships within society."[97] And as social hierarchy developed, the plethora of animistic nature spirits also became organized into a vertical pantheon of deities, with their own kings and queens and courts. Group rituals were replaced by exclusive ceremonies that could be performed only by the ruler or high priests.

With the early agrarian empires, the authority of rulers extended beyond politics because they were also at the apex of the religious hierarchy. According to Robert Bellah, "The king, whether as incarnation, son, or servant of the gods, is the key link between humans and the cosmos such that the weakness or absence of the king is a sign of profound cosmic and social disorder; the proper functioning of the king is the primary guarantee of life and peace."[98] This type of polity, which will be discussed in the next chapter, seems strange to us because the distinction between church and state, the sacred and secular realms, has become so basic to modern nation-states—at least in principle. Yet until recently the Japanese emperor was divine, and the Thai king still becomes a living god when he is consecrated. The official head of the Anglican Church remains the British monarch—only a ceremonial role today, but not during the reign of Henry VIII or his daughter Elizabeth. And given the role of Judaism in Israel, and Islam in many Middle Eastern countries, those cannot be considered secular states.

The religion of hunter-gatherers is nature itself: they worshiped the things they depended upon or feared, such as the sun, the moon, the winds, powerful animals, and so forth. With civilization the focus shifted from nature to nation. What Thorkild Jacobsen noticed about Mesopotamia applies to archaic empires generally: the cosmos came to be viewed as a state, and the state as an essential part of the cosmos.[99] Over time, most local shrines and sacred springs disappeared or were converted into temples and churches, as the old animistic gods transmuted into civic ones. Sargon's Enlil transformed into the deification of the Sumerian city of Nippur; the Nanna that his daughter served, originally a moon divinity, became the goddess of Ur; the water-god Poseidon eventually metamorphosed into the deity of Corinth; the olive goddess Athena came to symbolize Athens; and so forth. With such conversions the spirit world became more distant from the natural world, a bifurcation that would eventually evacuate nature of its intrinsic value, making it something for us to exploit rather than venerate.

As Arnold Toynbee put it, "the local communities became divinities, and these divinities that stand for the collective human power became paramount over the divinities that stand for natural forces. The injection of this amount of religious devotion into nationalism has turned nationalism into a religion, and a fanatical one." In his view, the most problematical form of groupism today is only a larger version of the Sumerian city-state nationalism that developed in the third millennium BCE. If, as Toynbee also claimed, "nationalism is ninety percent of the religion of ninety percent of the people of the Western world and of the rest of the world as well,"[100] then church is not actually separate from state because the state functions as a god. In effect, our national flag has become a religious symbol, which is why so many people are outraged when it is burned or otherwise "desecrated."

## Why Our Evolutionary Psychology Matters Today

With every year that passes it becomes more obvious that ecological catastrophe threatens the survival of civilization as we know it. So why does humanity continue to find it so difficult to respond appropriately? There are many issues, but the roots of the problem can be found in our psychology, which like our physiology is a product of biological and cultural evolution.

One contributing factor is the way we experience time: we have evolved to prioritize short-term problems over long-term ones. Whether we will eat tomorrow is less urgent than the bear that is sniffing around the entrance to our cave, but what we will have to eat tomorrow is more important than anything that may happen next year. For most of human history, our foresight did not normally need to extend much beyond one cycle of the seasons. Today the earth's changing climate—a comparatively abstract challenge—is naturally experienced as less threatening than the immediate physical and mental well-being of one's family. If you lose your job or one of your children is in the hospital, it's not the ecological crisis that you'll be worrying about.

Other answers are implicit in the overview of evolutionary psychology presented above. Let's begin by appreciating that you and I, like all other human beings living today, are offspring of many generations of parents who (obviously) survived to reproduce and raise their children, who, when they matured, were able to do the same. For you and me to be born, this had to happen successfully again and again, despite all the dangers of childbirth, starvation, predators, war, natural disasters—in short, against all odds. Anatomically modern humans developed about 150,000 years ago, which means there have been roughly 7,500 generations of *Homo sapiens*. The uninterrupted success of your and my ancestors required some luck, of course, but not only luck: to say it again, natural selection worked on genetic variation to produce and reproduce traits that have helped us survive and thrive. As biological evolution enabled cultural evolution, people who were better at living and working harmoniously with others gained an advantage that made them more likely to reproduce successfully. According to Nicholas Christakis,

> Once cultural transmission became possible, our species faced circumstances favoring brains that were capable of learning and teaching, including brains that could respect norms, copy models, or transmit information. In turn, as humans came increasingly to rely on the knowledge of others, they became even friendlier and kinder so that they could take full advantage of culture in order to survive. Culture builds on, and reinforces, our evolved capacity for making a good society.[101]

Important as this evolved capacity has been, it obviously has not replaced competition among individuals. As we have noticed, that rivalry might need to pause if one's group were fighting against another group, but it would reemerge when the external threat disappeared. "When within-group pressure is the stronger force, then evil triumphs over good. There is no warrant for a worldview that claims that nature writ large embodies goodness. Goodness only emerges when between-group selection pressures outweigh within-group selection pressures."[102] And that tension between within-group selection and between-group selection points to a big problem—in fact, it is *the* big problem: within-group selection did sometimes reward selfishness, greed, and aggression, all in the service of looking out for one's own individual interests. As those traits became encoded in our genome, along with different genes that promoted cooperation, the result was multilevel selection that promoted group competition or individual rivalry, depending on the situation.

Whether or not "greed, for lack of a better word, is good," does it "capture the essence of the evolutionary spirit," as Gordon Gecko famously proclaimed in the film *Wall Street*? To reinforce what was said earlier, the short answer is yes, in part because individual acquisitiveness sometimes rewards individual "fitness." In adverse conditions, for example, it could be advantageous to possess more stuff—and who knows when adverse conditions may occur? Is it a coincidence that during the COVID-19 pandemic many of us allayed our anxiety by buying more things? The same is true for aggression. The human propensity for violence (shared with most other primates) is not some blind, irrational instinct but an adaptation that is sometimes advantageous for achieving our goals, not only for capturing prey but also for fighting against other groups and sometimes against rivals, sexual and otherwise, within one's own group.

These two traits function in the way they do because they support two basic delusions that have been important to our evolutionary success: that *I* am special, and that *we* are special. Robert Wright explains the first one well:

> If inside me are genes that were selected because they've been good at getting copies of themselves into the next generation, then job one for these genes will be to take care of the vehicle that can carry them there—that is, my body. And that means my genes will build into my brain the idea that taking care of this body is much more important than taking care of other bodies (except, perhaps, when those other bodies belong to close kind). In other words, I'm special. My specialness lies very near the heart of natural selection's value system.[103]

Not only my specialness, but *our* specialness. This bias for both individual and collective selfishness, along with the two traits mentioned above, contributed to our reproductive success. Note an important but questionable belief built into both behaviors: that my own well-being is separate from that of others in our group, and that our collective well-being is separate from that of other groups. For biological evolution the bottom line has always been perpetuating one's genes, and if that involves exploitation and suffering—well, we remember that process does not prioritize the happiness of anyone involved.

Is it a coincidence that such acquisitiveness, aggression, and selfishness correspond closely to what Buddhism identifies as the three poisons: greed, ill will, and delusion? These three—also known as the three fires, or the three unwholesome motivations—are what Buddhist teachings highlight in place of the duality between good and evil emphasized in the Abrahamic religions. For Buddhism the basic problem is not sin but suffering born of ignorance. The Buddhist understanding of karma focuses especially on the role of one's intentions and basic motivations, due to the habitual actions that usually follow from them. To reduce suffering, the three poisons need to be transformed into more wholesome character traits: greed into generosity, ill will into loving-kindness, and the delusion of a separate self into the wisdom that appreciates our interdependence.

Traditional Buddhist teachings view the three poisons as personal problems, to be addressed individually by following the Buddhist path to self-transformation and enlightenment. Yet it is not difficult to think of historical instances when the three poisons have operated and cooperated on a social scale. A good example is European colonization of the New World. Technologies such as gunpowder enabled Europeans to conquer and exploit the Americas. Their aggression was in service of greed (initially for gold and silver) and rationalized by their assumption of cultural superiority. We are bringing Christian salvation to the heathen!

# The Three Poisons, Institutionalized

There is, however, no need to reach back half a millennium, because the same three collective poisons continue to function well today. In fact, greed, ill will, and delusion are more powerful than ever, because they have been institutionalized and, in the process, rationalized.

On an individual level insatiable greed—"never enough"—is readily perceived as immature or worse, but when systematized into corporate capitalism and consumerism we accept it as normal, and governments are of course preoccupied with economic growth. Personal aggression against other people is normally deplorable as well as illegal, even if they are not members of the tribe we identify with, but the violent militarism of one's own nation-state (and often the racism of one's own group) is acceptable and often lauded. While individual ignorance is recognized as an educational problem, today prominent segments of the media promote institutionalized delusion and collective anger, which by no coincidence tend to serve the goals of elites who seek to influence the political process in their own favor.

To understand what has happened, consider what is called "regulatory capture," when governmental agencies are dominated by the industries they are supposed to supervise. Their authority is thereby corrupted because special interests have priority over the general benefit to the public. Classic examples in the United States include the Federal Communications Commission (FCC), accused of acting on behest of media conglomerates, and the Securities and Exchange Commission (SEC), captive to the interests of Wall Street banks and hedge funds. But these instances of malfeasance are minor compared to what might be called "governmental capture," which occurs in two main forms. In less developed nations, where political institutions are often fragile, military coups are common. Western democracies are more susceptible to subversion by corporate power and extremely wealthy people, especially when there are few limits on their ability to influence the political process, such as financial contributions to elections and ownership of media. The United States is nominally a democracy, in that democratic institutions and processes generally still function (elections, division of powers, and so on), but academic research confirms what has become obvious, that political decision making today serves not what most people want, but what corporations and multi-millionaires want.[104] And what do they want?

The inconvenient but increasingly obvious truth is that prioritizing profit and economic growth is ultimately incompatible with solving the climate crisis. According to Naomi Klein, "What the climate needs to avoid collapse is a contraction in humanity's use of resources; what our economic model demands to avoid collapse is unfettered expansion. Only one of these sets of rules can be changed, and it's not the laws of nature."[105] Today it has become difficult for most of us to imagine an alternative to corporate capitalism, but our present economic system is only a few hundred years old. As Karl Polanyi explained in *The Great Transformation*, its development required a radically new way of understanding the world and our role in it: the earth became commodified into a source of resources (minerals, land for agriculture), people commodified into labor ("wage slaves"), and money into capital for investment (money breeds more money). In the process, each of them became revalued (or devalued) into a means contributing to the goal of increasing profitability and sustained growth.

Their collaboration has been sanctified as the best possible economic system: individuals acting in their own self-interest end up serving the best interests of society as a whole, as if Adam Smith's "invisible hand" were promoting the collective well-being. A less sanguine view has been proffered by John Maynard Keynes, who defined capitalism as "the astonishing belief that the nastiest motives of the nastiest men somehow or other work for the best results in the best of all possible worlds."[106] In either case, these commodifications are so familiar to us that we usually take them for granted, but our inability to control their interaction—to set limits on economic growth and make it more equitable—goes a long way toward explaining the ecological and social predicaments we face today. The basic problem is that this complicated process has taken on a life of its own: our economic system institutionalizes greed, our militarism is the foremost (but certainly not the only) example of institutionalized ill will, and for-profit corporate media institutionalize delusion.

If, as Aristotle said, acquisitiveness has no natural limit—if greed means *never having enough*—then, despite all its benefits, our now-globalized economy institutionalizes greed in several ways. Most obviously, corporations are never profitable enough, their market share is never large enough, and their share price is never high enough. People are conditioned into always wanting more, finding the meaning of life in shopping and consumption. And national GDP must keep increasing, of course. But why is "more and more" always better if it can never be enough?

It is important to realize that this "never enough" system is not created or maintained by some greedy individuals—although they have a role to play, of course. It's how corporations are designed to function. Even if the CEO of a transnational company wants to be socially responsible, he (it's usually a man) is limited by the expectations of stockholders. If profits are threatened by his concern for the environment, he is likely to lose his job. Corporations get their name because they are legally incorporated, which means they are social fictions, forms of *impersonal* collective self that are very good at preserving themselves and increasing their power, quite apart from any personal concerns of the individuals who serve them. This system molds the type of people it needs: those willing to do whatever is necessary to rise to the top.

The stock market functions to dilute responsibility for the actual consequences of the anonymized greed that fuels economic growth. Investors want increasing returns in the form of dividends and higher share prices. That's all that most of them care about or need to care about—not because investors are bad people, but because the system doesn't encourage any other kind of responsibility. This generalized expectation translates into an impersonal but constant pressure for profitability, preferably in the short run. The globalization of corporate capitalism means that this emphasis on profit and growth has become the engine of the world's economic activity. Everything else, including the health of the biosphere and the quality of most peoples' lives, tends to become subordinated to this demand for ever more, a goal that can never be satisfied.

Who is responsible for the pressure for growth, and who can reduce it? That's the point about institutionalization: this system has attained a life of its own. We all participate in this process, as workers, employers, consumers, investors, and pensioners, usually without any sense of responsibility for the larger consequences. Such awareness has been diffused so completely that it is lost in the anonymity of the economic system.

There are comparable problems with the second poison, institutionalized aggression. Critical race theory claims that racism is not simply a function of personal prejudice but is inherent in U.S. institutions—especially the criminal justice system, which incarcerates vast numbers of people, the majority of whom are poor or people of color or both. One could also point to our treatment of refugees and undocumented immigrants, but the most problematic example of systemic violence, by far, is militarism. Measured by the power of our military forces, and all the resources devoted to them, the United States is the most militarized nation in history. We continue to lavish as much money on our armed forces as the next dozen or so countries combined: if related budgets such as Homeland Security and Veterans Affairs are included, well over a trillion dollars a year. The need to "defend ourselves" apparently requires almost a thousand overseas military installations, as well as more than 900 domestic ones. No wonder relatively little is left for social services.

To justify its expense, the military needs an enemy. Thus the end of the Cold War with the Soviet bloc created a big problem for the Pentagon, but the "war on terror" solved it. It is already the longest war in our history, by far, and it may never come to an end. Using drones to assassinate suspects, along with any unfortunates who happen to be nearby, ensures that we continue to produce a dependable supply of angry people who have good reason to hate the United States. If terrorism is the war of the poor and disempowered, it is because war is the terrorism of the rich.

The ecological consequences of our militarism are often unnoticed but they are considerable. The Pentagon is the single largest consumer of energy in the United States, and probably in the world. While a non-nuclear aircraft carrier consumes 5,621 gallons of fuel per hour, a single F-16 jet (the U.S. Air Force has about a thousand of them) consumes about 1,700 gallons per hour—much more if the afterburners are engaged. In the 1990s the three branches of the military together used about 25 billion tons of fossil fuel per year, more than a fifth of total consumption in the United States and more than the commercial energy consumption of at least two-thirds of the world's nations. In addition to these carbon emissions, the Department of Defense continues to produce about 300,000 tons of toxic waste every year, which is more than the amount generated by the top five U.S chemical companies combined.[107]

Can all this expense and pollution be rationalized as the price of our role as "the world's policeman," unfortunate but necessary to preserve peace and foster democracy? Actually, we are okay with oppressive regimes and authoritarian rulers—for example, the kings of Saudi Arabia—as long as they do not obstruct our access to the minerals and other resources we covet. We did not invade Iraq in 2002 because Saddam Hussein threatened Europe with nuclear missiles; it was not a coincidence that Iraq just happens to have a lot of oil. The resource sought may be different from what the Spanish conquistadors wanted, but the parallel is otherwise valid.

The best account of this type of institutionalized aggression remains the extraordinary admission of Major General Smedley D. Butler, the most decorated marine in U.S. history, in his 1935 book *War Is a Racket*:

> I spent thirty-three years and four months in active military service and during that period I spent most of my time as a high class muscle man for Big Business, for Wall Street and

the bankers. In short, I was a racketeer, a gangster for capitalism. I helped make Mexico and especially Tampico safe for American oil interests in 1914. I helped make Haiti and Cuba a decent place for the National City Bank boys to collect revenues in. I helped in the raping of half a dozen Central American republics for the benefit of Wall Street. I helped purify Nicaragua for the International Banking House of Brown Brothers in 1902–1912. I brought light to the Dominican Republic for the American sugar interests in 1916. I helped make Honduras right for the American fruit companies in 1903. In China in 1927 I helped see to it that Standard Oil went on its way unmolested. Looking back on it, I might have given Al Capone a few hints. The best he could do was to operate his racket in three districts. I operated on three continents.[108]

No wonder he was never promoted to Commandant of the Marine Corps.

A better-known military figure, General Douglas MacArthur, spoke at the 1957 annual meeting of the Sperry Rand Corporation:

Our swollen budgets constantly have been misrepresented to the public. Our government has kept us in a perpetual state of fear—kept us in a continuous stampede of patriotic fervor—with the cry of grave national emergency. Always there has been some terrible evil at home or some monstrous foreign power that was going to gobble us up if we did not blindly rally behind it by furnishing the exorbitant funds demanded. Yet, in retrospect, these disasters seem never to have happened, seem never to have been quite real.[109]

What MacArthur said then is no less true today, of course: today the grave national emergency is called "the war on terror," which apparently will continue forever.

Institutionalized greed and institutionalized aggression supplement each other. Smedley Butler's challenge to the official narrative—that we are the good guys of history, peacemakers promoting justice and democracy—brings us to the third collective poison, the institutionalization of delusion. An evolutionary perspective confirms why truth can be so elusive: as mentioned earlier, our ability to reason developed not to enable us to derive the correct conclusions from available facts, but to help us (that is, our group) live together—and sharing the same beliefs (or delusions) can promote social harmony, as the history of religions amply attests. While each of us lives inside our own bubble of delusions about ourselves and the world, we also dwell together within a much bigger bubble that largely determines how we collectively understand what the world is and how to live in it. Today the institution most responsible for molding our collective sense of self is the media, which comprises our national and international nervous system.

Recently we have become all too familiar with "fake news," and the isolation of pandemic lockdowns induced many into online rabbit holes that led to QAnon conspiracies, ivermectin COVID cures, or the stolen 2020 presidential election. Nonetheless, and without detracting from the role of the internet in aggravating political polarization and the "culture wars," the most successful examples of institutionalized delusion remain advertising and nationalist propaganda.

Genuine democracy requires an independent and activist press to expose abuse and debate political issues, but that is not the main function of our media today. Since they are with few exceptions profit-making institutions whose bottom line is advertising revenue, it is never in their own interest to question consumerism, much less the inherent superiority of our economic system and the American way of life.

According to Alex Carey, the twentieth century was characterized by three important political developments: the growth of democracy, the growth of corporate power, and the growth of propaganda as a way protect corporate power against democracy.[110] The tension between democracy and corporate power remains the defining issue of our times, at least in Western nations, underlying our inability to respond appropriately to the ecological crisis, as well as aggravating the enormous and still increasing disparity between the wealthy and the poor everywhere.

This way of understanding the three poisons—how greed, ill will, and delusion have been institutionalized—connects our dangerous situation with the legacy of our evolutionary psychology. The problems that confront us now can be traced back to adaptations that developed over thousands of generations because they contributed to the evolutionary fitness of certain individuals and thereby the success of our species. But how can recognizing that relationship help us address our predicament today?

This book began with Noam Chomsky's warning that now is the most dangerous time in human history: the ecological crisis, threat of nuclear war, and rising authoritarianism mean that the risk of widespread social breakdown is serious and getting worse. These are collective dangers, created not so much by the unwholesome motivations of individuals as by the unwholesome functioning of impersonal institutions, as described above. Yes, each of us needs to take personal responsibility for reducing our carbon footprint, but this challenge calls for something more than individual responses.

Understanding this most dangerous moment as rooted in our evolutionary psychology can feel discouraging. If our predilections for greed, aggression, and delusion are genetically based, then they are part of our human nature. But that does not imply that they will necessarily dominate, for they are not the only part. The inclination for prosociality, promoting our ability to live and work together, is another aspect of our human nature that over time has become genetically encoded (remembering the Baldwin effect). Because humans are pulled both ways, that tension between them allows for choice and opens up the possibility of freedom. This is an especially important reminder that what we do is determined not by nature (genetics) or nurture (culture) but by their interaction.

That is the context for the next chapter, which will focus on one of the most important aspects of cultural evolution: religion. Understanding our evolutionary psychology—the consequences of natural selection for how our minds work—also helps us understand why religion has developed in the way it has. The historical conflict between religious belief and evolutionary biology has sometimes obscured the fact that religions also evolve. This chapter has already noticed one important example: the transformation of hunter-gatherer animistic gods (indifferent to human concerns) into the ever-watchful big gods of agrarian empires. As those earlier deities transmuted, their functions changed too, from natural forces to be propitiated to supernatural beings upholding the moral order by punishing transgressions and maintaining the hierarchical social structure.

During the first millennium BCE, a new type of religion originated in different places, which offered an innovative vision of the world and an alternative way of living in it. It took diverse forms in India, China, and the Middle East, but the similarities among them are so striking that they are often categorized together as *Axial Age* religions. They merit our attention because they can be viewed as attempts by cultural evolution to compensate for the psychological and social problems created by our biological evolution. Like it or not, acquisitiveness without limits (greed), aggression (ill will), and the belief that one is separate from others (delusion) have played significant roles in our evolution, but at this point in our civilizational and technological development these traits have become dangerous to our future—perhaps even to our survival. (That is in addition to the fact that, as psychologists emphasize, they do not make us happy.) Even as their individual versions are at the heart of our perennial personal problems, so their institutionalized versions are at the core of the collective problems that challenge us today.

So far, the Axial Age traditions—which still predominate today, of course—have had limited success in counterbalancing the three poisons. Evolutionary psychology can help us understand that, too: how those religions have ended up subverting their own original vision.

I used to think the top environmental problems were biodiversity loss, ecosystem collapse and climate change. I thought that with thirty years of good science we could address those problems. But I was wrong. The top environmental problems are selfishness, greed and apathy . . . and to deal with those we need a spiritual and cultural transformation . . . and we scientists don't know how to do that.

    **—Gus Speth**

The way we see the world shapes the way we treat it. If a mountain is a deity, not a pile of ore; if the forest is a sacred grove, not timber; if other species are biological kin, not resources; or if the planet is our mother, not an opportunity, then we will treat each other with greater respect. This is the challenge, to look at the world from a different perspective.

    **—David Suzuki**

Whatever we call reality, it is revealed to us only through an active construction in which we participate.

    **—Ilya Prigogine**

The greatest illusion in this world is the illusion of separation.

  —Albert Einstein

*Homo sapiens* can justly be called the mythopoeic species. Human beings must have an epic, a sublime account of how the world was created and how humanity came to be part of it. . . . Religious epics satisfy another primal need. They confirm that we are part of something greater than ourselves.

  —Loyal Rue

Until today mankind has lived by what happened during the Axial Period, by what was thought and created during that period. In each new upward flight it returns in recollection to this period and is fired anew by it. Ever since then it has been the case that recollections and reawakenings of the potentialities of the Axial Period—renaissances—afford a spiritual impetus.

  —Karl Jaspers

Half the people in the world think that the metaphors of their religious traditions, for example, are facts. And the other half contends that they are not facts at all. As a result we have people who consider themselves believers because they accept metaphors as facts, and we have others who classify themselves as atheists because they think religious metaphors are lies.

—Joseph Campbell

Praying to an otherworldly God is like kissing through glass.

—Paul West

For two thousand years man has been living in a dead or dying cosmos, hoping for a heaven hereafter. And all the religions have been religions of the dead body and the postponed reward.

—D. H. Lawrence

There are no unsacred places;
there are only sacred places
and desecrated places.

—Wendell Berry

The bad news is, there is no key to the universe. The good news is, it has been left unlocked.

—Swami Beyondananda

# 2
# What We Could Have Learned from Our Religions

## *How to Transform*

> It cannot possibly be an accident that, six hundred years before Christ, Zarathustra in Persia, Gautama Buddha in India, Confucius in China, the prophets in Israel, King Numa [Pompilius] in Rome and the first philosophers—Ionians, Dorians and Eleatics—in Greece, all made their appearance pretty well simultaneously as reformers of the national religion.
>
> **—Ernst von Lasaulx,**
> *A New Attempt at a Philosophy of History* (1856)

VON LASAULX WAS ONTO SOMETHING (and he could have added more names to his list). In the middle of the first millennium BCE, innovations both extraordinary and extraordinarily similar occurred in most of the world's major civilizations. Taken as a whole, they constitute the most important religious transformation in human history—even though it remains incomplete, never having been fully integrated into how we actually live. This momentous development also remains mysterious: How did it happen independently in places far apart from each other?

The Axial Age—to use the umbrella term Karl Jaspers later gave it—radically changed the ways we understand and practice religion. "It is there that we meet with the most deep-cut dividing line in history. Man, as we know him today, came into being. . . . Until today mankind has lived by what happened during the Axial Period, by what was thought and created during that period."[111]

If humans are bipolar apes, it is not surprising that our religions are also bipolar, vehicles for our best and worst tendencies. One way to understand Axial Age developments is that they were *attempts* by cultural evolution to compensate for problems created by our biological evolution. I emphasize *attempts* because our social and ecological predicament today reflects that ongoing struggle between biological inheritance and cultural development. Our present situation also reveals how unsuccessful the Axial spiritual traditions have been. If humanity survives the next thousand years, I suspect that our times will be viewed as a historic moment when the tension between biology and culture came to a head. One way or another, the consequences of their present encounter for the future of our species and our planet will be great.

A modern way to express an essential Axial point is that the sense of self we usually take for granted is a psychological and social construct that needs to be reconstructed. This is where religion comes in—or at least it should. Of course, religion today is usually understood more narrowly; it assuages our fear of death by reassuring us that we don't really die, and that if we do what we are told then we can qualify for a beatific afterlife. Ironically, our religious traditions often promote selflessness as a means to achieve a self-centered goal: my own blissful eternity with God in heaven, and so on. Nonetheless, Axial religions have offered guidelines and practices that can help us negotiate the tension created by our evolutionary legacy of (egocentric) individual selection versus (somewhat more altruistic) group selection.

Today, however, personal reconstruction needs to be accompanied by another realization: that our now-global civilization—including predominant economic and political institutions—also needs to be reconstructed. This is not a modern insight. Until recently, the quest for individual salvation and the struggle for a collective redemption—a recent example is Martin Luther King Jr.'s dream of a blessed community—have usually been two sides of the same Axial impulse to remake the world according to a transcendent vision. Although our now-individualized religions provide less guidance here, secular developments during the last few centuries show that such institutional makeovers are possible. And the urgency of our predicament today makes them necessary.

## The Axial Age

> Axial Age thinkers, such as Plato; the Hebrew prophets, Second Isaiah, Jeremiah, and Ezekiel; Confucius; Mencius; the authors of the Hindu Upanishads, and the Buddha, created alternative ideological systems to counteract and protest the empire and politics. They developed moral and legal systems outside the prevailing military and social structures of their day. These systems criticized the status quo and offered an ethical and often religious option rooted in humane values, such as personal responsibility to others, benevolence, virtue, compassion, justice, wisdom, and righteousness (dharma). This relativizing of the state and its cults brought human subjectivity and personal morality back into the center of religion—the covenant of the heart in Jeremiah, the Confucian virtuous gentleman, the Platonic wise sage, and the Buddhist enlightened monk—effectively undercutting rigid class stratifications and the power of temple cults.
>
> **—Rita Nakashima Brock and Susan Brooks**
> **Thistlethwaite,** *Casting Stones*

Because we have been living in the wake of the Axial (in the sense of "pivotal") Age transformation for over two thousand years and usually take it for granted, it can be difficult to appreciate what actually happened and how significant it was. We need to begin by recognizing the historical and cultural context within which Axial religions arose.

The previous chapter emphasized that, prior to these new spiritual traditions, religion as we know it today did not exist because it was normally indistinguishable from the state. The archaic civilizations of Mesopotamia, Egypt, India, and China—along with the pre-Columbian Inca, Maya, and Aztec empires later conquered by Europeans—did not differentiate between political and religious authority. Worldly monarchs were also sacred figures: often divine or semidivine, but in any case, functioning as the agents of gods. Commoners might worship lesser deities and nature spirits at local shrines, but their rulers served as the supreme mediators, conduits between human society and the major gods. According to Robert Bellah,

> He [the priest-king] was a god who was also a man, for he represented humans to the gods as well as the gods to humans. His arbitrary power and oppression of the common people over whom he ruled represent a remarkable breakdown of tribal egalitarianism and a return of a particularly harsh form of despotism, made possible by the increasing size of the social unit with its attendant loss of face-to-face community, by the increased surplus due to agricultural intensification, and by the rise of militarism now that there was so much to fight over.[112]

Shang China (ca. 1600–1046 BCE) exemplifies this fusion of church and state. The king was the son of Heaven (Tian), having inherited a mandate giving him special powers and responsibilities that he transmitted to his feudal subordinates. He was the only person permitted to approach Shangdi, the High God, to offer sacrifices and seek advice using oracle bone divination. After his death he too became divine, living with Shangdi in a vaguely defined heaven. Further west, Egyptian pharaohs were direct offspring of the sun god Ra. In Mesopotamia, Sargon of Akkade declared that in his conquest of Sumerian cities he was an agent of the wind-god Enlil, and he installed his daughter as high priestess at the shrine of the goddess Nanna in Ur.

The Egyptian language did not have a separate term for what we call religion, although it had many words for religious functions: gods, priests, worship, and so on. All aspects of daily life were infused with religious beliefs and symbolism. "Drama was religious in nature, tombs and temples were viewed as microcosms of a supernaturally animated universe and decorated accordingly."[113]

For pre-Axial civilizations the universe is not a function of something like scientific law but a manifestation of supernatural power, controlled by humanlike deities.[114] Unlike the all-powerful Abrahamic God of Genesis, who in the beginning made heaven and earth out of nothing, creation was usually understood as the construction of order out of primeval chaos, achieved by a heroic deity. The Babylonian epic *Enum Elish* tells the story of the storm god Marduk, who became king of the gods by defeating the sea goddess Tiamat and fashioning heaven and earth out of her dismembered body. But such victories were not permanent. The Shang king was preoccupied with maintaining the natural order of the universe with rituals that ensured human society was harmonious with the Way (Dao) of Heaven. As in Vedic India, Mesopotamia, Egypt, and with the civilizations of the New World, there was always the threat of disintegration back into chaos, which would happen without constant sacrifices and other rites to renew the depleted energies of the gods and the natural world they supervised.

Such ceremonies were how archaic cultures kept connection with the spiritual ground of the cosmos. They did more than reaffirm a collective understanding of the world: rituals did not just *symbolize* reality, they constructed and maintained it. "Ritual forms the naturally formless, it connects the inherently disconnected, and it heals the ontological disease of unreconstructed nature, the state toward which all created things and beings perpetually tend."[115]

Such rites fulfilled an important role. It was commonly believed that humankind had been created to serve the gods and preserve the precarious natural order they had created. In Egypt, rituals were conducted constantly, day and night. In principle this was the responsibility of the pharaoh but they were usually delegated to priestly deputies. The Aztecs believed that the violent end of their "fifth sun" era could be postponed by offering sacrificial victims to the sun god, feeding him daily with human blood. Most archaic civilizations believed in some type of afterlife but it was understood as a continuation of this world, not a radically transcendent reality. Instead of an ontological separation between heaven and earth, there was a continuum between the natural world, the realm of the gods, and human society—because they were understood to be different parts of a single unified cosmos.

For pre-Axial civilizations the hierarchical structure of society was an important part of that natural order because it replicated the world of the gods which is also organized hierarchically. As the Assyriologist Thorkild Jacobsen put it, the cosmos was seen as a state, and the state as an essential part of the cosmos. Thus archaic religions sanctified class and caste systems, with priests and nobles firmly embedded in the same institutional structure. There was little if any tension between one's social role and one's religious responsibilities because they were basically the same. Sacrificing to divinities was like taxation by rulers, many of whom had descended from heaven themselves. Every war was a sacred campaign ordered by the gods, and kings went to their temples to report victories.

In sum, the function of religion was to help maintain the status quo, politically as well as cosmologically. According to Gregory Riley,

> It was not obvious that the world needed a savior originally (or, in fact, that it even could be saved). According to the myths and sacred stories of the old monistic cultures, before there were souls and the Devil, there was nothing particularly wrong with the way things were; the world was not lost and did not need to be saved. . . . Internal conflicts, such as they were, were more or less under control and not life-threatening on a cosmic scale. The world was a small, closed system controlled by the gods and designed to last forever just as it was.

Moreover, before people came to understand that they had souls, salvation would not have been possible in the Christian sense: there were no souls to save.[116]

Predictably, the social ethics promulgated and enforced by such sacralized states served the interests of elites and preserved their dominion. To revolt against the powers-that-be would amount to challenging the sacred foundations of society and disrupting its collective project: continually enacting the sacrifices and other rituals that were necessary to keep the cosmos functioning. This meant that morality was communal, not personal. Insofar as people were believed to survive death, their postmortem fate usually depended less on their previous conduct than on the offerings made by living humans (usually their descendants).[117] The gods themselves were not paragons of virtue, nor were they all that interested in what humans did. But they expected to be fed.

These sophisticated Bronze Age cultures thrived for almost two thousand years and then abruptly collapsed. Beginning in the twelfth century BCE, all the major Mediterranean and Near Eastern civilizations broke down and retribalized, along with the complex network of international trade routes connecting them. Greece experienced a dark age that lasted until about 800 BCE, the survivors "living in the ruins of their former civilization, no longer able to read or write."[118] The Hittite empire and the kingdoms of Troy, Minoa, and Mycenae all crumbled, along with the Canaanites and Cypriots. Assyria and the New Kingdom of Egypt survived, though much weakened. Within a fifty-year period almost every important city in the eastern Mediterranean was destroyed. Some rebounded to become city-states but many never recovered.

Although the decisive causes of this widespread disaster remain unclear, there were interconnected natural and social factors: powerful earthquakes, a centuries-long mega-drought causing famine and political unrest, broken supply chains, roaming bands of pirates and bandits, and a mysterious confederation of seafaring invaders who became known as the "Sea Peoples."

Further east, two other Bronze Age civilizations suffered similar fates: the Indus Valley (Harappan) civilization in northwest India and the Shang Dynasty that ruled the Yellow River valley in China. After centuries of decline, the Indus Valley civilization finally ended about 1300 BCE. Again, the causes are obscure, but there too was evidence of a mega-drought and a series of earthquakes. The Shang dynasty was conquered by the Zhou in 1046 BCE, which ruled for several hundred years but with decreasing centralized control over feudal warlords, leading to centuries of internecine warfare.

Waves of violence eroded traditional values. The political and social chaos of this era, after a long period of relative stability and prosperity, led to widespread dissatisfaction with traditional worldviews. Earlier, a burgeoning population, along with economic growth and expanded trading networks, had impacted kinship bonds: people were living in a world of strangers. "[T]he enormously disruptive effects of large-scale and rapid urbanization and the intensification of warfare during the second half of the first millennium BCE created new human needs for ontological security, anxiety reduction, and release from suffering."[119] What had gone wrong? What have we done to deserve this? The ancient world was ready for new visions of cosmic and moral order. If they involved an escape from this vale of tears—perhaps even the possibility of a blissful immortality somewhere else—so much the better.

Alternative revelations appeared in an unexpected way: not from sanctified rulers or their institutionalized priests, but from marginal figures who had been transformed by personal encounters with something outside the official social structure. Their new understanding devalued ceremonial and political duties in favor of innovative *ethical* demands that emphasized the accountability of each human being to a sacred reality that encompassed but also transcended this world.

In pre-Axial cultures the important rituals were conducted by rulers and high priests; the role of everyone else was to support them. Because people were *members* embedded in society, and society was embedded in its cosmic role, even rulers were bound by the traditional functions of their position.

According to the new Axial spirituality, however, each person could and should have a personal relationship with the sacred. Individuating morality created something new: *individuals* who were no longer defined and delimited by their social functions. Now each of us is unique. "For the very first time individuals, not collectives, are told that there is only one universal God that reigns over the universe, but that this God seeks a relationship with every human being."[120] Not all the Axial religions were theistic, but identifying with the new supernatural ideal enabled some individuals to disidentify from their traditional roles within the established social order. Long-established *communal values* such as loyalty, tradition, and order were challenged by new *universal values* emphasizing compassion and justice for everyone.

In the process, human consciousness experienced an unprecedented growth in interiority. The price of this growth, however, was the unprecedented responsibility that accompanied this new relationship, which burdened each person with the task of integrating one's religious obligations into daily life. It was no longer simply a matter of maintaining the cosmos by performing one's institutionally prescribed duties, mainly rituals. Now there was a sacred demand that we transform how we live. Greater individual freedom became shadowed by a burgeoning sense of personal inadequacy, often experienced as sin and guilt.

This crucial development occurred because the divine became transcendent, creating a radical disjunction between ultimate reality (God, Brahman, Nirvana, and so on) and reality as we normally experience it. Now this world is "fallen" in the sense that there is something inadequate and unsatisfactory about it, and

> new types of ontological visions emerged and were institutionalized. The development and institutionalization of such conceptions of a basic tension, or chasm, between the transcendental and mundane orders gave rise in all these civilizations to attempts to reconstruct the mundane world—human personality and the sociopolitical and economic order—according to the transcendental vision.[121]

In India, what humans usually experience and assume to be real was declared to be *maya*, illusory appearance. The original impulse behind these religious revolutions involved "tearing apart the archaic unity of creation and dominion, or cosmic and political power," as religion became "a means of emancipation from the politico-cosmological power structure of the ancient world."[122] No longer comfortably integrated into a unified cosmos, human consciousness became aware of a tension between life here and now and the pull of something that transcends here and now. This Axial Age duality between a now-problematical world and an otherworldly realm remains at the heart of every major religion today, each offering its own explanation for our dissatisfaction here and a way to escape it.

In other words, Axial Age religions created a new spiritual goal: *salvation*. For archaic civilizations, as for hunter-gatherers, no redeemer was needed, only a good shepherd: "everything is founded on the conviction that home is already Eden and that exile must be avoided."[123] Time is cyclic, the golden age is in the past, and our task is to preserve or recover what is always in danger of being lost.

For the new salvation religions, however, the bad news is that the world we live in is no longer satisfactory; the good news is that there is a way to bring it into harmony with the holy realm that we are alienated from. It is not only individuals that need to be saved: all of humanity, indeed all of creation, needs to be redeemed from its fallen condition, a mandate that makes history—linear time—important and looks forward to the climactic event that will eventually bring history to an end: apocalypse.

In terms of evolutionary psychology, Axial Age religions instituted the realization that, both personally and collectively, we need to *transcend* the selfish and aggressive propensities built into the human genome by the constraints of our biological evolution. We do not overcome these predispositions with rituals and sacrifices, but we can do so ethically by practicing compassion and generosity. Instead of being motivated by individual ego ("What's in it for me?") or group-ego ("What's beneficial for our group?"), this more universalist perspective transformed and expanded the field of moral responsibility. According to Karen Armstrong,

> In one way or another, [the Axial] programs were designed to eradicate the egotism that is largely responsible for our violence, and promoted the empathic spirituality of the Golden Rule. This, they found, introduced people to a different dimension of human experience. It gave them *ekstasis,* a "stepping out" from their habitual, self-bound consciousness that enables them to apprehend a reality that they called "God," *nibbana,* Brahman, atman, or the Way.[124]

In relation to a supreme reality that so greatly transcends all of us, human social hierarchies become flattened (in principle, at least) because we are all subordinated to that reality. Rulers too are now subject to the same spiritual law promulgated by that higher power: a morality that enjoins compassion and benevolence.

Notice, however, that such egalitarianism depends upon a transcendence that equalizes us all only because it radically surpasses us all. The drawback here is somewhat similar to the evolutionary problem with prosociality: the challenge of something external is what binds us together. Without the threat provided by an adversary, members pursue their own personal agenda. What will happen to egalitarian principles, then, when the existence (and therefore the moral authority) of that transcendent reality becomes questionable?

# Script/ure

> More than any other single invention, writing has transformed human consciousness.
>
> —**Walter J. Ong,** *Orality and Literacy*

The Axial transformation was associated with major technological advances, especially the transition from bronze to iron, which requires much higher temperatures to smelt. Stronger iron weapons and tools changed warfare (making it more violent) and agriculture (more efficient), but no cultural development was more important than the spread of alphabetic script in the first millennium BCE. "It appears that societies move to later stages of religious evolution primarily when their populations become large, when they advance their level of subsistence technology, and when they acquire writing and record keeping."[125]

Writing itself—enabling *external memory storage*—was not new. Societies with shamanistic religions do not develop writing; instead it evolved independently in several agrarian civilizations. Mesopotamia created cuneiform to record agricultural produce and legal contracts, and Egypt devised hieroglyphics. Learning how to use either involved a lengthy education that created a highly specialized caste. Both incorporated pictographs that kept them visually connected to the sensory world and thus "retained a large measure of the animist magic of archaic perception. Like many ancient peoples, the Egyptians believed that a name captured the essence of a thing, but they also held that such supernatural power lived in the inscriptions themselves—that spelling was, in fact, a spell."[126]

Alphabetic script was different. By using a small number of simple symbols to represent sounds, in principle almost anyone could learn to read. Although near-universal literacy was not achieved until modern times, reading and writing became common enough among Axial Age elites to influence the ways they understood the world. Usually overlooked, however, are the profound implications for religion. Some scholars believe that alphabetic script was the most important factor promoting the Axial transformation. "Without the invention of writing, without the use of writing for the codification of cultural memory, and without the processes of canonization, the 'Axial Age' would have never occurred. The Axial Age is nothing else but the formative phase of the textual continuity that is still prevailing in our western and eastern civilizations."[127] It is no coincidence that every Axial civilization was a text-based culture.

As with the Axial Age generally, the consequences of script are difficult to comprehend because we live on the other side of that great transition. The way people in an oral culture experience their world has become foreign to us. According to David Abram,

> In indigenous, oral cultures, nature itself is articulate; it *speaks*. The human voice in an oral culture is always to some extent participant with the voices of wolves, wind, and waves—participant, that is, with the encompassing discourse of the animate earth. There is no element of the landscape that is definitely void of expressive resonance and power: any movement may be a gesture, any sound may be a voice, a meaningful utterance. . . . To directly perceive any phenomenon is to enter into relation with it, to feel oneself in a living interaction with another being.[128]

As the focus shifted to writing, "the stones fall silent. Only as our senses transfer their animating magic to the written word do the trees become mute, the other animals fall dumb."[129] But how miraculous script must have seemed to the first generations that learned it! In 1923 the anthropologist Lucien Levy-Bruhl wrote that the native peoples he was studying treated writing as magical, and "even when the native appears to have learnt what writing is, even if he can read and write, he never loses the feeling that a mystical force is at work."[130] And in some ways script has never lost that numinous quality for many people: religious books such as the Bible and the Qur'an are not only among the oldest but remain the most sacred and the most influential.

Script created scripture, shifting the focus from rituals to sacred texts that recorded spiritual revelations and eventually organized them into creeds and theology. The primacy of orthopraxy (performing ceremonies in the proper way) was gradually supplanted by orthodoxy (believing in the proper way). The beliefs that you profess—your faith—become more important. In contrast, cultures without script do not have doctrines; they have mythologies.

> A non-literate society has an oral religion where several versions of the most important myths usually circulate, where the extent of the religion is limited by the reach of the spoken word, and where there is no fixed set of dogmas that the faithful must adhere to. A literate society, on the contrary, usually has a written religion (often in the shape of sacred texts), with a theoretically unlimited geographic reach, with a clearly delineated set of dogmas and principles, and with authorized, "correct" versions of myths and narrative.[131]

Dogma readily becomes dogmatism, reminding us that the true source of heresy is orthodoxy: a strident quest for *the* correct belief system (for example, the Nicene Creed of fourth-century Christianity) that condemns divergent beliefs. Now there is a new mode of access to the sacred: the recorded *Truth*, which must be vigorously defended from error that might lead people astray. A pantheon of gods usually has room for one more, but monotheistic religions become intolerant of views that deviate from the official position. Polytheism encourages live-and-let-live: you have your god, I have mine. Monotheism is more arrogant and missionary: because *we* know what is true, you should join us—or else.

Pre-Axial traditions followed prehistoric animism (and most indigenous traditions today) in apprehending the sacrality of what we now call nature: sacred mountains, springs, trees, animals—even stones. That divine immanence became devalued in relation to canonized texts containing the word of God. "The codification of revelation leads to an expatriation of the holy from the worldly immanence into transcendence and into scripture. . . . Scripture requires a total reorientation of religious attention which was formerly directed towards the forms of divine immanence and is now directed towards scripture and its exegesis."[132]

As exegesis—studying and interpreting that Divine Word—became one of the most important religious activities, worship of natural phenomena became condemned as idolatry. The sacred is now found in *script*ure. But isn't veneration of holy books another type of idolatry? "An idol, in the theological sense, is a creation of man's hands, as the Bible says, in front of which we worship, and to which we attribute a power which transcends our own."[133] Then aren't the Torah, New Testament, and Qur'an examples of such creations? Spinoza criticized those who turn religion into superstition by "beginning to worship likenesses and images, that is, paper and ink."[134] As script began to speak to us and for us, the sacrality of our embedded life in a sensuous world was lost because we became unable to hear what the natural world is saying.

Script solidified custom into law. "Most non-literate societies are organized on the basis of kinship, while literate societies tend to be state societies where an abstract ideology of community, such as nationalism, functions as a kind of metaphorical kinship."[135] When law is written down it becomes impersonal and requires a powerful author or authority, such as a king or legislature. It is promulgated and enforced with specified procedures.

That difference reflects a larger one. Oral cultures are invariably focused on maintaining traditional ways of knowing and doing, which must be transmitted afresh—often memorized—by each new generation. Such societies are naturally conservative in the original sense, preoccupied with conserving what has been laboriously achieved. By preserving in a different way—storing externalized memory in books—script liberates us from that endless task of preserving and passing on knowledge, and encourages a second-order reflexivity that eventually creates a new kind of self: one that not only can learn to read silently—his contemporaries were shocked that Saint Ambrose could read without moving his lips!—but thinks privately about what is read. One's relationship with the sacred became internalized and thus individualized.

Such reflection provides a strong impetus for innovation. It was no coincidence that Luther's Protestant Reformation occurred soon after Gutenberg's printing press made the Bible more accessible, or that Mahayana Buddhism began to develop around the time that the orally preserved Pali Canon was written down. According to Thomas Ericksen,

> While the inhabitants of nonliterate societies tell myths about who they are and where they come from, literate societies have *history* to perform the same functions, based on archives and other written sources.
>
> Writing, in this way, has been an essential tool in the transition from what we could call a *concrete society* based on intimate, personal relationships, memory, local religion and orally transmitted myths, to an *abstract society* based on formal legislation, archives, a book religion and written history.[136]

The reference to history highlights another important difference in how time is understood. The introduction of script naturally distinguishes between those preliterate ancients and us literate moderns. Whereas nonliterate cultures almost always experience time as cyclic, as in the eternal recurrence of seasons or Indian *kalpas*, the distinction between older and newer ways promotes awareness of time as linear. This created the opportunity for *progress*, along with its shadow, the threat of decline and regression. Now the future might be very different from the past.

Among the cultural consequences of script is another intriguing possibility. Does writing imply that the transcendent reality discovered by Axial Age religions has all-too-human origins? "When the written word and the divine Word eventually joined forces they encouraged religions in which an invisible God was known by his Word alone."[137] Texts transcend this physical world, in the sense that they distance the originator of a thought from the person who receives it. Spoken words fly away as soon as they are uttered, but now thoughts are liberated from the person who wrote them down, with a meaning that achieves a life of its own. Now the written words actually speak to you: you *hear* them with your *eyes*! Vision became more dominant, subordinating our other senses.

Alphabetic script seems to offer a transcendent (from the Latin *trans* "across" and *scendere* "to climb") perspective because writing speaks to us of things and worlds that are no longer here and now. It creates a truth and reality that "rises above" any specific place or time. Written words are less susceptible to the decay that haunts everyone and everything else in our mutable material world. Although any particular papyrus or parchment scroll will eventually deteriorate, the text it records can be reproduced indefinitely, apparently achieving a timeless immunity to change.

The temptation to idealize such objectified meaning is quite understandable, along with the associated distinction between incorporeal souls and the messy world of physical bodies. According to David Abram,

> Transfixed by our technologies, we short-circuit the sensorial reciprocity between our breathing bodies and the bodily terrain. Human awareness folds in upon itself, and the senses—once the crucial site of our engagement with the wild and animate earth—become mere adjuncts of an isolate and abstract mind bent on overcoming an organic reality that now seems disturbingly aloof and arbitrary.[138]

Note that this sense of separation applies to alphabetic scripts, not to the kind of writing that developed in China, which was the only Axial civilization that did not develop an alphabet. Originally Chinese characters were religious symbols used in divination and other rites, and as they evolved they continued to function quite differently. Carl Becker explains:

> For written Chinese does not only *contain* symbols, to be deciphered by the reader—it *is* itself nothing but symbols. When one looks at words for fire, or water, or Pure Land in Chinese,

he does not first observe letters which he then mentally translates into sounds, and which then take on a meaning dependent on their context in the sentence. Rather, he sees pictures
of fire, water, purity, and land in front of his eyes in the hiero-
glyphic characters themselves. Reading Chinese is in many
ways more like scrutinizing a mural painting from one side to
the other than it is like putting together syllogisms.[139]

The Chinese language has a concrete flavor, abounding with similes
and metaphors, preferring particulars over universals. Such a script
does not encourage abstract thinking, such as distinguishing the
ever-changing phenomena perceived by our senses from some "higher
reality" that can be apprehended only by the mind. Nothing like Pla-
tonism ever developed in China. It is no coincidence that China's
conception of transcendence was also less dualistic than the sharp
ontological distinction that developed in the other Axial traditions.
The Dao (the Way) is neither a monotheistic supreme deity nor a
monistic absolute reality that transcends this illusory world, but it
instead refers to the way this-worldly phenomena unfold and flow:
the natural pattern or order that underlies all forms and shapes their
transformation.

In contrast to this Chinese qualification, there is no better example of the transformative power of script than the evolution of Judaism. "The invention of the phonological alphabet in the South Sinai
in the fifteenth century BCE almost certainly made the idea of an
abstract monotheistic God thinkable for the first time."[140] The story
of Moses receiving the Decalogue on Mount Sinai and destroying
the golden calf can be understood as representing a shift from graven
images (henceforth prohibited) to a God who is invisible but whose
pronouncements can be recorded and revered. The Ark of the Covenant, the original Holy of Holies, was believed to contain the ten
commandments transmitted to Moses by God, almost certainly in
the form of a parchment scroll. The earliest books of the Bible, form-
ing the Pentateuch, were written down in the eighth century BCE.

In 587 BCE Jerusalem was conquered and its temple was destroyed, with many of its residents deported to Babylon. During this "Babylonian exile" religious focus shifted from temple ritual to texts that were eventually collated into the Tanakh (Hebrew Bible). With the Roman destruction of Herod's temple in 70 CE and the eventual diaspora of the Jewish people, Judaism survived by becoming a portable religion emphasizing textual study. All its male members were expected to learn to read the sacred scriptures, and Torah study itself became one of their holiest obligations.

Of course, scripture is no less important for later Abrahamic developments such as Christianity and Islam. The apostle Paul became so influential because of his widely disseminated correspondence, much of it canonized into the New Testament. Christianity focuses on Christ, God incarnated as a man, yet (especially since the Reformation) the Holy Bible has become for most Christians the primary mode of access to the divine. Islam did not accept Jesus (or anyone else) as a divine messiah, emphasizing instead the Qur'an, the heavenly book dictated by the archangel Gabriel to Muhammad, God's illiterate prophet, who repeated what he heard for a scribe to record. For Muslims the real Qur'an is in heaven, being preexistent and uncreated, and summarizing God's previous revelations.

For all three Abrahamic religions God is formless and imperceptible, but we have access to the divine through God's *recorded* Word.

Indian religious traditions resisted the shift to literacy. The Bronze Age civilization of the Indus Valley (ca. 3300–1300 BCE) developed a script that has yet to be deciphered; after its decline, writing was little used before the reign of Ashoka in the third century BCE. The earliest and most sacred texts, the Vedas, were transmitted orally and (although Indian chronology is imprecise) not written down until after the fifth century BCE. Coincidence or not, this also seems to be about when the first Upanishads were composed. While the Vedas are preoccupied with sacrifice and ritual, the Upanishads are more reflective, providing the intellectual basis for later Hindu philosophy and its conception of a transcendent reality, Brahman.

There is an important parallel in the evolution of Buddhism from an oral tradition to a text-based one. Here too, it is probably no coincidence that this development coincided with a rupture between the Theravada tradition (still predominant in Southeast Asia) and the Mahayana (Central and East Asia). The dates for Gautama the historical Buddha remain uncertain, but he probably lived sometime in the fifth century BCE. His teachings were memorized and transmitted orally for three or four centuries before being written down and collated into the Pali Canon. The spiritual authority of monastics was originally based on their function as repositories of the Buddha's *Dharma*, a role that changed when those teachings were recorded.

Soon after the Pali Canon was written down, different ways of understanding the Buddhadharma appeared in Mahayana scriptures such as the Vimalakirti Nirdesa Sutra, the Lotus Sutra, and the Avatamsaka Sutra. This was accompanied by a shift from auditory metaphors ("Thus have I heard . . .") to the florid visual descriptions that abound in the new texts. This is also about the time that the first anthropomorphic representations of the Buddha appeared. Before then, the Buddha was never represented in human form, only symbolized with images such as a footprint or a wheel with eight spokes.

In place of earlier focus on *stupa* cults and relic worship, Mahayana began to emphasize devotion to its scriptures, to the extent that some of its sutras emphasized the immeasurable merit that could be gained by anyone who reproduced them. This textual focus incorporated a transformation in the way the Buddha was understood: no longer simply an awakened human, he became elevated into a transcendent being whose body, for example, could suddenly become radiant and illuminate all the world systems in the cosmos. We see again the connection between literacy, visual imagery, and a stronger sense of transcendence.

The great philosophical triumvirate of Socrates, Plato, and Aristotle also occurred during the Greek transition from orality to literacy. Socrates and Plato were among the earliest generations of Athenian boys who were taught to read. Like the Buddha and Jesus, however, Socrates himself wrote nothing, which was consistent with his dialogical style of inquiry. According to Plato, Socrates believed that writing transforms our living thoughts into lifeless objects in the physical world. Relying on what is written weakens our memory and ability to think. Genuine knowledge can emerge only from an active relationship between human minds.

Plato's written dialogues (notice the hybrid form) reveal more ambivalence. The *Phaedrus* agrees with Socrates that writing degrades memory, and that truth can be transmitted only orally, but Plato's scheme for an ideal society in the *Laws* requires that laws be recorded, and that all children learn to read and write—practices that, as Erik Davis notes, "extend our creative powers by amputating our natural ones."[141] As David Abram says,

> Writing creates an artificial memory, whereby humans can enlarge their experience beyond the limits of one generation or one way of life. At the same time it has allowed them to invent a world of abstract entities and mistake them for reality.[142]

Plato's dualistic metaphysics offers a prime example. Like the Abrahamic conception of God, it distinguishes this world, as we normally perceive and understand it, from a supernatural reality. The world as grasped by our senses, which is constantly transforming, is merely a copy or an image of an unseen and unchanging world of forms (*eide*) that can be grasped only by the intellect. "Like letters, Platonic ideas were immobile, isolated, and devoid of warmth and secondary qualities; they seem to transcend the world at hand."[143] Yet again, script and an invisible "higher reality" appear together, subordinating sense perception to an abstraction and supplanting the oral primacy of immanence.

With Aristotle's many treatises the transition to literacy became complete. "With their minds partly reformatted by alphabetic literacy, the rationalist Greek philosophers were able to detach their thoughts from the flowing surfaces of the material world. Nature became an impersonal and objective domain that could be dissected and analyzed in order to yield rational and general laws based on cause-and-effect explanations."[144] Reflecting on what was read is a philosophical version of transcendence—theorizing as another way of "rising above" what was perceived—and became the template for what would become, much later, a scientific revolution that enabled our modern world by objectifying it.

# Transcendence

Beware of the man whose God is in the skies.

—George Bernard Shaw[145]

The above discussion of the Abrahamic traditions, China, India, and Greece focused on the curious relationship between script and transcendence: cultures that developed script came to believe in another reality that transcends this one. By noting this correlation I do not mean to dismiss transcendence as a mere artefact of literacy. It does raise important questions about how we have been understanding transcendence, especially the ways we have reified the sacred into an *other* that is *up there*, rather than being an immanent dimension of *here and now*.

That perspective challenges our usual understanding of secularity and materialism. "[T]o project the experience of the sacred onto an immaterial God is to shortchange sacredness as a dimension of material life and turn it into an object of worship that is beyond our world and thus alien to life."[146] Having divided the world into discrete spiritual and physical components, and then put that spiritual component *somewhere else*—making heaven or nirvana a separate reality—we then found ourselves living in a spiritually impoverished world bereft of sacrality. Today we continue to struggle with the consequences of that dualistic legacy.

The concept of transcendence is essential to the Axial Age traditions, but it is important to distinguish its various versions. As noted above, the implications of the term are suggested by its Latin etymology: *trans* + *scendere*, "to climb over or beyond." Most generally, transcendence provides a "higher" perspective (also from Latin, *per* + *specere*, "to look through") on the given world. "Climbing beyond" our usual standpoint—becoming disembedded from one's physical and social nexus—enables us to see the world differently and frees us to relate to it differently. This allows the possibility of leverage over the given, something that the embedded members of pre-Axial civilizations did not have. Archimedes said that if he had a fulcrum sufficiently far away, he could use a lever to move the earth. Historically, that fulcrum has been provided by religious conceptions of transcendence, whether we understand them as pointing to another dimension of reality or as a product of the human imagination. As Ernest Renan said about the supernatural, the transcendent is "the way in which the ideal makes its appearance in human affairs."[147] We need ideals, but when we misunderstand their origins they can become chains.

This implies there are different types of transcendence, according to what is being transcended. The term can refer not only to some otherworldly reality but also to the role of ethical universalism, usually derived from such a "higher world"—for example, the Decalogue given to Moses by Yahweh. Such moral mandates have become secularized. "Even its most concrete form, the law code, implies a transfer of authority from the holders of office to the written rule [e.g., the U.S. Constitution]. Transcendental impulses therefore constitute, by definition, an implicit challenge to traditional authority and indicate some dissatisfaction with it."[148] In that sense—a transfer from the unchecked power of political elites to an objectified code of law—the transcendent is still very much with us, and indeed it is necessary to protect individuals from the state and to regulate one's relationships with others.

As the examples of Buddhism and Greece imply, writing—especially alphabetic script—enabled another type of transcendence:

by recording and thereby externalizing language, one could metaphorically "climb beyond" it by reflecting upon it. Myth still serves an important role in the Axial religions, but now texts could be analyzed and evaluated, eventually leading to demythologization in favor of the theorization that flowered as philosophy, theology, and science.

It is important to distinguish these versions of transcendence because different Axial civilizations emphasized different ones.

The *Abrahamic* religions (Judaism, Christianity, Islam) emphasize ethical monotheism, which combines the first kind of transcendence (a higher reality) and the second kind (a moral code derived from that higher reality). Although they all stress faith in a supreme being, transcendence is also experienced as an ethical demand: God wants us to live in a certain way. We will be punished if we sin, which is rebellion against God. The wages of sin is death, but if we behave ourselves the gift of God is eternal life (Romans 6:23).

The main Axial figures of *Greece* were philosophers who emphasized rationality. The crucial term *logos* originally meant "speech," but for pre-Socratic philosophers such as Heraclitus it referred to a universal law that structures the universe, which humans could discover. Pythagoreans believed in the harmony of the spheres—that heavenly bodies moved according to geometric equations, generating music normally inaudible to us—because they "believed that the principles of mathematics were the principles of all things," according to Aristotle's *Metaphysics* 1:5. Although Aristotle understood the *logos* more technically, as argument that employs reasoning (hence "logic"), the Stoics valued *logos* as a transcendent spiritual principle that pervades and animates the whole cosmos. The ambiguity of the term contributed to a general belief that the soul is harmonious when ruled by reason. For Greek philosophy, our basic problem is that we are not rational enough, being misled by our passions.

The *Indian* traditions, such as Hinduism and Buddhism, include ethical precepts, of course, but they emphasize more what might be called "epistemological enlightenment." There is an insight that each of us needs to realize, which is not accessible by reasoning alone.

Although we suffer the karmic consequences of unskillful actions, our root problem is that we do not know our own true nature or the true nature of the world. The fundamental issue is not immorality but ignorance. Addressing this usually requires some type of meditation practice, in which we *transcend* our usual ways of thinking—including rationality—by not identifying with the thoughts and other mental events that arise. That can lead to a nonconceptual understanding that liberates us from *maya* (illusion) and suffering.

As already mentioned, *Chinese* concepts of Heaven (Tian) and the Dao were not as transcendent as the Abrahamic God or Vedantic Brahman. They were never understood as referring to a separate reality, but to a dimension contiguous with this world and complementary to it. Although neither Confucians nor Daoists offered any serious challenge to the secular-cum-sacred institutionalized authority of political rulers, their authority was not unconditional: leaders were subject to the moral judgment of heaven and could lose the mandate of heaven if they ruled badly.

Elsewhere I have argued that our usual sense of self is a psychological and social construct, which makes it inherently insecure.[149] We normally experience this insecurity as a sense of *lack*, the feeling that "something is wrong with me," but what it is that is wrong with me (or us) can be understood in different ways. One way to view the above differences among the various Axial civilizations is that they have different explanations of what we *lack* and therefore offer alternative solutions, based on their different understandings of transcendence.

For monotheisms, we suffer because we disobey God (sin), which in some versions of Christianity includes our inheriting the original sin of Adam and Eve; but we can repent. For Greek philosophy, we will not be happy unless rationality rules the passions. For the Indian traditions, the root of our *lack* is delusion and ignorance: we need to "wake up" to the reality of who we really are and what the world really is. For the Chinese sages, self-cultivation can transform us into "superior humans" and help revive the old traditions, which promote social harmony (Confucianism) and harmony with the natural world (Daoism).

For pre-Axial civilizations the task was to preserve or recover what is always (in an oral culture) in danger of being lost. "[I]n mythological cultures, people live in an endless now where personal histories don't exist and life is lived within a narrow circle of birth, death, and rebirth. . . . Historical awareness introduces the idea that every event and every individual story is unique, finite, and unrepeatable."[150] Axial religions became future-oriented and often apocalyptic, looking forward to the day when the transcendent will irrupt into this world to purify it and the gap between the two realities will be healed forever. Our modern preoccupation with progress—an increasingly dubious concept today—is a secularized version of this future orientation unknown to pre-Axial cultures.

## The Birth of the Axial Age

> Religions exist primarily for people to achieve
> together what they cannot achieve on their own.
>
> **—David Sloan Wilson**[151]

The earliest known Axial figure may have been Zoroaster (also known as Zarathustra) in Persia.[152] I emphasize *may have been* because his dates are unknown. Estimates have ranged widely from somewhere in the second millennium to somewhere between the seventh and sixth centuries BCE.

In his time, Iranian people mostly followed the Ṛg Veda religion also practiced in India, which focused on ritual sacrifices to a polytheistic hierarchy of gods associated with the powers of nature, such as the sun, sky, earth, fire, and wind. According to the traditional biographies, the number of animal sacrifices required had become excessive and burdensome. Zoroaster, motivated by compassion for all the cattle being slaughtered, left home on a spiritual quest and at the age of thirty began to experience a series of revelations in which archangels and later Ahura Mazda ("the Wise Lord," a.k.a. the Supreme God) appeared "as pure light" to teach him the doctrines and duties of a new religion—not just another religion but the *true* religion. After some years of frustration, he was able to convert a prince in eastern Iran, and with royal support his new faith eventually grew to encompass most of Persia.

Zoroastrianism seems to have created the template that would be used and developed by the Abrahamic traditions:

> The concept of an all-powerful Creator God who is purely good, the personification of evil in an opposing being, the resurrection of the body after death, the judgement of the dead on the basis of their deeds while living, the existence of a heavenly paradise for the good and a hell of damnation for the evil, the expectation of a savior and a final cataclysmic battle in which good will ultimately triumph, as well as a universe populated by angels and demons, are all ideas that other religions acquired whether directly or indirectly from Zoroastrianism.[153]

In contrast to this familiar set of doctrines, spiritual teachings foundational to later Indian spirituality are not found in the Avesta or the Gathas, the primary Zoroastrian scriptures. These teachings include asceticism, renunciation of this world as a place of suffering, karma, reincarnation, meditation, and mysticism—including union with God or absorption in nirvana.

Zoroaster's vision initiated a basic tension that continues to afflict monotheistic religions: an omnipotent and benevolent God who nevertheless coexists with an evil deity. Ahura Mazda is opposed by the malevolent Angra Mainyu (a.k.a. Ahriman). Our world is their battleground. Mazda will eventually achieve final victory, but in the meantime Zoroastrianism introduced a novel responsibility: each of us must choose between them. Today such a spiritual requirement does not seem unusual, but at that time it was revolutionary in its focus on personal freedom and moral choice as the heart of religious practice, making individuals more accountable for their own conduct. This dualistic worldview transformed the pre-Axial myths of gods defeating monsters to create order out of chaos. The old power struggles were ethicized: now the war between light and dark takes place within each of us as well as in the world, supplanting the traditional emphasis on ritual and sacrifice. For Zoroaster, good people grew food, took care of the soil, and treated animals kindly. Evil people slaughtered animals.

Why is the difference between light and darkness so important? According to earlier beliefs recorded in the Hebrew Bible, and similar to the Greek understanding of Hades, after death everyone languishes in Sheol, a gloomy subterranean underworld. But the new emphasis on moral responsibility required a postmortem reward (or punishment) for one's deeds, since obviously not everyone gets what they deserve during their lifetime.

Zoroaster understood the cosmic struggle between good and evil to entail a religious obligation that applies equally to everyone, rather than being a doctrine associated only with particular social groups such as nobles and priests. This universalist and egalitarian innovation had important political implications. Zoroastrianism escaped the typical ethnic constraints of a specific culture to become the world's first missionary religion. That made it an attractive creed for an expansive empire, since members of conquered nations could be converted and incorporated into the new superstate. The pattern would be replicated: the world's most influential missionary religions—in historical order, Buddhism, Christianity, and Islam—were initially successful because each of them became the state religion of an empire. And, by no coincidence, all of them shifted their primary focus from temples to texts, which are more portable.

Zoroastrianism influenced the development of Judaism (and subsequent Abrahamic religions) through the Babylonian captivity of 597–38 BCE, when Jerusalem was conquered and many Judeans were transported to Babylon. After Cyrus the Great defeated the Neo-Babylonian empire, the exiles were allowed to return to Israel. It is not clear whether Cyrus himself practiced Zoroastrianism, but it soon became the state religion of Persia. Judean gratitude to Persia (Cyrus is praised in the Hebrew Bible) apparently included appreciation of its dynamic new religion and appropriation of some of its teachings. Zoroastrianism declined after Persia was conquered by Alexander of Macedon, but later it revived and became the state religion of the Sassanian Empire (224–651 CE). Today the largest surviving community of Zoroastrians is the Parsis in India.

Israel became fully monotheistic only as the result of a long and complicated process. J, the first biblical source according to scholars, imagined Yahweh sitting and talking with Abraham, but by the time of Ezekiel, God had become an overwhelming mystery. Elijah seems to have been the first prophet to insist on the exclusive worship of Yahweh, though he apparently did not doubt the existence of other gods such as Baal. For Elijah, Yahweh is not found in the natural world but dwells elsewhere, in a higher realm. The Hebrew word *kodesh*, usually translated as "holy," more literally means "set apart." For the Israelites divinity would henceforth be experienced not in nature but in history: in their developing relationship with God.

The first unequivocal assertion of monotheism is in *Deutero-Isaiah*: "I am the first and I am the last; apart from me there is no God."[154] Other early Axial Age figures in Palestine included the eighth-century BCE Hebrew prophets Isaiah and Jeremiah. Their promotion of ethical monotheism contrasted sharply with the polytheistic religions of their tribal neighbors. That development—from a Hebrew tribal divinity to the national God of Israel, and then to the One God who created everything—also created tensions that persist today: Does that God have a special relationship with the Jewish people? Or is he (the usual pronoun) a truly universal God that doesn't play favorites?

This evolution was mirrored by the deepening subjectivity and individualism that developed in all the Axial Age religions, an interiority that can also be described as the formation of an inner self—but a self that now needs salvation (from evil or Satan) or awakening (from ignorance or delusion). Expressed in theistic language, "Man becomes aware of himself *as man* in the encounter with the God who addresses him. This also entails a fundamental rupture between man and cosmos. The cosmos ceases to be divine in its own right, as it was (probably cross-culturally) in the millennia of early human history."[155]

This duality implied a crucial shift in the understanding of human destiny. Originally there was no focus on an afterlife. The tribal religion of the early Hebrews emphasized this world, with the rituals and sacrifices common to other pre-Axial traditions. Death involved descent into Sheol, an underworld where both the righteous and the unrighteous dwell. The earliest account of resurrection is in the book of Daniel, a second-century BCE prophetic eschatology set in the sixth century BCE, during the Babylonian exile. Just as God protected Daniel, even when he was thrown into a den of lions, so God will help the Israelites triumph over their enemies. "Then the sovereignty, power and greatness of all the kingdoms under heaven will be handed over to the holy people of the Most High. His kingdom will be an everlasting kingdom, and all rulers will worship and obey him."[156] Those who have already died are not forgotten: "Multitudes who sleep in the dust of the earth will awake: some to everlasting life, others to shame and everlasting contempt."[157] As later apocalypses emphasize, this would not be a transcendental event—no ascension into heaven—but an earthly reunion of the soul with its body.

> This is what the Sovereign Lord says:
> "See, I will beckon to the nations, I will lift up my banner to
>       the peoples . . .
> Kings will be your foster fathers, and their queens your nurs-
>       ing mothers.
> They will bow down before you with their faces to the
>       ground;
> they will lick the dust at your feet."[158]

Nonetheless, later Jewish sects disagreed about postmortem survival. Apparently Sadducees—who included most of the elite, although none of their own texts survive—did not accept any afterlife, but the Pharisees and Essenes both believed in the immortality of the soul and the resurrection of the dead. After the second temple was destroyed in 70 CE, it was Pharisaic beliefs that became the foundation of the Rabbinic Judaism that survived the diaspora.

In the Old Testament, God walked in the Garden of Eden, wrestled with Jacob, and Moses saw his backside. That was possible because in pre-Axial religions gods and humans are hewn from the same primal matter; in fact, the very concept of an immaterial transcendence would have made no sense. The Greek language, for example, had no term for "immaterial" until Plato invented it in the fourth century BCE. As monotheism developed it became revolutionary by sundering cosmic and political power. Religion became a way to free oneself from the power structures of the ancient world, in which sacred and secular authority reinforced each other. For the Israelites (and later Abrahamic traditions) a gap developed not only between humanity and God but also between our species and all others, clearly expressed in the creation story in Genesis, where only humans are created in the image of God.

As mentioned before, the individuation promoted by such transcendence emphasized morality—how one acts in everyday life—more than the rites and rituals that predominated in pre-Axial religion. Prophets denounced the privileges of the priestly caste. All of us are equal before God, and kings cannot do whatever they want, for they too are subject to the divinely ordained moral code. According to Karen Armstrong,

> The pagan gods depended upon the ceremonies to renew their depleted energies; their prestige depending in part upon the magnificence of their temples. Now Yahweh was actually saying that these things were utterly meaningless. . . . Isaiah felt that external observance was not enough. Israelites must discover the inner meaning of their religion. Yahweh

wanted compassion rather than sacrifice: "You may multiply your prayers, I shall not listen. Your hands are covered with blood, wash, make yourselves clean. Take your wrong-doing out of my sight. Cease to do evil. Learn to do good. Search for justice, help the oppressed, be just to the orphan, plead for the widow."[159]

In the first century BCE, Hillel the Elder famously summarized the whole of Judaism "while standing on one leg"—that is, most concisely: "That which is hateful to you, do not do to your fellow. That is the whole Torah; the rest is commentary."[160]

Notice again, however, the price of understanding God (the source of everything sacred) as wholly transcendent. The rest of the world—the world we live in—loses its divinity. The myriad nature gods of animism are replaced by incorporeal spirit. The ultimate meaning of life is detached from everyday experience and projected into another reality. "This dualistic conception applies equally to morality. The determination of whether something is good or bad comes not from one's own experience but from whatever God has decided."[161]

In other words, the Axial Age was a double-edged sword: the sacred transcendence that freed us from being wholly embedded in social roles did so by alienating us from our earthly home, now devalued into a means for achieving an otherworldly goal. Modern rejection of transcendence has not solved this problem, insofar as its disappearance (as the source of life's meaning) has left us susceptible to this-worldly nihilisms that exalt power or are preoccupied with sense gratification.

Jesus was an observant Jew who, like other Abrahamic figures, emphasized the moral law. Far from intending to establish a new religion, he was a wisdom teacher and apocalyptic prophet who expected the kingdom of the Jews to arrive soon. Only in the Gospel According to John—the last of the New Testament's canonical gospels to be composed, some 60–70 years after Jesus' death—does he identify himself with God: "I and the Father are one."[162] Many mystics have made similar assertions about nonduality, without being acclaimed as the only begotten son of God the Father. Much of the responsibility for that claim falls on Paul, who never met Jesus but apparently knew better than anyone else the true meaning of Christ's ministry. In Paul's letters the teachings of Jesus on how we should live became overshadowed by his role as the messiah and locus of salvation. Christ was sent by God to save the entire world, atoning for the sins of everyone by his sacrifice on the cross. This was blasphemy for many Jews, but Paul had bigger ambitions: to make salvation through faith in Christ available to pagan Gentiles as well as observant Jews.

The New Testament proclaims a universalism that is not bound by any ethnic or class identity. The Sermon on the Mount remains unsurpassed in its emphasis on unconditional love:

> You have heard that it was said, "Love your neighbor and hate your enemy." But I tell you, love your enemies and pray for those who persecute you, that you may be children of your Father in heaven. He causes his sun to rise on the evil and the good, and sends rain on the righteous and the unrighteous.[163]

Nevertheless, here Jesus the devout Jew was speaking to other Jews. Another famous teaching is more explicit in its transgression of ethnicity. The context is important: "an expert in the Law" tested Jesus by asking what he must do to inherit eternal life. Jesus replied "What is written in the Law? How do you read it?" and the expert cited a well-known teaching: "Love the Lord your God with all your heart and with all your soul . . . and love your neighbor as yourself." Jesus approves of this response but the interrogator persists: "Who is my neighbor?" Jesus replies with the parable of a traveler who is attacked by robbers, stripped of clothing, and left half dead alongside the road. A priest and a Levite pass by, both ignoring the injured man. Then a Samaritan takes pity on the hapless traveler, bandages his wounds and takes him to an inn, promising to pay for any caretaking expenses. "Which of these three do you think was a neighbor to the man who fell into the hands of robbers?" "The one who had mercy on him," replied the expert. "Go and do likewise" was Jesus' immortal response.[164]

Although ethnically related, Samaritans and Jews often disliked if not despised each other, so this teaching extends the imperative "love your neighbor as yourself" to include everyone, Jew and non-Jew alike. Because it is found only in Luke, some scholars wonder if this story is a later addition to the gospels, but Paul reinforces its implications in his Letter to the Galatians: "There is neither Jew nor Gentile, neither slave nor free, nor is there male and female, for you are all one in Christ Jesus."[165] God's plan of salvation was intended for all of humankind. There is an important parallel here with the community of spiritual renunciates established by the historical Buddha: the sangha was open to members of all castes, and he also created a sangha for women, because male and female have the same potential to awaken.

There is another remarkable parallel between what Jesus says in Matthew 25 and what the Buddha teaches in the Kucchivikara-vatthu of the Mahavagga, part of the Pali Canon. Jesus describes what will happen when "the Son of Man" comes in his glory and sits on his throne. He welcomes those who are blessed by the Father and will inherit the kingdom prepared for them. "For I was hungry and you gave me something to eat, I was thirsty and you gave me something to drink, I was a stranger and you invited me in, I needed clothes and you clothed me, I was sick and you looked after me, I was in prison and you came to visit me." The righteous are puzzled: "Lord, when did we see you hungry and feed you? . . . When did we see you sick or in prison and go to visit you?" And he answers: "Truly I tell you, whatever you did for one of the least of these brothers and sisters of mine, you did for me."[166]

The Buddha was on an inspection tour of lodgings when he came across a monk ill with dysentery, lying in his own urine and excrement. With the help of his attendant Ananda he washed the monk and placed him on a bed. Then he had the other monks assembled and asked them, "Why don't you attend to him?" "He doesn't do anything for the monks, which is why they don't attend to him." The Buddha responded: "Monks, you have no mother, you have no father, who might tend to you. If you don't tend to one another, who then will tend to you? Whoever would tend to me, should tend to the sick."[167]

Despite such universalism, Christianity soon developed ambivalence toward our physical bodies, based on its dualism between a transcendent reality and this "fallen" material world. In the Gospel of John Jesus says that his followers "are not of the world, even as I am not of it,"[168] and in his first epistle John declares that "everything in the world—the lust of the flesh, the lust of the eyes, and the pride of life—comes not from the Father but from the world. The world and its desires pass away, but whoever does the will of God lives forever."[169]

Thus the split between this world and that which transcends it is also a split within us, between the "higher" part of us that yearns for better realms, and a "lower" part that is bound to the earth. Paul's letters distinguish two modes of existence: living according to "the flesh" and subject to sin and death, or living according to the Spirit, when we are reborn in Christ, which frees us to live a virtuous life here and offers the possibility of immortality hereafter. According to this dualism, the flesh and its desires are naturally evil, in contrast to redeemed life, which transcends our physical bodies.

In Genesis God "formed a man from the dust of the ground and breathed into his nostrils the breath of life, and the man became a living being."[170] For Homer too the soul (*psyche*) was the breath, a common view at the time. For Aristotle *psyche* was the life-principle that actualizes the body; other living beings have different types of souls. For Christianity, however, only humans have souls, which are our personal connection to divine transcendence. This link distinguishes us from all other forms of life. According to Rosemary Reuther,

This human-animal split is reinforced by the soul-body split. These splits reinforce a view of the essential human as a transcendent, disembodied, immortal "soul" that can kick aside the physical world of bodily life. Its destiny is not an integral part of this bodily world. Thus despite the official continuation in Christianity of certain Hebraic concepts of the resurrected body and redeemed earth, operative Christian eschatology for the most part is one of an immortal soul that escapes from and is not limited by the mortal fate of earth's creatures.[171]

Three centuries later Augustine of Hippo reinforced this duality. His early Neoplatonism influenced his later emphasis on God's immaterial transcendence, in contrast to lower things such as our physical bodies that have lesser being and goodness. "The soul is utterly superior to the body, and that which gives each one of us his being is nothing else but his soul, whereas the body is no more than a shadow that keeps us company."[172] The spiritual path involves ascending from material things to the incorporeal Being that is God. For Augustine, as for Paul, our immortal souls survive in disembodied form after death, although at the time of resurrection and the Last Judgment they will be rejoined with our lowly bodies, now transformed "so that they will be like his [Christ's] glorious body."[173]

This perspective seems to view the earth simply as a means to a superior transcendent goal. It is merely the theater where the drama of human salvation is enacted. However, recent developments in Christian thought have attempted to nuance this dualism, most notably in the 2015 encyclical *Laudato si'* of Pope Francis, which criticized consumerism, unfettered economic growth, and human destruction of the planet.

Islam generally fits into the same Abrahamic perspective, also much influenced by the Hebrew Bible. But there is no trinity of divine persons: the most important teaching is *tawhid*, that God is one. Allah (*Al-ilah*, literally "the God") is omniscient and omnipotent, eternal and transcendent, the uncreated creator of everything, although this is emphasized without denying or minimizing God's immanence—divine presence—in the natural world that is his handiwork. Like Yahweh in Judaism, Allah in pre-Islamic Arabia was originally the supreme deity in a pantheon of lesser gods. Muhammad's teaching was revolutionary because he emphasized that Allah is the same singular and unitary God that Abraham encountered. Muhammad himself was not an incarnation of God, but is considered "the Seal of the Prophets," the last in a series of messengers that includes Adam, Noah, Abraham, Moses, and Jesus.

For Muslims there is no Augustinian dichotomy between the sacred and the profane. The Qur'an tells us that we should appreciate nature as God's primary miracle, which continually testifies to the reality and benevolence of its creator.

Of the many attributes of God, by far the most important is compassion. With one exception, all 114 chapters of the Qur'an begin with the same verse: "In the name of Allah the compassionate, the merciful . . ." Nonetheless, our life here is a test from God, and we will be held accountable for what we do and what we don't do. Islam too emphasizes the afterlife: after death souls enter a state of waiting until bodily resurrection on the Day of Judgment. Paradise (*Jannah*, "a garden,") awaits believers and those who live righteously, while unbelievers and evildoers will suffer in hell. Again, our life here and now has a postmortem goal.

Greek popular religion remained polytheistic while its Axial turn occurred politically (democracy), scientifically (including, for example, Euclidean geometry), and philosophically (Socrates, Plato, and Aristotle, among many others). We trace the origins of Western civilization back to classical Greece because the Greeks discovered the momentous difference between *physis* (the natural world) and *nomos* (human convention). That distinction overturned the archaic pre-Axial worldview that justified traditional hierarchies by embedding the social order within the natural order. Now we are freed to determine for ourselves how to live together.

This points to another important aspect of the Axial revolution: the yearning for personal salvation and the quest for social utopia are two sides of the same transformative impetus. At a critical time in Athenian history, Cleisthenes reorganized its four family-based tribes into ten districts, replacing kinship identity with place of residence; later, Pericles extended the access of citizens without wealth (*thetes*) to public office. The result was a provocative—although limited, since women and slaves were excluded—experiment in direct democracy. Political authority was transferred from traditional elites to all free male citizens.

Greek Axiality also emphasized the discovery (invention?) of what we now understand as *rationality*, an analytic process that offered a different challenge to the narrative *mythos* of pre-Axial cultures. As a reflective activity that thinks about thinking, logical reasoning is a "second order" mental process that transcends (objectifies) the world in attempting a conceptual assessment of it. Such an overview had important ethical and social implications. For example, Plato extrapolated his tripartite understanding of the human *psyche*—consisting of a thinking part, a spirited (emotional) part, and an appetitive part—to argue that the ideal state would also have three classes: philosopher-kings, warriors, and citizen-workers.

The development of Greek Axiality was much influenced by the astonishing mathematical discoveries of Pythagoras and his school. Mathematics for us is a science, but "the father of numbers" was as much a mystic as a mathematician, and in fact our usual distinction between them would have made no sense in his time. Pythagoreans believed that numbers are the ultimate reality and that everything could be measured and predicted according to their laws and patterns. "The so-called Pythagoreans, who were the first to take up mathematics, not only advanced this subject, but saturated with it, they fancied that the principles of mathematics were the principles of all things."[174] Pythagoreans also believed in the transmigration of souls, which are fallen (corrupted) divinities imprisoned in bodies but capable of recovering their divine status. They practiced Orphic-like purification rites to help the psyche ascend to higher, presumably mathematical, realms. All very Axial.

Today we have lost the strangeness of the astounding realization that our world is a function of mathematical relationships whose truth is not dependent upon any particular physical arrangements. This suggests a more abstract reality—another type of transcendence—that is distinct from anything the senses can experience, and invulnerable to decay and mortality: the laws of science. The groundwork for that perspective was provided by Plato, the doorway to whose Academy announced: "Let no one ignorant of geometry enter herein." For Plato this world is unreal and human imagination is mimetic and derivative, subject to the ravages of time. His philosophy seeks instead the *Eidos* (immutable Forms) that manifest timeless Being, which are accessible only by reason. Everything in the physical world is an imperfect copy of such eternal essences. In the famous parable of the cave (*Republic* book 7) one can escape the illusory shadows here to experience the changeless Being symbolized by the Sun—that is, the One or the Good. The purifying practice of philosophizing can free us from the appearances of things to realize the reality behind them. True justice or beauty cannot be experienced by our fallible senses but could be comprehended using the reasoning abilities that characterize our immaterial souls. This too involves spiritual ascent to a higher reality. Plato used the language of the Eleusinian and Dionysian mysteries when he explained the process of illumination and recollection. For Plato, as for Pythagoras and Parmenides, reasoning at its best is a mystical activity.

Aristotle did not believe in Plato's *Eidos* and was not as influenced by mathematics, but he agreed that what distinguishes humans from all other beings is *theoria*, our ability to think rationally. "The life according to reason is best and pleasantest, since reason, more than anything else, is man."[175] Our divine and immortal intelligence (*nous*) links us to the gods, for it gives us the ability to grasp the highest truth. In fact, *noesis noeseos* ("thinking about thinking") characterizes the nature of Being itself, which is an Unmoved Mover: the highest divinity is pure *nous*, self-absorbed and self-sufficient.[176] Yet again, the goal of life is to experience a reality that transcends this material world.

It is difficult to generalize about Hinduism, a religion that did not exist until the early nineteenth century. I am alluding, of course, to the fact that the English term is a modern colonial neologism used

a describe a diverse collection of beliefs and practices, an amalgama-
tion of various Indian traditions whose origins are mostly unknown.
The Vedas acknowledge many gods such as Agni (fire), Aditya (sun),
and Indra (king of the gods), and like most other polytheisms they
emphasize ritual ceremonies. In India, too, sacrifices were needed to
keep the universe going, and ritual activity sustained the world. "The
offerings that the priest made into the fire kept the sun from going
out; if no one sacrificed, the sun would not rise each morning."[177] This
changed as the Vedic tradition evolved into the Vedanta (literally "the
end of the Vedas"). As with other Axial religions, later texts such as
the Upanishads are strongly opposed to ritual. One of the oldest, the
Brihadaranyaka Upanishad, declares that anyone who worships a deity
other than one's innermost self or soul (*atman*) is a domestic animal
of the gods. Sacrifice came to be understood allegorically. Instead of
slaughtering a horse, one should renounce the universe, which is visu-
alized as the image of a horse.

Although Varuna was originally a sky god, by the time of the Rg
Veda his main responsibility had become punishing those humans
who transgress the *dharma* (sacred law). His role was not the only one
to evolve. Vedic polytheism developed into *henotheism* or "serial monotheism": worshiping a number of deities, although regarding each as
the supreme god, or even the only god, while you are relating to him or
her. Nonetheless, such a profusion of gods became difficult to manage
and eventually they were absorbed and organized into the *Trimurti*, a
trinity of supreme divinity: Brahma the creator, Vishnu the preserver,
and Shiva the destroyer. Other deities became their various manifestations. Krishna, for example, is one of the major avatars of Vishnu.
Another, according to Hinduism, was Gautama Buddha.

In place of Abrahamic beliefs (a creator god, sin, apocalypse, and
a final judgment leading to heaven or hell), the Upanishads emphasize concepts and practices that became central to Indian (not only
Hindu) philosophy: karma and rebirth, renunciation and meditation,
samsara and *moksha* (spiritual liberation). Most of India's orthodox
religious traditions, which accept the authority of the Vedas, came to

believe in an all-pervasive and eternal ultimate reality named *Brahman*, an impersonal creative principle that itself does not change but is nonetheless the source and ground of everything that exists, including humans.

Needless to say, Brahman itself, being incorporeal and immutable, transcends this world. The central issues of Hindu philosophy became the relationship between *atman* (one's true Self) and Brahman, and the relationship between Brahman and this world. The predominant view is that *atman* and Brahman are identical: to dispel ignorance and realize one's true nature is to realize that each of us has always been Brahman, and that the rest of the world is also a manifestation of Brahman. For those who are unenlightened, however, this world is *samsara*—a place of suffering, craving, and delusion into which we are repeatedly reborn after death, according to our karma. The ultimate spiritual goal is release from samsara, revealing that one's true self is *satchitananda*—reality, which is pure consciousness and blissful.

This release may be the ultimate goal for serious spiritual practitioners, but escape from this world was not an aspiration that appealed to everyone. Belief in karma and reincarnation provided another possibility: rebirth into a wealthier family in one's next lifetime, if not winning the lottery this time. This ambivalence reappears in Buddhism and continues to thrive today in the difference between what is sometimes called nirvanic Buddhism and karmic Buddhism. Does one emphasize the path of meditation or focus on accumulating merit by making offerings to monastics and temples? Unlike the Abrahamic heavens, which our resurrected bodies can enjoy eternally, ending rebirth by realizing one's nonduality with an immaterial transcendent absolute—whatever that might mean—is not necessarily attractive to those who prefer to appreciate what sensory experience has to offer.

*Ahimsa* ("nonviolence") is one of the central virtues in Hinduism (and India generally). Notably, this applies to all living beings, not just humans. Nonetheless, it does not entail the moral egalitarianism that one might expect, as the recalcitrant caste system shows. Another crucial Hindu concept, *dharma* (not to be identified with Buddhist dharma), refers to the duties and behaviors that we should practice because they sustain harmony in the world. Hindu dharma is about the right way to maintain *rta*, the cosmic order that regulates the way the universe operates. But not everyone has the same dharma: people born into different castes, due to their karma from past lives, have different roles in society. According to the Rg Veda, *brahmins* (priests) are the mouth of Brahma, *ksatriyas* (kings, warriors) are his arms, *vaishyas* (merchants and traders) his thighs, and *shudras* (peasants and workers) his feet. It is important that each caste perform its own duties and not encroach on the responsibilities of others. In particular, only Brahmin priests (all male) should enact sacred rituals and offer sacrifices. Instead of promoting universal human rights, this status differentiation rationalized social hierarchy and enshrined class discrimination. It is a good example of what is sometimes called "incomplete Axialization": the coexistence of Axial developments such as Vedantic monism with pre-Axial beliefs and practices.

Not all Indian spiritual traditions accepted the authority of the Vedas. Non-orthodox schools—most notably Buddhism and Jainism—did not. They are the best-known examples of the renouncer ascetic movements that arose in the middle of the first millennium BCE, about the same time that the most important Upanishads were composed.

According to the Pali Canon, the Buddha ("the awakened one") said that he was not a god but a human who has awakened. He had achieved *nibbana* (*nirvana* in Sanskrit), although descriptions provided in the earliest texts are not altogether clear about what that means, being mostly either metaphorical (the refuge, a safe harbor) or negations ("The destruction of lust, hatred, delusion: this is called Nibbana.")[178]

Note the difference between *nibbana,* which the Buddha experienced in his thirty-fifth year while meditating under the bodhi tree, and *parinibbana*, which the Buddha attained when he died at the age of eighty (according to traditional accounts). The distinction is important: Is *nibbana* itself complete and final salvation? Or does it simply indicate that final salvation will occur with *parinibbana*, because the

Buddha will not be reborn into samsara after this, his final lifetime? End of rebirth seems to imply extinction, but florid descriptions of his death in the Parinibbana Sutta—an account of his last days—suggest attainment of some transcendent reality.

Nonetheless, Buddhist teachings explicitly reject both possibilities, since annihilationism and eternalism both presuppose a real self, which is either destroyed or survives death. According to Buddhism such a self does not exist and never has: although we have a *sense* of a self that is separate from others, it is a delusion—or, in modern language, a psychological and social construct. In that sense there is nothing to gain, just something to realize. (You can see why the prospect of a more comfortable rebirth might be more attractive to most people.)

In short, the nature of the final goal remains ambiguous, with important implications. If the ultimate aspiration is *parinibbana*, Buddhist salvation is not that different from the dualistic focus of other Axial religions: to transcend this inferior and unsatisfactory realm. But if *nibbana* here-and-now is salvation, that implies the possibility of a *this-worldly* transcendence: that what needs to be transcended is not this world but our usual ways of experiencing it.

The Pali Canon abounds with examples of monastics and even laypeople who awakened (attained *nibbana* or lesser stages of enlightenment) after hearing a talk by the Buddha or one of his main disciples. Eventually, however, *nibbana* became "transcendentalized" in the sense that it was generally understood to be something extremely difficult to achieve, requiring thousands if not millions of lifetimes of arduous meditation practice. Today most monastics in South Asia have a more modest aspiration: scrupulously following the many rules and regulations that make them "fields of merit" deserving of the material support (*dana*) of laypeople. And most Buddhist laymen and laywomen understand their primary spiritual role as making offerings to monastics and temples, because the merit accumulated by doing this can lead to a better rebirth.

According to the Hebrew prophets, Yahweh wants compassion, not sacrifices. The Upanishads are also critical of Vedic ceremonies and sacrifices. The Buddha too emphasized that rituals (including sacrifices) are among the four types of grasping that we should let go of, along with sense objects, speculative opinions, and theories about the self. (Notice that only one of the four involves nonattachment to something physical.) When the Brahmin Sundarika Bharadvija advised the Buddha to bathe in the holy Bahuka River, which can wash away one's evil deeds, the Buddha responded that bathing in rivers could not cleanse anyone of their moral impurities; one should bathe instead in moral teachings about how to live.[179] (The nun Punnika later remarked that if water had such salvific power, then frogs, turtles, and crocodiles would all go to heaven!) Jesus later made the same point: "Nothing outside a person can defile them by going into them. Rather, it is what comes out of a person that defiles them."[180]

In the Dhammapada the Buddha applies this emphasis on ethical behavior to redefine what it means to be a Brahmin:

> Not by matted hair, not by clan,
> Not by birth does one become a Brahmin.
> The one in whom there is truth and Dharma
> Is the one who is pure, is a brahmin.
>
> Fool! What use is matted hair?
> What use is a deerskin robe?
> The tangled jungle is within you
> And you groom the outside![181]

In contrast to the Hindu caste system, the *sangha* (community) of spiritual renunciants that the Buddha created did not discriminate between members according to caste; the *Vinaya* rules that regulate monastic activity even forbid any reference to someone's former station in life. In the Agganna Sutta the Buddha teaches that such status discriminations are not a result of birth differences determined by a creator god (as most Hindus believed) but are nothing more than social conventions: cultural constructs created by humans. Buddhist scriptures do not call upon us to renounce the world. What should be renounced is one's role in a particular social order.

The Buddhist path has two pillars: wisdom and compassion. As in many Asian traditions, wisdom is insight into the true nature of the world. Living according to that realization involves practicing compassion and related virtues.

According to one story, the Buddha instructed a group of monks to meditate in a particular forest, but they became frightened by some resident earth spirits (*devas*) who did not appreciate their intrusion. In the Metta Sutta the Buddha taught the monastics how to placate such spirits by cultivating unconditional goodwill for the well-being of all living creatures, including *devas*: "May all beings be happy. . . . Cultivate an all-embracing mind of love for all throughout the universe, in all its height, depth and breadth—love that is untroubled and beyond hatred and enmity."[182]

In another text, the Tevijja Sutta, a group of young Brahmins consulted the Buddha on how to attain union with the god Brahma. He responds by teaching them how to attain the four *Brahmaviharas*, the metaphorical "abodes of Brahma": loving-kindness or basic friendliness (*metta*), compassion (*karuna*), empathetic joy (*mudita*), and equanimity (*upekkha*). These are also known as the four immeasurables, because developing them makes one's mind immeasurable, like the mind of Brahma himself.[183]

During the first century BCE a different type of Buddhism developed: the Mahayana, with its own sacred scriptures, philosophies, and practices. Mahayana expanded the status and role of the historical Gautama Buddha. He became "transcendentalized" into a godlike figure, one of a group of powerful and long-lived buddhas that ceaselessly work for the salvation of all beings. In the Pancavimsatisahasrika Sutra, for example, the Buddha's body becomes radiant, illuminating all the many world-systems in the universe with rays of light emanating from his "divine eye," toes, legs, ankles, thighs, hips, navel, arms, fingers, ears, nostrils, teeth, and eyes—even from his pores!

The Mahayana tradition critiques preoccupation with one's own enlightenment and expands the role of compassion: the *bodhisattva* path focuses less on one's own liberation (becoming an *arhat* who has achieved individual nirvana) and more on helping to liberate other sentient beings, which is what buddhas do. According to a more devotional type of Mahayana, however—Pure Land Buddhism, the predominant form of Buddhism in East Asia—when adherents die Amitabha Buddha can facilitate their rebirth into his blissful *buddha field*, where it is much easier to practice and attain full enlightenment. His Pure Land is only an intermediate realm, yet it is much better than where we are now. As with other Axial spiritual traditions, a superior place awaits us after we die . . .

China is, again, the odd one out—but in a way that (like some forms of Buddhism) suggests an alternative to problematic types of transcendence. What can be confusing is that Chinese Axiality developed more naturally out of its archaic past, without the clear break that occurred elsewhere. In Confucianism, particularly, there is no quest for otherworldly salvation, no priesthood or asceticism; there is no creator God or Satan, no reference to afterlife immortality in a heaven or hell.

Early China actually began with a monotheistic paradigm quite similar to the Abrahamic. During the Shang dynasty (1766–1040 BCE) it was believed that everything is created and controlled by the all-powerful Shangdi ("Celestial Lord"). Shang rulers were descendants of Shangdi and their rituals could influence what happens on earth. After we die we return to his spiritual realm.

That changed when the Shang were overthrown by the Zhou dynasty (1040–223 BCE), who claimed the "mandate of heaven" when Shangdi became transformed into an impersonal heavenly realm, Tian. Although sometimes anthropomorphized and identified with Shangdi, Tian evolved into a cosmological force that generates and regulates the ways that the earth's natural processes change, such as the perennial cycle of seasons. During the Warring States period (ca.

481–221 BCE), philosophers of the Hundred Schools came to prefer the term Dao ("the Way") to signify the underlying natural order of the cosmos.

Despite different nuances in their understanding of the Dao, Confucianism, Daoism, and (to a lesser extent) Chinese Buddhism—the three main religions, widely believed to be essentially the same—all focused on a *this-worldly* salvation that involves realizing something about here and now, and embodying that realization by living in harmony with the moral order.

Confucian morality cherished an idealized way of life that supposedly prevailed in the past. Confucius emphasized that he was "a transmitter who invented nothing," merely reviving traditional customs, especially rites that had been forgotten or gone out of fashion. Social harmony required respecting hierarchical roles but now the roles were mostly familial: father-son, husband-wife, older-younger siblings, ruler-subject. Filial piety included venerating ancestors, especially by procreating sons to continue the family line. Unlike the Hebrew prophets or Indian renouncers or Greek sophists, Chinese literati such as Confucius and his followers apparently supported the social hierarchy in ways that inhibited universalist reforms. There is nothing very Axial about any of this, so in what sense was Chinese Confucianism Axial?

In two important ways. Both involved experiencing "the secular as sacred"[184]—to say it again, a *this-worldly transcendence.* The first is that Confucianism did recognize a heaven that exercised moral judgment over this world, particularly evaluating its rulers who could lose the Mandate of Heaven if they governed badly. The nature of Tian, like Buddhist *nibbana,* is ambiguous. Unlike the Abrahamic God, Tian does not appear or speak to humans, or create a covenant with special people. Nonetheless, Confucius and others understood it as a divine will that not only judged rulers but supported the ruler's redemptive mission, which sought to reform the state but focused most of all on self-cultivation. Confucius always advocated a normative standard by which to evaluate existing reality, both personally and collectively.

That emphasis on individual self-transformation is the other way that China has been unambiguously Axial, resonating with the teachings of other Axial founders. According to Benjamin Schwartz,

> [Confucius's] description of these evil tendencies which impede the achievement of the good is strikingly similar to the diagnoses made by prophets, wise men, and philosophers in all the high civilizations of this period. The unbridled pursuit of wealth, power, fame, sensual passion, arrogance, and pride—these themes figure centrally as the source of "the difficulty." The language of the vices lends itself comparatively easily to translation into the vocabulary of Gautama Buddha, Plato, and the Hebrew prophets. . . . For them the divine no longer dwelt in the manifestations of power, wealth, and external glory.[185]

According to Confucius, anyone could become a "superior man" (*junzi*, literally "ruler's son") by cultivating one's innate *ren*, or "humanness," with five main virtues: earnestness, generosity, sincerity, diligence, and kindness. His two most prominent disciples, Mencius and Xunzi, disagreed about whether human nature is inclined to be good or evil, altruistic or selfish, yet for all Confucians our nature (*xing*) is not something predetermined but better understood as our potential for development.

What is distinctive about Confucianism is that human salvation is found not in rebirth or some other postmortem reward, but here and now in how one relates to other people. In that way self-cultivation can lead to a relationship with the ultimate moral order and uphold it as a normative standard, no matter how dire one's own historical time may be or whether one's efforts have any political impact. (Confucius and his immediate followers had very little.) The important point is that, unlike pre-Axial civilizations, China too developed an insightful critique of how we humans so often go wrong, and how we can correct ourselves. In that way China generated and sustained the basic Axial tension between the ideal and the real.

Daoist sages such as Lao-tzu and Chuang-tzu claimed a more intimate experience of the Dao, and their critique of society was less an attempt to reform social relations than to justify withdrawing from them. For early Daoists the alternative was not political reform but being co-opted and corrupted by the powers-that-be. There was nonetheless the same emphasis on self-cultivation in pursuit of harmony. In their case, however, the transformation that was sought prioritized harmony with the natural world.

## The Good, the Bad, and the Ugly

> In every single one of the religions of the Axial Age, individuals have failed to live up to their high ideals. In all these faiths, people have fallen prey to exclusivity, cruelty, superstition, and even atrocity. But at their core, the Axial faiths share an ideal of sympathy, respect, and universal concern.
>
> —**Karen Armstrong,** *The Great Transformation*

This chapter began with the claim that the Axial Age was the most important religious transformation in human history. Although it began over two thousand years ago, it is best understood as a developing process that is far from over. But enough has happened to offer a provisional evaluation.

### *Transcendence Pro*

None of the greatest conquerors and revolutionary leaders [e.g., Alexander, Julius Caesar, Genghis Khan, Napoleon, Stalin, Mao] can even remotely compete with these apostles of love in the magnitude and durability of the change brought about by their activities.[186]

Arguably, the most important practice that promotes self-transformation—emphasized in every Axial tradition—is living according to an ideal so simple, even obvious, that we tend to take it for granted, which, of course, does not mean that we actually follow it: the ethic of reciprocity, more popularly known as the Golden Rule. This ethic is not unique to the Axial Age religions, but they emphasized it more and at their best universalized it beyond one's own clan or social network. According to Robert Jensen,

> In the first century BCE, the *Jewish* scholar Hillel was challenged by a man to "teach me the whole Torah while I stand on one foot." Hillel's response: "What is hateful to you, do not do to your neighbor. That is the whole Torah, while the rest is the commentary thereof; go and learn it." In *Christianity*, Jesus phrased it this way in the Sermon on the Mount: "So whatever you wish that someone would do to you, do so to them; for this is the law and the prophets" (Matthew 7:12). In *Islam*, one of the Prophet Muhammad's central teachings was, "None of you truly believes until he loves for his brother what he loves for himself" (Hadith 13). In secular Western philosophy, *Kant's* categorical imperative is a touchstone: "Act only according to that maxim whereby you can at the same time will that it should become a universal law."[187]

Jensen's examples are Abrahamic, but many other Axial versions can be added. *Zoroastrianism*: "That nature alone is good which refrains from doing unto another whatsoever is not good for itself" (Dadestan-i Denig). *Hinduism*: "This is the sum of duty: Do naught unto others which would cause you pain if done to you" (Mahabharata). *Jainism*: "Persons endowed with intelligence and purified selves, should always behave toward other beings after the manner of that behavior which they like others to observe toward themselves" (Acaranga Sutra). *Buddhism*: "Hurt not others in ways that you yourself would find hurtful" (Udanavarga). *Confucianism*: "Is there one maxim which ought to be acted upon throughout one's whole life? Surely it is the maxim of loving-kindness: Do not unto others what you would not have them do unto you" (Analects). *Daoism*: "Regard your neighbor's gain as your own gain, and your neighbor's loss as your own loss" (Taishang Ganying Pian).[188]

Although ethical reciprocity and universalized compassion may be the most widely appreciated Axial teachings, they are only the most conspicuous parts of a more radical program. Relating to something that transcends the given social order liberated members from identification with the heretofore sacralized state, and a more personalized responsibility to that transcendence ultimately implied *reconstruction* of the individual, a task considerably more important and difficult than ritual observances. If the legacy of our evolutionary psychology has left a genetically based tension between predispositions that support one's own reproductive fitness (what's good for me and my offspring) and predispositions that encourage altruism (what's good for my group), now the struggle between those tendencies assumes a new form, in principle both individualized (I should reconstruct myself) and universalized (everyone should do it).

The goal of such self-cultivation was self-transformation, and self-transformation implied a different relationship with one's society, which could also be transformed. In addition to the implications for our individual behavior, many other modern values and institutions have Axial roots. Western civilization originated in the interaction between Judeo-Christian transcendence (ethical monotheism) and the very different types of transcendence that developed in ancient Greece (mathematics, philosophy, replacing godlike rulers with democracy).

Appeals for social justice can be traced back to the Hebrew prophets, who criticized rulers for afflicting the poor and powerless. Isaiah complained about those who "deprive the poor of their rights and withhold justice from the oppressed of my people, making widows their prey and robbing the fatherless."[189] The prophets spoke truth to power because they believed they were on a divine mission, speaking on God's behalf when demanding justice for the oppressed.

This Abrahamic emphasis, in combination with the Greek realization that society can be restructured, eventually resulted in the modern Western concern to pursue both social justice and personal liberty—the preeminent value of individuals—by reforming political and economic institutions. Since the Renaissance there has been the progressive development of religious freedom (the Reformation), political freedom (democracy), economic freedom (class struggle), colonial freedom (independence movements), racial freedom (anti-slavery and civil rights movements), and most recently sexual freedom and gender equality (feminism, LGBTQ rights, transgender fluidity).

All these historical transformations are social processes that remain contested, to various degrees, but taken together they manifest values and ideals ultimately rooted in the Axial traditions that flowered in Athens and Jerusalem. We can add to these Euro-American examples the type of liberation that the Axial religions of South Asia and East Asia have emphasized: not freedom for the self but freedom *from* the self—from the cravings and sufferings of an isolated and insulated ego-self, and ultimately from ignorance about its true nature.

While we cherish all these freedoms, the legacy of the Axial Age is more complicated and problematic.

## Transcendence Con

The influence of Axial traditions will continue to decline as it becomes ever more apparent that their resources are incommensurate with the moral challenges of the global problematique. In particular, to the extent that these traditions have stressed cosmological dualism and individual salvation we may say they have encouraged an attitude of indifference toward the integrity of natural and social systems.

—**Loyal Rue,** *Everybody's Story*

We must begin by acknowledging our collective failure to live up to the ideals promulgated by the Axial traditions. But are the Axial religions themselves partly responsible for this? Perhaps some of the problem is that Axial emphasis on personal self-cultivation has continued to be overshadowed by institutional preoccupation with external forms: for example, Catholic sacraments, or Ramadan fasting and Meccan pilgrimage for Muslims, or Buddhists accumulating *punya* (merit) for a better future rebirth. Although such observances sometimes promote positive individual transformation—for example, fasting as self-denial—they can also be viewed as updated versions of pre-Axial preoccupation with ritual. But can any institutionalized religion dispense with ceremonial practices?

As we have seen, the biggest problem with the Axial Age traditions is their emphasis on cosmological dualism, a type of transcendence that tends to devalue this world. On the beneficial side, however, what greatly transcends us all thereby promotes egalitarianism down here. Belief in transcendence could and sometimes did disrupt the all too familiar human preoccupation with amoral grasping at power and wealth, by offering a different perspective and a different value system.

In place of the usual group identities and animosities, our shared subordination to something "higher" makes us all brothers and sisters. Hobbes claimed that, to avoid a constant war of all against all that makes life "solitary, poor, nasty, brutish, and short," we need "a common power to keep them [people] all in awe." He was thinking of secular power—the need for a sovereign who could keep the peace—but it works just as well, or better, if we all believe in an all-powerful deity who is watching us. Jesus taught that we should love our enemies and do good to those who hate us, if we are to be children of our Father in heaven.[190] The Buddha emphasized the practice of generating *metta* (unconditional goodwill) for the well-being of all living beings.

Nonetheless, transcendence comes at a cost. The most obvious is preoccupation with what happens after we die, which makes our brief earthly existence into a disposable *means* to attain a much more important postmortem *goal*. For the Christian and Islamic traditions, the ultimate meaning of life becomes the task of avoiding everlasting damnation and qualifying for eternal bliss. For Hinduism and Buddhism, the ultimate spiritual objective is not to be reborn into *samsara*, this world of suffering—or at least to achieve a better rebirth. This encourages an alternation between fear and hope that can make us behave ourselves here, but it can also cast a long shadow over the ways we can experience joy and happiness now.

Sex is one example. The dualism between this desacralized world and a better place is often reproduced in our present embodied life. That division is also a split within us, between the higher part that yearns for postmortem salvation and a lower part that is bound to the earth. As Epictetus put it, "you are a little soul carrying around a corpse." Pauline Christianity distinguished between the flesh—subject to lust, sin, and death—and the spirit, a sharp dichotomy reinforced by Augustine, who wrote that we must ascend from physical things to the immaterial Being that is God. As Freud noticed, worshiping an invisible God "signified subordinating sense perception to an abstract idea: it was a triumph of spirituality over the senses."[191] Bodily desires are a distraction at best, when not a trap to be avoided. So Catholic clergy and Buddhist monastics, among others, are expected to be celibate.

But let's acknowledge the appeal of a higher and better reality: after all, this world *is* a place of suffering and death. That is why we don't want to be part of nature. Those carcasses our souls are carrying around have expiration dates. Much of the attraction of the Axial religions is that they offer a solution to mortality—the dread of which also explains many cultures' fear and degradation of animals as well as women, who bleed and remind us that we are conceived and born like other animals.

The dualism between this devalued world and that-which-transcends-it has also rationalized hierarchies, most notably patriarchy (every Axial tradition is patriarchal: women are identified with the physical, men with the rational), clerical superiority (over the laity), and human supremacy over all other species (the Bible especially has often been used to justify not only slavery but our exploitation of the rest of the biosphere).

Eventually, however, the Greek emancipation of reason from religious myth facilitated the development of something that came to question transcendence: a scientific and technological revolution that offered secular explanations for this world and how it functions, including an evolutionary understanding of how life developed on this planet. These new ways of understanding have been so successful because they provided us with extraordinary power to control the earth and each other. In the process, the soul became the mind (initially still viewed as quite different from the physical body), and more recently the mind has become understood as a function of the human brain—the most complex structure in the known universe, but now viewed as a completely material one.

It is important to realize that the secularity many of us take for granted today is not simply the here-and-now world where we live, but a specific, historically conditioned understanding of where and what we are: not reality "as it really is in itself," but an interpretation of reality. Secularity was originally one half of a duality, and it remains haunted by the loss of its other half. Modernity developed out of the split that appeared between God's transcendence and a de-spiritualized material world. Until recently God was believed to be the ultimate source of meaning and value, so when transcendence disappeared—because scientific explanations didn't need it—we were left to cope as best we could with what remained: a desacralized mechanistic universe. Our usual understanding of the secular is thus a defective worldview, distorted by the fact that the other half, the spiritual, is missing. In trading mystery for mastery, what are we overlooking?

Of course, many people today would not agree that God has disappeared. They continue to accept conventional religious doctrines, often taken literally: this world is where we qualify for the next, and so on. This understanding provides their lives with meaning that is difficult to relinquish, for what is the alternative? Loss of belief in transcendence can lead to a nihilism where life becomes meaningless, insofar as traditional understandings of meaning have been grounded in transcendent teachings about how we should live.

Where both responses agree, in effect, is that there is something unsatisfactory about this world; it is deficient in some way. But is there a third possibility? Is the problem this world, or the ways we have been understanding and experiencing it? Is the challenge to *resacralize* our life on this earth? The final chapter looks at what that might involve.

## The Ugly

Karl Jaspers noticed a collapse that occurred in all the Axial civilizations beginning about 200 BCE, when "great political and spiritual unifications and dogmatic configurations held the field." He described this as "a loss of consciousness. Only a few suitable intellectual possibilities and spiritual figures from the bygone Axial Period were seized upon to impart spiritual community, luster, and concordance to the new state authorities. The imperial idea was realized in forms founded on religion."[192]

In Greece the political breakdown began a little earlier, when Alexander conquered it in 335 BCE and ended Athens' short-lived experiment with democracy; his empire did not long survive his death and in 146 BCE Rome annexed the whole peninsula. Israel became a Roman vassal during the reign of Herod and then a Roman province in 6 CE. Ashoka (ca. 304–232 BCE), the third Mauryan emperor and the first ruler to unify almost the whole of the Indian subcontinent, promoted Buddhism, but after his death the Mauryan empire declined and was overthrown in 184 BCE by Pushyamitra, who founded the Shunga empire; he is believed to have persecuted Buddhism and reestablished Brahminism, including the animal sacrifices that Ashoka had forbidden.

In China the chaotic Warring States period ended when the militaristic kingdom of Qin succeeded in unifying China in 221 BCE. The new emperor, Shi Huang, had no interest in the morality or compassion taught by Axial sages such as Confucius and Chuang-tzu, and their classic texts were fortunate to survive a massive book burning in 213. What we know as Christianity was a product of the Roman empire: the church that resulted—with the Pope as something like an ecclesiastical emperor—owes more to that empire's institutions than anything Jesus taught. What became Islam evolved politically and theologically as the new Arabian state unified by Muhammad expanded aggressively to become one of the largest empires in history.

Ironically, the revolutionary teachings of the new Axial Age traditions were appropriated by rulers who wielded them to justify their own power and superiority: "Our universalism is better than yours!" Like Zoroastrianism before them, the three most successful missionary religions—Buddhism, Christianity, and Islam—each became institutionalized by an empire. In effect, the new state religions reverted to the pre-Axial unity of secular and sacred authority—enshrining, for example, the divine right of European kings. Even today the British monarch is legally the "supreme governor" of the Anglican Church, and the king of Thailand is a *devaraja*, or "divine ruler," as well as a Buddhist bodhisattva whose authority is triply grounded in his religious role, moral example, and pure dynastic blood.

Those who claim to represent the transcendent and speak on its behalf assume power that can be used in different ways. European Christendom, with its history of antisemitism, inquisitions, heresy and witchcraft trials, militaristic crusades, and imperialistic oppression of other religions, offers a particularly regrettable example of how an Axial religion—ostensibly based on the teachings of Jesus—can go wrong. But it is hardly unique. Even a supposed peace-loving religion such as Buddhism provides many counterexamples, most recently in Sri Lanka, where the Buddhist establishment supported the ruthless crushing of a Tamil independence movement, and Myanmar, where some Buddhist monks have supported similar violence against Muslim Rohingya.

Jaspers concluded that the Axial Age was "an interregnum between two ages of great empire, a pause for liberty, a deep breath bringing the most lucid consciousness."[193] Despite their political eclipse, however, the fact that all the Axial traditions were script-based meant that post-Axial empires absorbed these profound developments into themselves as holy scriptures, cultural time-bombs that always threatened to explode into radical social movements. When English Puritans did something hitherto unthinkable by executing King Charles in 1649, they were motivated in part by how they understood the Bible, especially predictions in the Book of Revelation. The teachings of Jesus and the life of Francis of Assisi have continued to inspire people up to the present day. The same is true, of course, for other Axial founders and many of their followers. Now we urgently need to ask: What can be recuperated from the teachings of the Axial Age that can help us respond to our dangerous situation today? And in what ways do those teachings need to be updated?

## Why This Matters

> The process of transmission of religious tradition is potentially the most confining among human institutions, creating for some a kind of cultural prison, or the most liberating because religious commitment permits the individual to stand within a tradition that calls into question all traditions, including ultimately aspects of itself.
>
> **—Raymond B. Williams**[194]

This chapter began with the claim that the Axial Age can be understood as cultural evolution attempting to compensate for problems created by our biological evolution. The Axial religions did that by offering universalistic teachings and practices that address the deep-rooted tension between egocentric tendencies (What's in it for me?) and more altruistic ones (What serves the well-being of our group?).

Of course, religions perform many other functions. As noted above, they usually assure us that we don't really die, which assuages our deepest fear. As Arthur Schopenhauer put it, religion is the metaphysics of the masses: religious creeds and communal practices bind us together into communities that share beliefs and values. Because we are social animals, we learn from each other what is real and what is important, how to live and how to love.

In that sense, religions provide the ultimate security, explaining our place and role in a world that is otherwise intimidating and mysterious. It is no coincidence that atheism is most common when political and economic well-being is high: then it becomes an option that people can psychologically afford.[195] A lack of this-worldly safety often induces us to seek a transcendent refuge.

Religion also legitimates social institutions. Most obviously, it sanctified the political and spiritual hierarchies of pre-Axial archaic civilizations, but we have noticed that Axial religious institutions have continued to rationalize and consecrate social hierarchies.

Today many Western cultures pride themselves on separating church from state, a distinction that remains contested because the nature of secular authority is inherently problematic: Unless physically compelled, why are we obligated to do what the state wants us to do? "Religion *mystifies* institutions by explaining them as *given* over and beyond their empirical existence in the history of a society." It imposes a fictitious inexorability upon a social world that is actually our human construct.[196] Ursula K. Le Guin famously stated,

> We live in capitalism, its power seems inescapable—but then, so did the divine right of kings. Any human power can be resisted and changed by human beings.[197]

Religions can also *de-legitimize* institutions by withdrawing the sanctity previously assigned to them. Arguably, something like that is happening right now. Belief in Christian nationalism and other forms of American exceptionalism has been justified by understanding the United States as a country especially favored by God, a "beacon of hope" to the world. Today, however, increasingly acrimonious conservative-versus-liberal political divergence is raising questions about American politics and our international role. For better and worse, the legitimacy of that system—its right to our acquiescence—is no longer something that can be taken for granted.

Le Guin's reference to capitalism highlights another institution that has become suspect. The creativity and energy of Anglo-American capitalism has led to extraordinary comfort and freedom for many people, but its fruits have not been well distributed. Campaign contributions and "dark money" have subverted our political system into something better described as a plutocracy that uses and abuses democratic forms for the benefit of an increasingly wealthy elite. Short-sighted corporate focus on growth and profitability continues to exploit and damage ecosystems, while resisting the reforms necessary for us to become a civilization that lives in harmony with the rest of the biosphere.

For some people, questioning something as basic as our economic system—"the greatest in human history," we are told—implies that one must be an atheistic, God-hating communist. "When the socially defined reality has come to be identified with the ultimate reality of the universe, then its denial takes on the quality of evil as well as madness."[198] In the 1980s British prime minister Margaret Thatcher famously declared "There Is No Alternative" to neoliberal free-market economics. I haven't conducted a survey, but it seems to me that those who accept traditional religious views about God are also the most likely to normalize, if not sanctify, capitalism and American exceptionalism. And why worry so much about problems here—including social injustice and ecological devastation—if the apocalypse is imminent and our ultimate destiny is elsewhere?

But what if we have misconstrued the nature of transcendence? The French Surrealist poet Paul Eluard is said to have declared "There is another world, but it is in this one." Or is that other world actually (the true nature of) *this one*? What alternatives open up if and when Axial Age teachings are understood not as pointing to some "higher" reality, but as saying something important that we have been overlooking about the nature of this one?

\* \* \*

I have read somewhere of an old Chinese curse: "May you be born in an interesting time!" This is a *very* interesting time: there are no models for *anything* that is going on. It is a period of free fall into the future, and each has to make his or her own way. The old models are not working; the new have not yet appeared. In fact, it is we who are even now shaping the new in the shaping of our interesting lives. And that is the whole sense (in mythological terms) of the present challenge: we are the "ancestors" of an age to come, the unwitting generators of its supporting myths, the mythic models that will inspire its lives.

  —Joseph Campbell


The central quality of the evolutionary process is creative emergence.

  —Willis Haman and Elisabet Sahtouris


The most remarkable feature of this historical moment is not that we are on the way to destroying our world—it's that we are beginning to wake up—as if from a millennia long sleep.

  —Joanna Macy

The ultimate hidden truth of the world is that it is something we make and could just as easily make differently.

—**David Graeber**

My point, once again, is not that those ancient people told literal stories, and we are now smart enough to take them symbolically, but that they told them symbolically, and we are now dumb enough to take them literally.

—**John Dominic Crossan**

There is a dream dreaming us.

—**Australian Aborigine and Kalahari Bushman saying**

"Appearance" is a funny sort of word. It means some kind of surface thing, but with something else called "reality" that is behind it. "Presence" is a much better word. Something is presenting by itself, whose essence is emptiness. What appears is the phenomenal world, but it is empty because it has no real substance.

—**Traleg Kyabgon Rinpoche**

God is an utter nothingness,
Beyond the touch of time and place:
The more you grasp after him,
The more he flees your embrace.

> **—Angelus Silesius**

God made everything out of nothing, but the nothingness shows through.

> **—Paul Valery**

You never know the world aright till the Sea floweth in your veins, till you are Clothed with the Heavens, and Crowned with the Stars; And perceive yourself to be the Sole Heir of the Whole World; And more so then, because Men are in it who are every one Sole Heirs, as well as you. Till you are intimately Acquainted with that Shady Nothing out of which this World was made; Till your spirit filleth the whole World and the Stars are your Jewels; Till you love Men so as to Desire their Happiness with a thirst equal to the zeal of your own.

> **—Thomas Traherne**

The emptiness cannot be destroyed; it can only be filled by love.

    —**Michael Ende**

I really love transcendence only as my love transfigures the world.

    —**Karl Jaspers**

The world doesn't want to be saved. It wants to be loved. That's how you save it.

    —**Richard Brendan**

Heaven is my father and earth is my mother and even such a small creature as I finds an intimate place in its midst. That which extends throughout the universe I regard as my body and that which directs the universe I regard as my nature. All people are my brothers and sisters and all things are my companions.

    —**Chang Tsai**

# 3

# What We Need Today

## *A Spirituality That Loves This World*

Most of us who grew up in a religious family naturally took that religion for granted, at least while we were children. Only much later, if at all, do we become aware that its doctrine, rituals, and institutional organization are historically conditioned, products of complicated social influences that could have developed differently—and, in some cases, need to become different today.

In particular, the origins of the world's major religious traditions are more convoluted than usually recognized, and that includes the formation of their sacred texts. For example, many Christians believe that the four gospels of the New Testament record the original words of Jesus. Many Theravada Buddhists believe that the Pali Canon faithfully reproduces what the Buddha taught. Scholars today challenge both claims, and the early history of both religions raises important questions about how basic teachings develop and solidify into doctrines.

Stories in the Hebrew Bible (Tanakh) were written down long after the events they purport to describe, and many of them have been preserved because they are edifying, not because they actually happened. There is, for example, no historical evidence in Egypt or Israel for the existence of Moses, the most important Jewish prophet. Most biblical archaeologists consider his accomplishments to be legends that may have become influential because they support the claim of the Israelites to their Promised Land.

Unlike most of the other major religions, Christianity originated at a time when literacy was widespread enough in the Mediterranean world that we have many accounts of its early development. Those first few centuries provide perhaps the best recorded example of how diverse views compete and some doctrines eventually become canonized as orthodox (literally, "correct opinion"), while others are condemned as heretical. Immediately after the death of Jesus his followers apparently expected him to return soon, within their own lifetimes, which meant there was little motivation to write anything down or construct a theology. But as eyewitnesses began to die, concern grew for future generations, and different understandings of his life and mission began to proliferate.

The Ebionites, one of the earliest Christian sects, believed that Jesus of Nazareth was not divine but conceived and born like other humans (no virgin birth), and only at his baptism was chosen by God to be a messianic prophet. He was a Jew fulfilling Jewish law and died as a martyr urging other Jews to repent.

According to Marcion of Sinope, however, Jesus was not human at all but a divine being who only appeared to be born and to suffer on the cross. Marcionites rejected Judaism, distinguishing the jealous and vengeful God of the Old Testament from the teachings of Christ, who emphasized love and mercy. While the Ebionites considered Paul an apostate, Marcion regarded Paul's letters as expressing the essence of Christ's teachings.

Like the Marcionites, Christian Gnostics believed that this world was created by a malevolent god, and that our incarceration here is a cosmic catastrophe. Matter is evil, spirit is good, and our souls are divine sparks that need to be liberated from their physical bodies. Jesus was a divine emissary sent down by a different and more benevolent God to impart the spiritual truth that can save us. For the Gnostics, unlike the Marcionites, the fundamental issue is not repenting for our sins but obtaining the esoteric knowledge that dispels illusion.

All three of these early movements (along with others such as Arianism and Montanism) were eventually condemned as heretical, most notably in 325 CE at the First Council of Nicaea summoned by the Roman emperor Constantine. A convert who ended centuries of Christian persecution, Constantine disliked the social instability that religious controversy fostered. He instructed the bishops to formulate a theological consensus that he would enforce. The result was the Nicene Creed, which affirmed one God, the Father Almighty, with Jesus Christ (both fully human and fully divine) his only-begotten Son, born of a virgin, who was crucified but arose again and ascended into heaven; at the future resurrection of the dead he will return to judge everyone and decide where each of us will spend eternity.[199]

From a modern perspective, the story of a god who dies and is resurrected seems distinctively Christian, but at the time there was plenty of competition. According to Randel Helms,

> In the first century of the Common Era, there appeared at the eastern end of the Mediterranean a remarkable religious leader who taught the worship of one true God and declared that religion meant not the sacrifice of beasts but the practice of charity and piety and the shunning of hatred and enmity. He was said to have worked miracles of goodness, casting out demons, healing the sick, raising the dead. His exemplary life led some of his followers to claim he was a son of God, though he called himself the son of a man. Accused of sedition against Rome, he was arrested. After his death his disciples claimed that he had risen from the dead, appeared to them alive, and then ascended to heaven. Who was this teacher and wonder-worker? His name was Apollonius of Tyana; he died about 98 A.D. and his story may be read in Flavius Philostratus's *Life of Apollonius.*[200]

Jesus was not the only god born of a virgin. Other examples include the Egyptian deities Ra and Horus (the son of Isis), as well as the Greek hero Perseus and the god Asclepius. According to some accounts, Dionysus, the Greek god of wine, fertility, and religious ecstasy, was virgin-born, performed miracles such as changing water into wine, descended into the underworld, was resurrected, and later ascended into heaven, where he joined the other Olympians. And you didn't need to be a god: some people believed that Plato and Alexander of Macedonia were born to virgins. According to the traditional story, Gautama Buddha's mother was not a virgin but became pregnant when she dreamed of a white elephant that entered her right side.

As the Roman Empire declined, the Christian version of a resurrected god became the most popular, perhaps because it offered the possibility of resurrection for believers too. We don't really die! At least not forever . . .

The orthodox Nicene view is the one that most Christians today are familiar with, but its doctrinal success was by no means inevitable. It is generally compatible with the four gospels of the New Testament—although the earliest, Mark, does not mention the virgin birth and its description of Jesus's baptism implies that only then did he become the unique Son of God. Its earliest version was very short, ending at 16:8: "Trembling and bewildered, the women went out and fled from the tomb. They said nothing to anyone, because they were afraid." But over the next few decades there were several attempts to expand Mark's bare-boned story. Those efforts included the gospels of Matthew and Luke, both of which incorporated almost all of Mark, editing and adding to fit their doctrinal agendas. None of those three mention that Jesus considered himself God incarnate. Only in the most theologically sophisticated gospel, John—the last to be written—does Jesus assert his divinity.

Despite their traditional titles, all four gospels are anonymous and none was an eyewitness account. Each derived from collections of oral teachings and miracle stories eventually written down between 66 and 110 CE—later than the epistles of Paul. It was generally believed that interviews and other historical research were not necessary, since everything that had happened in the life of Jesus was "according to the scriptures" of the Hebrew Bible, which was replete with oracles about the imminent appearance of a messiah.[201]

There are at least twenty other apocryphal gospels that were not incorporated into the New Testament, including those attributed to Thomas, Peter, Mary, and Judas, with varying perspectives on Jesus and his mission. Today we know little about the Ebionites, Marcionites, or Christian Gnostics because their writings were condemned and little survives, except as quoted by Irenaeus and other Church Fathers who criticized them—although the discovery of the Nag Hammadi manuscripts in 1945 brought to light several long-lost Gnostic texts.

What is sometimes called Mariolatry—veneration of the Blessed Virgin Mary—developed relatively late. Four beliefs about Mary were much debated in the Middle Ages and eventually became official dogma of the Catholic Church: her role and status as Mother of God (declared at the Council of Ephesus, 431 CE); that she remained a virgin before, during, and after the birth of Jesus (Synod of Milan, 389 CE); her Immaculate Conception (Mary herself was conceived and born "without sin," 1854); and that she did not physically die but at the end of her life ascended directly into heaven. The last dogma was not affirmed until 1950.[202]

The essential point from all this is that what we take for granted today as Christian doctrine is in fact the result of a complex intellectual and historical process that, had circumstances been different, might have resulted in a different creed. Is that true only for Christianity? Muslims today believe that the holy text of Islam, the Qur'an, is both the verbatim word of God and God's unalterable final revelation to humanity. Nothing in it can be changed in any way—but that was not always the case. Various versions circulated prior to the third caliph, Uthman ibn Affan, who standardized one particular version in 652 CE and had all other variants destroyed. This was controversial at the time: one of Muhammad's close companions, Abd Allah ibn Mas'ud, complained that Uthman's scribes had added three extra *suras* (chapters) and made numerous other changes to the original text. He described Uthman's version as a "deceit," yet, once again, political power played a major role in how the religious institution developed and how its teachings became canonized.

Another important example is the early history of Buddhism. It is important to note that the role of belief in most Buddhist traditions is quite different from Christianity and Islam, because Buddhism does not highlight faith in the same way: the emphasis is on morality and contemplative practice, and the teachings are adjuncts to that. The Buddha compared his Dharma to a raft, useful for reaching the "far shore" of enlightenment, but not something to be grasped (carried around on one's back afterwards).[203] With the exception of Pure Land Buddhism—a late devotional development—unenlightened people can expect to be reborn according to their karma, regardless of what they believe. It is also difficult to compare the origins of Buddhism with the origins of Christianity, because while Christianity became a text-based religion within a few generations, Buddhism remained an oral tradition for over 250 years. According to the Pali Canon, after the Buddha's death his attendant, Ananda, recited from memory all the teachings that the Buddha had presented. That story is somewhat implausible for several reasons, including the fact that the Pali Canon is several times the length of the whole Bible. We do not know what teachings may have been lost, added, or altered during those centuries of oral transmission, which means we cannot hope to recover the original words of the founder, and therefore can never know how faithfully any Buddhist tradition today preserves what Gautama Buddha actually taught.

As Bhikkhu Anālayo has pointed out, in an oral tradition the difference between the "source text" and later commentaries is naturally porous. When reciting a memorized passage to an audience, speakers naturally attempt to explain what may not be clear to listeners; over time, helpful clarifications tend to become part of the original teaching. In that way the initial corpus can expand significantly, but there is always the possibility of misinterpretation. The speaker's understanding may be quite different from the Buddha's. That is especially problematic for a tradition that emphasizes personal insight—enlightenment—over mere intellectual comprehension.[204]

Textual analysis has enabled scholars to distinguish different strata in the Pali Canon, and one of the earliest teaching collections—mentioned by name in at least three other suttas—was the Atthaka-vagga (Book of Eights). What is particularly interesting about this text is that it lacks almost all the doctrines now considered essential to Buddhism: the four noble truths, the eightfold path, the three characteristics, the four foundations of mindfulness, the seven factors, and the four stages of awakening; even the concepts of no-self and rebirth are absent. The Atthakavagga also does not distinguish this conditioned world of suffering (*samsara*) from an unconditioned transcendent reality (*nibbana*). Instead, it highlights a peace that can be found here and now. To attain that serenity the Atthakavagga emphasizes letting go of all views, avoiding sensual craving, and developing the characteristics of sagehood.[205]

We cannot draw firm conclusions from this single example, but it reinforces what other Buddhist texts emphasize: the impermanence and insubstantiality of everything—including the Buddhadharma itself.

There are other curious parallels with early Christianity, including docetism, the belief that the founder's physical body was not real but only an apparition. As Buddhism grew from a cult into a popular religion, doctrinal schisms developed, eventually resulting in at least eighteen different schools. According to the Lokottaravada "Transcendentalists" and some of the Mahayana schools that arose later, Gautama the historical Buddha was not human but a supramundane being whose bodily manifestation was illusory, who knew everything and taught ceaselessly while nonetheless meditating nonstop. As both spiritual teachers receded into the past, Christ and the Buddha became superhuman to the followers who never knew them personally.

As also happened with Christianity, one of the main reasons why Buddhism became so successful is that it gained the patronage of an emperor. For Buddhism it was Ashoka (ca. 304–232 BCE), whose Mauryan empire incorporated almost all the Indian subcontinent. Although historical records are sparse, Ashoka is credited with calling the Third Buddhist Council, which purged the monastic community of apparently heretical monastics who were accused of joining in order to enjoy royal patronage. According to Theravada sources, Ashoka favored the monk Moggaliputta-Tissa, who founded the Vibhajjavada school that later evolved into the Theravada tradition. With his help Ashoka promoted extensive missionary activities that included sending his own son and daughter (both ordained) to Sri Lanka, where they helped to establish Buddhism. Although it later disappeared from India, Buddhism in Sri Lanka and Southeast Asia remains primarily Theravada, with significant doctrinal differences from the Mahayana Buddhism that predominates in East Asia and Central Asia.

Why are these histories important? Because they remind us, again, that every religious tradition, no matter how consistent and cohesive its teachings may be today, is a complex social product. The supposed "pure origin"—the original words of the founder—can never be recovered. The problem goes beyond the fact that the most important religious innovators did not themselves write about their encounters with the sacred. Every major religion is founded on the special religious (usually mystical) experience of its founder, who shared what he (yes, *he*) experienced—or more precisely, who taught what he had learned from the experience. Founders being so great—either divine or divinely inspired—no questions can be raised internally about any possible distortions caused by their subjectivity, with no concern that there might be a difference between what actually happened and how that was understood after the fact. In particular, religious traditions ignore how easy it would be to (mis)understand a different way of experiencing this world as the temporary irruption of another, "higher" reality into this one. It would also be tempting to conclude that this newly revealed transcendent reality offers an escape from the sufferings of the "lower reality" that is this world: best of all, maybe even the exciting possibility of postmortem survival in a superior place.

Are such misunderstandings examples of what Joseph Campbell and John Dominic Crossan describe as religion getting stuck in its own metaphors and interpreting them literally rather than symbolically?

The idea that we experience things the way we do because of the ways our minds work—that the world we usually take for granted is a psychological and social construct—was first expounded in Europe by the German philosopher Immanuel Kant in the late eighteenth century. It is also implicit in Buddhist teachings, with the additional corollary that such a construct can be deconstructed and reconstructed, in which case both our sense of self and the world we live in become different too.

The previous chapter argued that the Axial Age in the first millennium BCE can be understood as a response to a widespread social crisis—the collapse of Bronze Age civilizations—that led to the development of a new religious and social paradigm. Today we face another, even greater, crisis: a polycrisis with multiple ecological, technological, economic, social, and political dimensions. Our dangerous situation today can be viewed as a consequence of our failure to embody Axial principles such as universal compassion and self-transformation. But that critique overlooks the basic problem: those ideals were rooted in a worldview that has become problematic. Axial religions were for the most part based on a defective paradigm, a cosmological dualism that made sense two thousand years ago but is less plausible now. Although transcendence is necessary, today more than ever, the challenge is not to transcend this world but to transcend our usual ways of experiencing it. Instead of trying to qualify for some after-death salvation, we need a spiritual path that focuses on transforming ourselves so that we realize the true nature of this world (including our own true nature).

It is important to recognize that this is not a new idea. Rather, this perspective addresses an internal tension found within each of the Axial Age traditions. We need only turn our attention to what many saints, gurus, sages, and enlightened masters have taught, often at odds with the orthodoxy maintained by mainstream religious institutions. Many traditionalist Muslims today, especially revivalist Wahhabis and pietistic Salafis, consider Sufism—the most influential mystical development in Islam—as heretical. Some of the teachings of Meister

Eckhart, arguably the most important mystic-philosopher of medieval Christianity, were condemned by the Catholic Church. I do not remember my own teacher, Zen Master Yamada Koun, ever talking about physical rebirth after we die, an essential teaching of conventional Buddhism; the Zen path is about letting go of oneself *now* in order to realize something life-transforming about *here*.

At the risk of oversimplifying, I might try to summarize the most important point of this book by comparing the three primary worldviews competing for our allegiance today. The first continues to have the most adherents, although its influence is declining in the developed world: traditional religious versions of cosmological dualism, including the promise (or threat) of individual postmortem salvation (or damnation). Today their main competition is a second worldview: secularism, supported by the physical sciences, which offers a naturalistic understanding of the world that does not support any afterlife transcendence.

The third worldview regards the earth and its creatures as sacred, without the need for a "higher reality" to have created them. Humanity is one of the manifestations of a self-organizing cosmos that, according to some versions, is evolving to become more self-aware. Theistic traditions describe *theophanies*, when divine beings appear, and *hierophanies*, a more general term for any manifestation of the sacred. According to the nondualist paradigm, however, everything is a hierophany, which we can experience when we wake up from the delusion of being a separate self in an objectified world.

Given our fear of death, it is not surprising that the prospect of postmortem survival continues to be so attractive. Ironically, though, the predominant alternative—secularism—is not simply the everyday world we live in when we let go of questionable beliefs about creator gods and immortal souls. A secular perspective remains conditioned by the very duality it denies: it merely removes one half (spirit) without considering what that means for how we experience the other half (matter) of the duality.

Our modern world developed out of the split between a transcendent spiritual reality (God, to use theistic language) and a material realm that was thereby de-spiritualized—that is, God created it but is separate and "higher" than it. God's ongoing role in this duality is to be the external source of goodness and meaning. He (to use the traditional pronoun) tells us why we are here and how to live while we are here. Belief in God thereby situates our morality and mortality within the larger context that he provides. Our striving serves an essential role within his grand plan for us, and our efforts affect our ultimate destiny.

The evolution revolution that Darwin initiated became a mortal blow to that God. An all-knowing and all-powerful Being was no longer necessary to create the extraordinarily complex organisms, including us, that compose the web of life. But God's disappearance left us stranded in the remaining half of the duality: in a desacralized universe that has lost the traditional source of its value and meaning. Now human beings serve no function in the grand scheme of things, for a mechanistic cosmos, ruled by impersonal physical laws, is indifferent to us and our fate.

So it seems . . . but is it true? Having projected all sacrality onto an imperceptible God and then banished that deity, along with immaterial souls and all other aspects of spirituality, we find ourselves abandoned in a world of atoms and physical laws that is apparently unconcerned about the things we are concerned about. We may accept that way of understanding the world, coping as best we can, but when we realize that way of experiencing is also historically conditioned, then other options appear. These include the possibility of revaluing this undervalued world, which would involve (among other things) no longer treating it as a disposable means to qualify for somewhere better. The question then becomes, How might such a reappraisal change the way we experience here-and-now? Can the notion of a *this-worldly transcendence* reincorporate the sacrality that has been lost?

This chapter explores the implications of such a nondualist paradigm. In contrast to the cosmological dualism of Axial traditions, the sacred is not imported from somewhere else but is the true nature of this world, and the impermanent phenomena we experience are the manifold ways that the sacred assumes form and reveals itself.

According to this paradigm, there are (at least) two different ways to experience the world, but we are normally aware of only one of them, which we mistakenly believe to be "the way the world really is." We usually perceive it as a collection of separate, self-existing things that interact in objective space and time, one of those things being *me*. We learn to understand the world this way as we grow up, socialized into relating to it in the same fashion that everyone else does. Living this way has served the evolutionary process by contributing to our survival and success: once we identify things and their functions, we can utilize them for doing and getting what we want. So this way of perceiving serves an important role in our lives. But it is not the only way to experience and understand the world, or ourselves.

Our preoccupation with recognizing and using objectified things means that we usually overlook something important about them: the world experienced this way is a psychological and social construct. That points to the role of deconstructive practices such as meditation and non-petitionary prayer, which can lead to a more nondual way of experiencing the world, in which supposedly separate beings (including ourselves) are actually hierophanies revealing the sacred. In theistic terms, everything can be perceived as a theophany of God, who is nothing other than the true nature of the universe. By this account, "God" is not an invisible, super-powerful being who created everything but instead a form-less nothing (or *no-thing*) that manifests as all the phenomena we experience. According to Paul Tillich,

> God is not a reality that may or may not exist, but God is the most common Western name for "what is," for "ultimate reality," for "the ground of being," for "Being itself," for "isness."[206]

This paradigm is not new: it corresponds to what many of the great mystics in each religious tradition have been pointing at when they talk about *experiencing* God or Brahman or the Dao, and so on. It is no coincidence that all three of those names for ultimate reality share the same characteristic of having no identifiable characteristics of their own, which is why each can be understood as a pure, "empty" potentiality that assumes various forms.

*Mysticism* is a broad term that refers to a variety of spiritual experiences, but its most influential versions all involve unmediated awareness of a supreme reality here and now. In such encounters the usual duality between a self *inside* and an external world *outside* dissolves when I "let go" of myself. That is possible because the sense of a discrete self that is distinct from what it experiences—the subjective side of our dualistic experience—is also delusive. In modern language, it too is a psychological and social construct that can be deconstructed. And that is what happens in meditation, when one cultivates letting-go of the habitual thought patterns that constitute and sustain the illusion of a separate self. This can lead to the most important realization of all: that we are not separate from, or other than, the ultimate reality that is revealed. Each of us is a theophany.

So it is no coincidence that the principal mystical traditions—including the Abrahamic theistic as well as Asian nondualist—agree that the fundamental obstacle to God-realization or enlightenment is the ego-self, the subjective pole of the self/other duality. Perhaps we should not be surprised that nondualist Asian traditions such as Mahayana and Vajrayana Buddhism, Advaita Vedanta, Kashmir Shaivism, and Daoism emphasize "forgetting" the sense of self. What is more remarkable is that so many theistic mystics have also highlighted the importance of "extinguishing" the self. According to the Jewish Kabbalah: "When a man attains to the stage of self-annihilation he can thus be said to have reached the world of the divine Nothingness [*Ayin*]. Emptied of selfhood, his soul has now become attached to the true reality."[207]

One of the most famous Christian expressions of nonself is found in Paul's letter to the Galatians: "I no longer live but Christ lives in me."[208] Meister Eckhart encouraged the same self-emptying (*kenosis*): "If you could naught yourself for an instant, indeed I say less than an instant, you would possess all." This is different from an intellectual understanding. For Eckhart the best way to serve the world is by not-knowing, which is essential to self-emptying: letting-go of what we know, or think we know. "To him who knows nothing, it appears and reveals itself."[209]

An ancient inscription carved on the door of St. Paul's monastery on Mt. Athos reads, "If you die before you die, you will not die when you die." When the self lets go of itself, it dies—but not literally, because it was always an illusory construct, without any discrete reality of its own. We are in the realm of metaphor: the ego-self lets go so that something else can be reborn. Is this the way to understand the crucifixion and resurrection at the heart of Christianity?

Within the Abrahamic traditions, Sufis emphasize this death of the self perhaps more than anyone else. In *The Conference of the Birds* Attar of Nishapur has the hoopoe declare, "So long as we do not die to ourselves, and so long as we are identified with someone or something, we shall never be free." Rumi agrees: "If you could get rid of yourself just once, the secret of secrets would open to you. The face of the unknown, hidden beyond the universe, would appear on the mirror of your perception."[210] To achieve this extinction (*fanaa*), Sufis use ritual prayer and devotional exercises (*dhikr*) such as reciting the names of Allah. According to al-Ghazali, persistent repetition can lead to ascending levels of spiritual experience, and in the third stage—the *dhikr* of the "innermost heart"—one is absorbed into the divine.

As these examples suggest, not only is this third worldview not new, it can be found in almost every major religion, although rarely emphasized or even publicly acknowledged because usually it is in tension with more orthodox doctrines that understand cosmological dualism more literally. To explore that tension, let us take a closer look at some of the most important traditions.

## Shamanism

We begin with a nod to the spiritual traditions of indigenous peoples, including those often described as shamanistic. *Shamanism* has become a controversial term, but it remains a useful way to describe a religious practice widespread among native, precolonial societies, especially hunter-gatherer cultures. A shaman uses altered states of consciousness (often with the help of plant medicines such as ayahuasca or psilocybin mushrooms) to interact with a spirit world—not a transcendent reality but a dimension of this world that we are normally unaware of. The goal is usually to learn something or bring something (such as spiritual energies) back into our physical world, to heal or otherwise help human beings.

Aspiring shamans can offer themselves to the spirit world, but the spirits choose whom they will, and sometimes they select people who did not ask for the role. In every shamanic culture, candidates must endure an arduous trial, out of their control and often violent, involving regression to an undifferentiated condition: dissolution, ego-death, and rebirth.

> The shamanic crisis brings the potential shaman to the brink of annihilation, forcing him to walk the boundaries between life and death. During the process, he is stripped of everything that makes him an individual and must totally relinquish his ego; all that restrains him in this is experienced as monsters that devour him—manifestations of fears, doctrinal beliefs, hang-ups and so on. Usually this is only possible when the candidate becomes ill to the point of death, or suffers what feels like endless pain and suffering, sometimes with visions of torture and spirit battles. . . .
>
> There is always a point where the potential shaman remains for a time on the threshold, experiencing the primal void—a

state of un-being—and its greatest mysteries. Only when he has surrendered himself utterly can he be reborn.[211]

It is the traditional alchemical formula: *solve et coagula*—dissolve and congeal! Become nothing and then re-form. According to the Yanomami shaman Davi Kopenawa, the body that has been dismembered is resurrected but not as physical:

> The spirits do not content themselves with dancing for you! When they arrive, they also hurt you and cut up your body. They divide your torso, your lower body, and your head. They sever your tongue and throw it far away, for it only speaks ghost talk. They pull out your teeth, considering them dirty and full of cavities. They get rid of your guts, full of residues of game, which disgusts them. Then *they replace all that with the images of your own tongues, teeth, and entrails.* That is how they put us to the test![212]

In this ordeal one's material body is cast aside and replaced by "images." What can that possibly mean, since shamans do not become ghosts that fade away into the night but still function as members of their society? To anticipate the discussions that follow, one way to understand this transformation is to use theophanic or nondualistic language: one's reborn body is now experienced as empty and insubstantial, because it is actually a manifestation of something else.

If that doesn't make much sense, well, stay tuned.

A repeated theme in the rest of this chapter is the emphasis on realizing nonduality, especially seeing through the delusion that the world is composed of discrete subjects and objects. The mystical Abrahamic and Asian traditions offer more convoluted theological and philosophical critiques of such dualism, but they have no monopoly on the experience of nonduality, as indigenous peoples remind us:

We cannot speak of our relation to the land . . . because we *are* the land. We are the land made human. They have tried to turn us into persons. But we have chosen to remain natural as part of the earth.[213]

Also:

It is lovely indeed, it is lovely indeed.
I, I am the spirit within the earth . . .
The feet of the earth are my feet . . .
The legs of the earth are my legs . . .
The bodily strength of the earth is my strength . . .
The thoughts of the earth are my thoughts . . .
The voice of the earth is my voice . . .
The feather of the earth is my feather . . .
All that belongs to the earth belongs to me . . .
All that surrounds the earth surrounds me . . .
I, I am the sacred words of the earth . . .
It is lovely indeed, it is lovely indeed.[214]

## Judaism

A close reading of the Jewish Tanakh and the Old Testament of the Christian Bible reveals that the earliest Israelites were neither monotheistic nor concerned with an otherworldly salvation. Religious activities were originally organized around the Temple and only later (after expulsion from Jerusalem in the second century CE) did the focus shift to communal worship, when group prayer replaced ritual sacrifice.

The historical development of Judaism—the earliest Abrahamic tradition—shows a gradual evolution from a polytheistic tribal religion to an ethical monotheism that nonetheless continued to emphasize orthopraxis (what one must do) more than orthodoxy (what one must believe). A variety of beliefs about God were (and continue to be) allowed, as long as one followed the customary dietary laws, circumcised male infants, avoided work on the Sabbath, and attended synagogue.

By the time of Jesus many Jews were ready for a messiah (an "anointed one," not necessarily divine) sent by God, who would be their savior. Salvation remained controversial: while some expected an eternal kingdom here on earth, belief in a "higher world" was becoming more widespread. Judaism survived its diaspora by refocusing from the Temple to the Torah—script is portable! Priests who officiated at ritual ceremonies became rabbis who taught the Torah and functioned as community leaders.

Early Jewish *merkabah* (chariot) and *hekhalot* (palace) mysticism was based on prophetic visions found in the Hebrew Bible, which involved ascending to the Throne of Yahweh (as in Ezekiel 1 and Isaiah 6). Kabbalah, the most influential version of Jewish mysticism, developed in southern Europe during the medieval period. Its esoteric doctrines and practices offer a more metaphorical and symbolic way of understanding traditional teachings. In place of a God outside the world, who created it and sometimes intervenes in its affairs, Kabbalah speaks of emanation: everything is manifesting God, flows out of him, and in fact there is nothing but God—although God too is nothing, or not-a-thing. "The Kabbalistic approach emphasizes that God is No Thing. But it still affirms an absolute existence—even if ineffable."[215]

According to Schneur Zalman of Liadi, the first Rebbe of the Chabad-Lubavitch movement, the famous saying *ein od milvado* (Deuteronomy 4:35), usually translated as "there is no god but God," is more correctly rendered as "there is nothing other than God." God is the only and ultimate reality. Objects and events in the world have no independent existence.

Humans are a divine microcosm of the divine macrocosm, and what humans do is extremely important for damaging or redeeming that macrocosm. "Spiritual magic or theurgy was based on the idea that one could reach God in an ascent up the scale of creation made possible by a rigorous course of prayer, fasting and devotional preparation."[216] That is because it is possible to reverse the creative process whereby we have emanated from God. Special meditative practices enable us to achieve mystical union with God, which requires *bittul,* a complete nullification of the sense of self. One opens up to experience the *shekhinah*, the "in-dwelling" of God in a place—ultimately, in every place.

The most important Kabbalist was the sixteenth-century rabbi Isaac Luria, who described the initial process of creation as *tzimtzum,* the self-contraction of God's infinite light in order to provide space for apparently objective and independent things to exist. That is the Fall: our exile from God's presence, which according to some metaphorical interpretations is only a illusion, but one that involves a lot of suffering. After *tzimtzum*, God created vessels (*HaKelim*) in the emptied space, but when he began to pour his light into them they were not strong enough and shattered (*Shevirat*). The shards became *qelippot* (shells or husks), demonic forces that conceal the sparks of God's light beneath them. The third and final step, *Tikkun* (repair), is the process of recovering and raising up the sparks of divinity that were scattered when the vessels shattered.

Understood symbolically, this myth expresses the relationship between our usual, constructed way of experiencing the world—as a collection of separate things, including us, that interact in objective space and time—and how this world appears when the sense of self has been negated and "the whole earth is filled with his glory" (Isaiah 6:3). As the Zohar, the most important Kabbalistic text, repeats many times, "God fills all the worlds and surrounds all the worlds." The nineteenth-century Hasidic master Menahem Nahum elaborated: "The Creator's glory fills the whole earth; there is no place devoid of Him. But his glory takes the form of garb; God is 'garbed' in all things." All things in this world are the forms he takes. How can we experience this?

Seek to make yourself into a vessel for God's Presence. God, however, is without limit; "Endless" [*Ein Sof*] is His name. How can any finite vessel hope to contain the endless God?

Therefore, see yourself as nothing; only one who is nothing can contain the fullness of the Presence.[217]

According to another Hasidic master, Nahman of Bratslav, "When one finally is included within *Ein Sof*, his Torah is the Torah of God Himself, and his prayer is the Prayer of God Himself."[218] Hasidism, which developed in the eighteenth century in eastern Europe, brought these teachings down to earth by emphasizing their ethical implications: how they can be integrated into one's life. Its founder, the Baal Shem Tov ("Good Master of the Name"), emphasized the responsibility of each individual to remember and serve God in every aspect of daily life. Moshe Idel describes the quintessence of Hasidism "as the sequence of an inner, mystical experience that consists of a cleaving to God, often preceded by a self-induced feeling of 'nothingness'—that is an expansion of consciousness, and the subsequent return to this world and drawing down into it the divine energy by performing the ritual and then distributing the energy to others."[219]

According to the Kabbalah, there has never been any gulf between humans and God, just the illusion of a separation. If the whole earth (including us) is God's luminous hierophany, we do not need another world and we do not need to return to this world, because even when cleaving to God we never leave it. Instead of transcending this world, we are offered an immanent mysticism that reveals its true nature.

## Christianity

Although the historicity of Jesus has sometimes been doubted, today virtually all scholars of antiquity agree that a Jesus of Nazareth lived in first-century Judea. Most scholars also agree that he was baptized by John the Baptist and became a spiritual teacher who was crucified for being a public nuisance, on the order of Pontius Pilate. (Contrary to the synoptic Gospels, however, apparently Jewish priests were not implicated.) Aside from those basic facts, however, the rest of the story becomes unclear.

The historicity of other events in Jesus's life is controversial, especially (for our purposes) his resurrection and the eschatology that he proclaimed. But there is more than one way to understand them. Death-and-resurrection is the paradigmatic spiritual metaphor: the ego must let go of itself and die, in effect, for rebirth to occur—for something deeper to come to life. That does not require an empty tomb. Does this point to the original meaning of baptism: to die symbolically and be reborn anew? Justin Martyr, a second-century Christian philosopher, wrote that baptism is "illumination, because all who receive it are illuminated in their understanding."[220] (It is difficult to square that view with the baptism of newborns, which became customary).

According to the Gospels, Jesus predicted an apocalypse during the lifetime of his generation, beginning with a period of great destruction and distress.

> Then will appear the sign of the Son of Man [Jesus] in heaven. And then all the peoples of the earth will mourn when they see the Son of Man coming on the clouds of heaven, with power and great glory. And he will send his angels with a loud trumpet call, and they will gather his elect from the four winds, from one end of the heavens to the other.[221]

The last book of the Bible, the Revelation of St. John the Divine, elaborates on what would soon happen—except it didn't. So was it all a big misunderstanding?

According to John Dominic Crossan, the predicted Second Coming of Christ was a distortion of his teachings added later. The Kingdom of God was not an imminent end of the world, but a reality here and now, a "realized eschatology" for those who are able to perceive it.

> Once, on being asked by the Pharisees when the kingdom of God would come, Jesus replied, "The coming of the kingdom

of God is not something that can be observed, nor will people say, 'Here it is,' or 'There it is,' because the kingdom of God is in your midst.[222]

The Gospel of Thomas adds, "what you look forward to has already come, but you do not recognize it" and "the kingdom of the Father is spread out upon the earth, and people do not see it."[223]

Was Jesus (the son of) God?

As mentioned earlier, only the fourth canonical gospel, John, the last to be written, and controversial in its day—includes an unambiguous assertion of the divinity of Jesus, who calls himself "the light of the world": "No one comes to the Father except through me. If you really know me, you will know my Father as well."[224] Does this supplant all the spiritual teachings in the other gospels, including the parables and the beatitudes in the Sermon on the Mount? The Gospel of John makes Jesus himself the message, rather than anything he taught. What saves us is accepting Jesus as our savior, in contrast to what the Gospel of Thomas emphasizes, that "the Kingdom is inside you, and outside you. When you come to know yourselves, then you will be known, and you will realize it is you who are the sons of the living Father."[225] But Thomas was repressed and rediscovered only when a buried manuscript was found in 1945 near Nag Hammadi, Egypt. Instead, the Nicene Creed (formulated in 325 and revised in 381) explicitly affirmed Jesus as the only "Son of God," of the same substance as the Father. With the addition of the Holy Spirit, this trinity became an orthodoxy enforced by the emperor Constantine and many Christian authorities after him.

According to Crossan, assertions of the divinity of Jesus need to be understood in their historical context. There was, in fact, a much better-known contemporary who was also called a god, and sometimes "the son of God," whose titles included Lord, Redeemer, and Savior: Caesar Augustus, the Roman emperor at that time. Crossan believes that, by adopting such language, the early Christians were comparing Augustus unfavorably to the true savior. "They were taking the identity of the Roman emperor and giving it to a Jewish peasant."[226] If so, this may be another example of the problem Joseph Campbell warned against: taking metaphors literally.

If Jesus was a Jew who never intended to start a new religion, Paul becomes the most important figure in the development of early Christianity. He often receives bad press because some of the letters attributed to him endorse slavery and the subordination of women, while condemning homosexual behavior—views that have been used throughout Christian history to rationalize social discrimination and oppression. But only half of the fourteen letters usually attributed to him are considered genuine by most scholars, and at his best Paul emphasizes the spiritual transformation that Christ modeled for us when he "emptied himself" or "made himself nothing."[227]

With this transformation we die to our old identity and are reborn into a new one. "I have been crucified with Christ and I no longer live, but Christ lives in me. The life I now live in the body, I live by faith in the Son of God, who loved me and gave himself for me"[228] Now "in him we live and move and have our being."[229] Christ resurrected shows us the way to a new life, "so if anyone is in Christ, the new creation has come: the old is gone, the new is here!"[230]

As Augustine famously put it three centuries later: "You must be emptied of that of which you are full, so you may be filled with that of which you are empty."

Notice that this does not refer to some postmortem transcendent salvation, but to a spiritual rebirth that can happen now—in fact, it can only happen here and now. The sign of this transformation is a life motivated by faith, hope, and love, knowing that "the greatest of these is love."[231]

> The love of which Paul speaks is a spiritual gift, not simply an act of will, not something we decide to do, not simply good advice for couples and others. Rather, as a spiritual gift love is the most important result (and evidence) of a Spirit transplant. As the primary fruit of the spirit, it is also the criterion by which the other gifts are evaluated. . . . The social form of

love for Paul was distributive justice and nonviolence, bread and peace.[232]

The Christian mystical tradition that developed later was much influenced by Pseudo-Dionysius the Areopagite, an anonymous Greek author in the early sixth century who emphasized the *via negativa*: letting go of all our ideas about God in order to experience his "pure being" beyond any forms or particular attributes. Perhaps the most important figure (of many!) was the German theologian Meister Eckhart, who emphasized that "God is closer to me than I am to myself."[233] How can one realize that? Because God is nothing—that is, not a thing—we must also become nothing in order to experience God.

> But if God is neither goodness nor being nor truth nor one, then what is He? He is pure nothing: He is neither this nor that. If you think of anything He might be, He is not that. (Sermon 23)

> Since it is God's nature not to be like anyone, we must come to the state of being nothing in order to enter into the same nature that He is. (Sermon 7)

> For you to know God in God's way, your knowing must become a pure unknowing, and a forgetting of yourself and all creatures. (Sermon 103)

To know God is still dualistic: the self (subject) knows something else (an object). "So I pray God to rid me of God." Thus Eckhart distinguishes God (*deus*) from the Godhead (*deitas*), when we are not aware *of* God because we are one with God. By cultivating detachment from everything else—having nothing, knowing nothing, willing nothing—we can come to realize that "God's ground is my ground, and my ground is God's ground" (Sermon 5b).

So, when I am able to establish myself in nothing, and nothing in myself, uprooting and casting out what is in me, then I can pass into the naked being of God, which is the naked being of the Spirit. (Sermon 7)

You must know that this is in reality one and the same thing: to know God and to be known by God, to see God and to be seen by God. In knowing and seeing God we know and see that He makes us know and see. (Sermon 76)

Eckhart was masterful at manipulating language to make it say what he wanted, and he was not afraid of apparent contradictions. Sometimes he contrasts the "nullity" of all creatures with the being of God, in which case it is not that God has being, or even that God is being, but that being *is* God (*esse est deus*). At other times he turns that upside down: if God is nothing it is because he is our nothingness, and if we are nothing it is because all our being is actually God's.

Eckhart's most famous statement baldly and boldly asserts our nonduality with God: "The eye that I see God with is the eye God sees me with. My eye and God's eye is one eye, and one sight, and one knowledge, and one love."[234] This, however, was too much for the thought-police of the Church. The inquisitional authorities accused Eckhart of presenting sermons "that can easily lead simple and uneducated people into error." Eckhart died before a final judgment was made, but his way of understanding God was not unique. Two centuries later, St. Catherine of Genoa (1447–1510) wrote: "Once stripped of all its imperfection, the soul rests in God with no characteristics of its own, since its purification is the stripping away of the lower self in us. Our being is then God."[235]

Jakob Boehme (1575–1624), arguably the most important Protestant mystic (and the first German philosopher, according to Hegel), echoed these teachings in describing his own experiences:

Lastly, Whereas I also said, Whosoever finds it, finds Nothing and All Things; that is also certain and true. But how finds he Nothing? Why, I will tell thee how. He that findeth it, findeth a Supernatural Supersensual Abyss, which hath no Ground or Byss to stand on, and where there is no Place to dwell in; and he findeth also Nothing is like unto it, and therefore it may fitly be compared to Nothing; for it is deeper than any Thing, and is as Nothing with Respect to All Things, forasmuch as it is not comprehensible by any of them. And because it is Nothing respectively, it is therefore free from All Things; and is that only Good, which a Man cannot express or utter what it is; there being Nothing to which it may be compared, to express it by.[236]

This archaic translation reproduces the awkwardness of Boehme's original German, but also reproduces the important point: God is an incomprehensible groundlessness, a nothing free from all things. This no-thingness-in-itself is what enables the divine to manifest freely as the multitudinous forms of this world, including us.

Once again, notice that none of these Christian teachings refers to or presupposes a postmortem transcendent salvation in a better place, which transports us to some higher reality. Instead, the spiritual challenge is to realize the true nature of this world, including us. In contrast to the otherworldly deliverance that Western Christianity came to focus on, Greek and Russian Orthodoxy still emphasize "the transfiguration of this world," which began when the whole cosmos was transformed by God becoming flesh. Salvation for the Orthodox traditions means "awakening to the whole world illumined by the brilliance of divine presence," which returns "the world to the beauty in which it was first created."[237] When we are transformed, our world is transformed too.

Thomas Merton offers a contemporary version:

Life is this simple: we are living in a world that is absolutely transparent, and God is shining through it all the time. This is not just a fable or a nice story. It is true. If we abandon ourselves to God and forget ourselves, we see it sometimes, and we see it maybe frequently. God shows himself everywhere, in everything—in people and in things and in nature and in events. It becomes obvious that God is everywhere and in everything and we cannot be without Him. It's impossible. The only thing is that we don't see it.[238]

## Islam

For Muslims there is no duality between the sacred and the profane, because all things come from God and therefore everything is holy. The spiritual task is to help all beings, including ourselves, to realize their sacred potential. There is no denigration of this world, no hostility to sexuality or the flesh. The Qur'an declares that God is everywhere: "Wherever you turn, there is the face of God" (2.115). As one of the most famous *hadiths* (aphorisms attributed to Muhammad) says: "Revile not the world for the world is God." Natural phenomena are his[239] *ayat* ("signs" or "similitude"), and the Qur'an repeatedly tells Muslims that they should view the earth's beauty and harmony as revealing God's love for the world. "Have you not considered the extraordinary bounty of nature? . . . Let man consider the food he eats! We pour down abundant water and cause the soil to split open. We make grain grow, and vines, fresh vegetation, olive trees, date palms, luscious gardens, fruits and animal fodder—all for you and your livestock to enjoy."[240]

Instead of focusing on an *incarnation* into this world (such as a divine son of God born into it), for Islam the whole world is an active, continuous hierophany of God's imaginative power. According to Ibn 'Arabi (1165–1240), perhaps the greatest Muslim mystic-philosopher, the unity-of-being (*waḥdat al-wujūd*) means that nothing is real except God. "He is named by every name, described by every attribute, qualified by every description. . . . There is nothing in Being/existence but God, while the entities [objects in this world] are non-existent."[241] Everything is his self-disclosure. The things of this world reveal him while also concealing him, because he transcends them all. The Real (al-ḥaqq) manifests itself only "from veil to veil," yet every veil is also a window into the Real. God's essence is unknowable, but we know him through his names—that is, the forms that he assumes. So God is both transcendent (without any qualities) and immanent (manifesting as all qualities).

Yet again, there is the paradoxical emphasis on God's nothingness. For Ibn 'Arabi, God is distinguished from his creatures by the negation of all attributes, not their affirmation. God is like water, which seems to take the color of the vessel that holds it.

> My heart has become capable of all forms.
> It is a meadow for gazelles and a monastery for Christian
>     monks,
> A temple for idols and the pilgrim's Ka'aba,
> The Tables of the Torah and the book of the Koran.
> I profess the religion of love
> Wherever its camels turn, there lives my faith.[242]

The spiritual path is therefore *via negativa*: letting-go of everything that we normally identify with. As Rumi says, the whole world has taken the wrong way, for they fear nonexistence, while it is actually their refuge. Sufis practice *dhikr* (remembrance), such as repeating the names of God (Allah, the merciful, the generous, the wise, and so on) in a devotional, single-pointed way. According to William Chittick,

> The *dhikr* in this meaning is a spiritual state in which a mystic concentrates all his bodily and spiritual powers on God in such a way that his whole existence is united with God completely, without any residue. When a mystic attains to this state, the distinction between the subject (who exercises the

concentration of the mind) and object (upon which his mind is concentrated) naturally disappears, and he experiences the immediate "tasting" of the essential unity with the Absolute.[243]

Now "the one who 'witnesses' and the object 'witnessed' become completely unified. At this stage it is no longer the human heart that 'witnesses' its object; but it is the Absolute itself 'witnessing' itself in itself."[244] When the ego-self is thus annihilated, we realize that we have never been separated from God because we have never been other than God: "I Myself am [both] the Seeker and the Sought."[245] According to another Sufi saying, none knows God but God.

Human beings are unique in that we alone of God's creation have all his attributes, being the most perfect self-manifestation (compare Genesis 1:27, where God creates man in his own image). It is only with humanity that the universe can achieve its full potential, because each of us is a microcosm of the macrocosm: *al-kawn al-jami*, "a being that gathers together [all the other beings]." Nonetheless, the perfect human is, like God himself, nothing specific. Being no thing in particular—achieving *maqam la maqam*, "the station of no station"—is what enables us to be anything and everything.[246] Everyone else has a defined identity that distinguishes them from everyone else. "The people of perfection have realized all stations and states and passed beyond these to the station above both majesty and beauty, so they have no attribute and no description."[247]

Although Arabic has no word that corresponds to the English word *consciousness*, the Qur'an repeatedly says that God is "the Seeing and the Hearing." Most Muslims naturally understand it to mean that God sees and hears everything that happens in the universe, but Sufis such as Ibn 'Arabi understand it more literally: God *is* seeing itself and hearing itself, which is consistent with the belief that we too are nothing other than *ayat* of God. "There is no Existent Being save He. So it is He who hears, and He is the hearing. So also is the case with the other faculties and perceptions. They are nothing but He."[248] The resonance here with Eckhart is difficult to miss. Like Eckhart,

Ibn 'Arabi makes the strongest possible assertion of our nonduality with God.

> The soul gains awareness that it "sees" God not *through* itself, but *through* Him; it loves only *through* Him, not *by* itself; it contemplates God in all other beings not *through* its own gaze, but because it *is* the same gaze by which God sees them . . . the soul itself is *His* organ of perception. The soul's vision of its divine Lord *is* the vision which He has of the soul.[249]

According to another famous hadith: "I was a hidden treasure, and I desired ['loved'] to be known. Hence I created the creatures and thereby made Myself known to them. And they did come to know Me."[250] As Ibn 'Arabi puts it, God felt distress within himself at the nonexistence of things, so he exhaled: "Our only word to a thing, when We desire it, is to say to it 'Be!' and it is."[251] All the countless types of individual things in the world can be understood as the letters, words, sentences, and books that God expresses with his all-merciful breath.

It turns out that God needs us as much as we need him. "We have given Him the power to manifest himself through us, Whereas He gave us (the power to exist through Him). Thus the role is shared between Him and us. . . . If He has given us life and existence by His being, I also give Him life by knowing Him in my heart." God provides us with existence, we provide him with appearance: all things (including and especially us) are how God presences. "By knowing Him, I give Him being."[252]

Ibn 'Arabi uses the analogy of a mirror to express our interdependence (or "interbeing") with God. God is *our* mirror (in which we contemplate ourselves and realize who we are) but at the same time we are God's mirror (by which he contemplates himself as his "divine names," the ways he manifests in the universe). "He who has recognized himself has recognized his Lord," according to a hadith that Ibn 'Arabi is fond of quoting. As Corbin puts it, God describes himself to us through ourselves.

More than that, human beings are the self-polishing of the mirror that is the universe. God becomes self-aware through our (awakened) awareness, which is both our own self-awareness and our awareness of him—they are the same thing. This invites comparison with the seventeenth-century German mystical writer Angelus Silesius: "God nothing is at all; and if he something be, / Only in me it is, having chosen me. . . . I am as important to God as He is to me; I help Him to maintain His being, and He helps me to maintain mine."[253]

Notice the lack of any intermediary such as a salvific messiah (Christ) or a priest to administer sacraments. If God is the All-Merciful and the All-Compassionate, what does our nonduality with him mean for the role of compassion in our own lives? When we are most in need of compassion, what does God do? *He makes us compassionate.* "Those to whom God remains veiled pray [to] the God who in their belief is their Lord to have compassion with them. But the intuitive mystics ask that divine compassion be fulfilled through them."[254] It is then that we are fulfilling our potential as vessels of God.

One more important doctrine of Ibn 'Arabi deserves mention: that the universe is continually recreated at each instant. What we call matter is an illusion insofar as it seems to self-exist, but it actually has no existence apart from the absolute reality that is God. "If the world were to remain in a single state for two units of time, it would possess the attribute of independence from God." While only God is real, everything else—the whole cosmos—is constantly changing, like the evanescent images in a dream. In fact, this cosmos *is* God's dream, what Ibn 'Arabi describes as his "nondelimited imagination."[255]

This is not a dualistic ontology. For Sufism this world is not devalued in comparison with some other reality that we aspire to attain. Again, the spiritual challenge is not to transcend the world but to polish it—our mirror—by practicing *dhikr*. By letting-go of the sense of self, here and now, we can realize the true nature of this world, which is also our own true nature: a manifestation (*ayat*) of God, whom we see in our mirror even as the same mirror reveals God to himself.

# Vedanta

Asian traditions such as Vedanta, Buddhism, and Daoism use different language than the theistic religions discussed above. Nonetheless, the similarities in worldview are so remarkable that it becomes difficult to avoid the tired metaphor of different fingers pointing at what seems to be the same moon.

According to Heinrich Zimmer, in Hindu cosmology "there is nothing static, nothing abiding, but only the flow of a relentless process, with everything originating, growing, decaying, vanishing."[256] That is an accurate description of Buddhism, with its emphasis on impermanence and insubstantiality, but only half true for the Vedas, the oldest Hindu scriptures that understand Brahman as the ultimate reality from which the universe originates: infinite, all-pervasive, eternal, and in itself unchanging.

Vedantic texts (*Vedanta* means "the conclusion of the Vedas") provide a variety of viewpoints on the relationship between Brahman and the individual self, and on the relationship between Brahman and the rest of the world. Some Upanishads assert that this world is only an appearance, with no reality of its own. Others declare that the world is real and distinct from Brahman. This diversity of views enabled several different Vedantic philosophies to develop. All of them agree that Brahman is the ground of the cosmos, but they offer different perspectives on its relation with the ever-changing world as we usually experience it.

Orthodox Hindus sometimes view Shakyamuni, the historical Buddha, as a Vedic heretic: one of the avatars (incarnations) of the god Vishnu who nonetheless became an apostate by founding a different religion. In fact, the influence was mainly from the other direction. Gaudapada (fifth century CE) and Shankara (seventh century), the two most important expounders of Advaita ("Nondual") Vedanta, were both accused of being crypto-Buddhists. Gaudapada even quoted from the two most important Mahayana philosophies, Madhyamaka and Yogacara. It is a classic example of the often-porous boundaries between coexisting religious traditions.

According to Gaudapada and Shankara, Brahman alone is real, this world is unreal, and the individual soul or true self is not different from Brahman. Shankara distinguishes impersonal Nirguna Brahman (formless and without characteristics) from Saguna Brahman (with characteristics, manifesting as a personal god to devotees). There is no contradiction between these two aspects of Brahman, only a difference of perspective due to *maya*, a mysterious power that makes the unreal seem to be real. The world as we usually experience it is due to super-imposing *maya* on Brahman, just as when we mistake a coiled rope for a snake. We perceive the everyday world as real (self-existing) due to our ignorance (*avidya*), but when true knowledge dawns we are freed from the delusion of individuality and wake up to our true nature, which is that we have always been nondual with Brahman. Because the phenomenal world is merely an appearance, the things we per-ceive (including ourselves!) are not real, which also means there is no real birth or death. According to Gaudapada, "No creature whatever is born, no origination of it exists or takes place. This is that highest truth where nothing whatever is born."[257]

The most famous expression of our nonduality with Brahman, in the Chandogya Upanishad, is the assertion *Tat Tvam Asi*: "*That* is what you are." *Atman* (one's true self or soul) is not other than Brahman.

How do we wake up from the dream of *maya*? Although some later Advaitins introduced meditation practices, for Shankara there is no gradual path to liberation. Either awareness delusively identifies with particular forms such as one's body, self-image, or possessions—or it doesn't. The Upanishads emphasize *neti, neti*, "not this, not that," as a way for us to let go of everything and realize Brahman. Our true form-less nature is revealed when awareness rests serenely by itself, with-out any characteristics of its own. Just as a bubble becomes one with the ocean when it bursts, so our sense of self merges with Brahman when it becomes aware of Brahman. Actually, of course, the water that composes the bubble has always been one with the sea, and the same is true for us and Brahman.

Ramanuja (eleventh century) formulated another school of Vedanta called Vishishtadvaita 'Qualified Nondualism,'" because it combines *advaita* (the nonduality or oneness of God) with *vishesha* (characteristics). For Shankara all the forms and characteristics that we perceive are unreal superimpositions, delusive *maya* that obscure Brahman. For Ramanuja, however, these modes (*prakaras*) of Brahman are better understood as the ways that Brahman manifests. The world and its creatures are related to Brahman in the same way that my physical body is related to my mind: it is dependent upon the mind but not reducible to it. Ramanuja's Brahman is not an impersonal Absolute but a personal God with many characteristics, including infinite love. The path to liberation involves cultivating devotion (*bhakti*) and complete self-surrender to God, who can shower grace on devotees.

The type of Vedanta easiest for most Westerners to understand is the Dvaita (dualistic) school founded by Madhva (thirteenth century). True to its name, it emphasizes differences, especially those between God (Saguna Brahman, or "Brahman with characteristics"), the self or soul, and the world. Early scholars believed that Dvaita must have been influenced by Christianity, because there are many similarities, but there is no evidence for that. According to Madhva, God, the Supreme Being, is the only independent reality, creating and ruling the world including the souls in it. Nonetheless, the material stuff (*prakrti*) of which the world is made is not an illusion. Subject and object, the knower and the known, are not nondual. All objects, including our physical bodies, are composed of *prakrti*. When God energizes *prakrti*, creation happens and the world evolves. Liberation occurs only through the grace of God, when one realizes the true nature of God and the self.

The main difference among these three types of Vedanta is their attitude toward the phenomenal world. How real is it? For Advaita this world is only *maya*, an illusion that obscures the true nature of Brahman. For Vishishtadvaita this world is the way that Brahman manifests. For Dvaita this world has been created by God and is real, although it remains dependent upon him. Take your pick: Is the world real, unreal, or something in between? How does one adjudicate among these views? Do they result from different spiritual experiences, or are they different ways of conceptualizing the same realization?

Advaita Vedanta has been the preferred darling of Western interpreters, but one could argue that Vishishtadvaita is actually more nondual. Shankara distinguishes a "pure" Brahman from the world created by *maya*, but then he cannot explain the origin of *maya*, which he acknowledges is mysterious, like a magic show. Ramanuja has no such problem with *maya*: this world is the body of Brahman, and the specific things that we experience are its modes (*prakaras*) and accessories (*sesha*). Although Brahman is the only substance—the only real thing—names and forms are the ways it expresses itself. Again, this perspective seems quite similar to the views of the Abrahamic mystics already discussed.

# Buddhism

For Buddhism the usual duality between subjectivity and objectivity is an unconscious and problematic psychological construction that can be deconstructed. The result of that deconstruction is an awakening that experiences this world differently. The delusion of separation is due to craving, which leads to clinging. The act of clinging creates the sense of a self that is *doing the craving* and at the same time reifies what is perceived into *that-which-is-craved*. The earliest Buddhist texts, in the Pali Canon, emphasize four types of clinging: to sensual pleasures, to views, to rules and observances, and to the notion of self. Notice that only one of them is physical.

In response, a meditation or mindfulness practice involves letting go of whatever thoughts, feelings, and desires that arise—that is, not identifying with them—which leads to the cessation of clinging. One discerns that feelings of pleasure are fleeting and not to be relished or grasped. One becomes disenchanted with sense objects, including ideas that arise in the mind. "Being disenchanted, he becomes dispassionate. Through dispassion [his mind] is fully liberated. When it is liberated, there comes the knowledge: 'It is liberated.' He understands: 'Birth is destroyed, the holy life has been lived, what had to be done has been done, there is no more coming to any state of being.'"[258]

The Pali term for such liberation is *nibbana* (Sanskrit, *nirvana*). How does someone who has attained this liberation experience the world? What is special about his or her life? The earliest teachings offer different accounts. Many of them are metaphorical: *nibbana* is an island, a harbor, the refuge, the other shore, and so on. Some explanations are apophatic, describing what *nibbana* is *not*: it is the end of greed, ill will, and delusion (the three poisons); the end of karma; the end of mental fabrication (*papanca*) and ignorance. Other descriptions emphasize positive qualities: a pure and radiant mind, serene and equanimous, effortlessly compassionate.

The diversity of these early expressions, apparently based on the personal experience of practitioners, offers a notable contrast to the more abstract and philosophical views that became important later, which are more concerned to describe the nature of ultimate reality.[259] However, such differences in themselves do not answer the most important question: Is *nibbana* transcendent, in that it involves experiencing another (and better!) dimension of reality? Or does it mean experiencing *this* world differently?

*Nibbana* is the end of *samsara*, the cycle of repeated rebirth into this place of suffering, craving, and delusion. It literally means "blown out," like snuffing a candle flame—but what is blown out? Given the Buddhist teaching of *anatta* (nonself), one answer is the extinction of self, but for Buddhism a discrete self has never existed, so there is nothing to be extinguished. *Nibbana* is described as a middle way between annihilationism and eternalism, two extreme views both wrongly assuming that there is a self, which either is destroyed or survives death.

It is more correct to say that *nibbana* involves "blowing out" the three poisons of greed, ill will, and delusion—also known as the three fires or the three roots of evil—but that by itself is not very help-ful. There seems to be some tension within the early texts between emphasizing either the *nibbana* "with remainder [retaining a physical body]" that the Buddha experienced under the bodhi tree when he was thirty-five years old, or his *parinibbana* when he died about the age of eighty, knowing that he had ended physical rebirth. This too corresponds with different views regarding the nature of the final goal. Did the Buddha attain some transcendent salvation from this world when he finally passed away, or is the more important point that he had already realized the true nature of this world?

As Buddhism developed into a religion, the Buddha became more transcendental or "supramundane" (*lokottara*), with a full panoply of supernatural powers and qualities including limitless life. However, what are believed to be the oldest parts of the Pali Canon collected in the Suttanipata—and therefore the earliest of all Buddhist texts—present a more modest view of enlightenment. According to Gil Fronsdal,

> The peace that this text [the Suttanipata] holds at its center is one to be experienced here and now, without any reference to the ultimate metaphysical and religious realities often taught as fundamental to Buddhism. In this text, reality is not divided into a conditioned, worldly realm and an unconditioned, tran-scendent realm far removed from the contingent world of ordinary human life. Instead, the teachings point to a peace that can be found in this life in this world. . . .
>
> No mention is made of most of the familiar numbered lists such as the Four Noble Truths and the Eightfold Path—teachings that are often considered to be the essence of Buddhism.[260]

Nor is there any reference to rebirth, or the different stages of enlight-enment. Instead, the Suttanipata focuses on four basic (and this-worldly) themes: letting go of views, avoiding sensual craving, the qualities of a sage, and the training to become a sage. Special psychic powers and transcendent states of consciousness are not mentioned, while ethical behavior and the development of virtuous character traits are emphasized.[261]

In some later *suttas* the Buddha offers teachings about "the all":

> Bhikkhus, I will teach you the all. . . .
>
> And what, bhikkhus, is the all? The eye and forms, the ear and sounds, the nose and odors, the tongue and tastes, the body and tactile objects, the mind and mental phenomena. This is called the all.
>
> If anyone, bhikkhus, should speak thus: "Having rejected this all, I shall make known another all"—that would be a mere empty boast on his part. If he were questioned he would not be able to reply and, further, he would meet with vexation. For what reason? Because, bhikkhus, that would not be within his domain.[262]

The passage that follows emphasizes that this *all*—the eye and the visual forms it sees, and whatever arises from eye-contact, repeated for ear, nose, tongue, body, and intellect—is a phenomenon to be "abandoned," leaving . . . what?

> Then there remains only equanimity, purified and bright, malleable, wieldy, and radiant . . . he does not cling to anything in this world. When he does not cling, he is not agitated. When he is not agitated, he personally attains *nibbana*.[263]

The most-quoted line from a much later text, the Diamond Sutra, encapsulates this teaching in one sentence: "Let your mind come forth without fixing it anywhere." The Platform Sutra of the sixth Chan (Zen) patriarch, Hui-neng, emphasizes the same point: "When our mind works freely without any hindrance, and is at liberty to 'come' or to 'go', we attain liberation." Such a mind "is everywhere present, yet it 'sticks' nowhere." Hui-neng emphasized that he had no system of Dharma to transmit. "What I do to my disciples is to liberate them from their own bondage with such devices as the case may need."[264] Someone who does not identify with anything is "immeasurable" and their activity is *signless*: "his track is hard to find, like that of birds in the air." We are reminded of Ibn 'Arabi's way of characterizing the perfect human: someone who is nothing (no-thing) in particular, having achieved "the station of no station." In ninth-century China, Chan master Linji spoke in a similar way about "the true man of no rank" who seeks nothing and has "nothing to do."

Perhaps the most important person in the history of Buddhism, after the Buddha himself, was the Indian philosopher Nagarjuna (ca. 150–250 CE). His extremely influential text, the *Mulamadhyamaka-karika* ("Root Verses on the Middle Way"), was foundational for the Mahayana tradition that later predominated in Central and East Asia. Its chapter on nirvana argues that nirvana is not another reality but the true nature of this reality:

> There is no specifiable difference whatever between nirvana and the everyday world. (25:19)
>
> That which, taken as causal or dependent, is the process of being born and passing on, is, taken non-causally and beyond all dependence, declared to be nirvana. (25:9)
>
> Ultimate beatitude [*shiva*] is the coming to rest of all ways of taking things, the repose of named things; no truth has been taught by a Buddha for anyone, anywhere. (25:24)[265]

Language divides up the world into a collection of separate but interacting "named things" that we can use (causally) to obtain what we desire. Once I identify something as a "cup," for example, I know how to use it and barely notice it until I want a sip of coffee. (Even then I may hardly notice it!) In everyday life this automatized way of relating to the world is often necessary, but in the process we are overlooking something important about the true nature of the world in itself, which can be realized when we let go of intention-driven behavior and thus our usual ways of "taking things"—of perceiving and interacting with them. Instead of offering truths to be embraced, all Buddhist teachings are heuristic, enabling followers to practice and experience for themselves.

Mahayana Buddhism became the only Indian spiritual tradition to thrive north of the Himalaya. In contrast to Indian Buddhist preoccupation with karma and rebirth, Chinese Buddhism was less concerned about qualifying for a better place after we die. The aspiration of Chan (Zen) practice is not so much to qualify for some higher reality as to become aware of the true nature of this one. "Everyday mind is the Way [*Dao*]" according to the eighth-century master Nanchuan. Before enlightenment, fetching water and chopping wood; after enlightenment, fetching water and chopping wood. One doesn't need to go anywhere else or do anything different—but one does it *differently.*

The shift of focus from an afterlife to this world and this lifetime allows for ambiguity about our postmortem fate. When the influential eighteenth-century Japanese Zen master Hakuin was asked, "What happens to a Zen master after he dies?" he responded, "Why do you ask me?" "Because you are a Zen master." "Yes, but not a dead one."

Given our natural fear of death, such agnosticism regarding one's own demise is not an ignorance to be deplored but a rare achievement, the fruit of a maturity that focuses on self-transformation here and now. That attitude does not imply there is no transcendence, but it can challenge literal understandings that have become dogma. Do we need to transcend samsara, this place of suffering and craving, by qualifying for somewhere better, or is the important thing to transcend our usual egoistic ways of experiencing it and relating to it? If the world as we know it now is psychologically and socially constructed, how might it be deconstructed and reconstructed? And to what effect? What will be different about the ways we experience it then?

One of the best (and briefest) summaries of the Buddhist path is by the Japanese Zen master Eihei Dogen (1200–1253) in his "Genjo Koan":

> To study the way of enlightenment [Buddhadharma] is to study the self. To study the self is to forget the self. To forget the self is to be actualized by myriad things. When actualized by myriad things, your body and mind as well as the bodies and minds of others drop away.[266]

To forget the self is not something that the self can intentionally do, anymore than I can make myself fall asleep, but the self can *let go* of itself indirectly, by focusing wholeheartedly on its meditation practice.[267] According to the traditional story, when Dogen became enlightened he exclaimed, "I came to realize that mind is nothing other than mountains and rivers and the great wide earth, the sun and the moon and the stars."[268] The delusion of a self that is separate from the rest of the world evaporates as we realize our nonduality with it. According to Hakuun Yasutani,

> There is a line a famous Zen master wrote at the time he became enlightened which reads: "When I heard the temple bell ring, suddenly there was no bell and no I, just sound." In other words, he no longer was aware of a distinction between himself, the bell, the sound, and the universe. This is the state you have to reach. . . .
>
> Stated negatively, it is the realization that the universe is not external to you. Positively, it is experiencing the universe as yourself.[269]

Perhaps there is nowhere else to go, nothing else that needs to be achieved? As Hakuin concluded his "Song of Zazen":

> Truly, is anything missing now?
> Nirvana is right here, before our eyes,
> This very place is the Lotus Land,
> This very body, the Buddha.[270]

The tension between a more literal understanding of the Buddhist goal (transcending this world) and a more metaphorical understanding (transcending our usual ways of experiencing it) is also found in the Pure Land traditions of Mahayana Buddhism, which offer a more devotional path than the familiar emphasis on meditation. According to the predominant "western direction" Pure Land teachings of the Chinese masters Tanluan, Daochuo, and Shandao, the Pure Land is another realm where one can be reborn if one has faith in Amitabha Buddha. In contrast, for "mind-only" Pure Land, *this* world is in fact the Pure Land. We perceive it as impure only because of our own impurities, which we project onto the world. The way to realize the Pure Land, then, is to purify our minds.

The most important controversy in Buddhist philosophy is about *shunyata*, the Sanskrit term usually translated into English as "emptiness" and sometimes (mis)understood nihilistically. In the Pali Canon and Theravada Buddhism, the focus is on denying the reality of a self, which is an *empty* construct—without any substantive reality of its own—composed of interacting ways of thinking, feeling, and acting. Mahayana Buddhism enlarged the concept by emphasizing that all phenomena are empty of self-existence, because everything is dependently originated and thus an impermanent manifestation that arises according to causes and conditions—and disappears when those conditions are no longer operative.

Other Buddhist schools have understood *shunyata* more metaphysically. The Tathatagarbha (Buddha Nature) sutras, in particular, portray *shunyata* not simply as denying something but as a positive way to express an important insight about the inherent nature of the world. According to this school of Buddhism, buddha nature refers not only to our own true nature but also to an unconditioned, self-arisen primordial reality from which the whole phenomenal world originates, an eternal realm of luminous serenity and joy. This buddha nature is empty in that it has no specific forms or characteristics of its own, being the imperceptible ground from which all forms arise. According to the Dalai Lama, "When talking about the fundamental nature of reality, one could sum up the entire understanding of that nature in a simple verse: 'Form is emptiness and emptiness is form.'"[271]

Of course, this way of understanding *shunyata* suggests comparisons with the Abrahamic mystical traditions discussed earlier, which also emphasize an imperceptible, inscrutable primordial reality but give it a different name: God. The buddha nature teaching is even more similar to its Indian sibling, the Vedantic tradition of Hinduism as discussed in the previous section.

Historically, both Buddhists and Vedantins have been very concerned to differentiate themselves from each other. Buddhism emphasizes that there is no self, but Advaita and Vishishtadvaita Vedanta insist everything is the self, now deserving of being capitalized: the Self! Note, however, that these apparently contradictory claims are the two ways to negate the delusive duality between self and nonself, subject and object. In the end, it becomes difficult to distinguish a pure being with no characteristics of its own from a nonbeing—a nothing or no-thing. In both cases, the spiritual path does not emphasize qualifying for a postmortem escape from this world. The task is to wake up from the delusion of separation and realize the true nature of this reality right here.

## China

If one presupposes that religion is about transcending this world, China seems to be the least religious of the major premodern civilizations. Although a sacred (literally, celestial) dimension was not denied, the spiritual goal usually taught and sought in China was not a postmortem supernatural salvation. In his *Lunyu* ("Analects") Confucius famously admonished a disciple who asked about "the ways of heaven."

> Chi Lu asked about serving the spirits. Confucius said, "If you can't yet serve men, how can you serve the spirits?" Lu added,

"May I ask about death?" Confucius said, "If you don't under-stand what life is, how will you understand death?"[272]

In contrast to the more mystical Indian traditions, which often encouraged world-renunciation, Chinese spirituality emphasized this-worldly harmony with the Dao, "the Way." Confucians focused on social harmony, while Daoists focused more on harmony with the natural world.

One particular parallel with Buddhism should not be overlooked. The Buddha said that a true Brahmin is not someone born into a par-ticular caste but crafted by self-cultivation. "Whoever lets passion, aversion, conceit, and hypocrisy fall away . . . I call a Brahmin."[273] Confucius made the same point: a genuine *junzi* (gentleman) is not born to that rank but a product of cultivating virtues that develop one's full humanity, such as benevolence and filial piety. How can this be achieved? "Overcome selfishness and keep to *li* [propriety]." (*Li*, is the moral law of heaven.) Confucianism did not support monasticism: family life is not an obstacle to personal transformation because proper family relations are what need to be cultivated. Each member is taught to live for the well-being of the whole. "Now the *ren* [benevolent, humane] man, wishing himself to be established, sees that others are established, and, wishing himself to be successful, sees that others are successful."[274]

Instead of an ontological duality between this reality and another one that transcends it, early Chinese thought understood this world using the double concept of *t'i-yung* (essence-function). *T'i* refers to essence or basic principle of things, including the inmost dimensions of the human mind. *Yung* means activity or function—in this context, how a foundational principle is expressed or takes form. The important point is that *t'i* and *yung* need each other: a principle means nothing unless it is manifested, and manifestations are manifesting something that is otherwise latent.[275] Note that these concepts do not involve any reference to anything supernatural.

As Mahayana Buddhism became absorbed into Chinese culture, many of its doctrines were reformulated into the language of essence and function. In particular, the pivotal Heart Sutra assertion that "form is emptiness, emptiness is form" became understood as a version of *t'i-yung*. Although the impermanent things of this world lack inherent existence, they are how that emptiness (*t'i*) manifests. By no coincidence, the Tathatagarbha claim that an unconditioned primordial buddha nature generates the phenomenal world received more attention in China than in its Indian birthplace. As the Vishishtadvaitin Ramanuja might put it, *yung* is the manifest functioning of imperceptible Brahman. And for Daoists, the Dao is not a transcendent reality but the ineffable ground of all worldly phenomena, the pattern of their emergence, interaction, and transformation.

> When we try to see it, it cannot be seen, so it is called
>     formless.
> When we try to hear it, it cannot be heard, so it is called
>     inaudible.
> When we try to grasp it, it cannot be held, so it is called
>     subtle. . . .
> Unceasing, unnamable, it returns to nothingness.
> Thus you can know the beginning of things,
> Which is the essence of the Way.[276]

In terms of what we can actually perceive, the Dao is indeed nothing, or no-thing, but not in a negative or passive sense. It is the inexhaustible womb of all life, "an empty vessel that yet may be drawn from without ever needing to be filled": a Nonbeing pregnant with Being.[277] And becoming no-thing is how we return to the source from which all things, including us, originate:

> There is somewhere from which we are born, into which we
> die, from which we come forth, through which we go in; it is

this that is called the Gate of Heaven. The Gate of Heaven is that which is without anything; the myriad things go on coming forth from that which is without anything. Something cannot become something by means of something, it necessarily goes on coming forth from that which is without anything; but that which is without anything is for ever without anything. The sage stores away in *it*.[278]

Having achieved this, the sage can "let his heart-mind [*xin*] roam with other things as its chariot," by responding appropriately to whatever happens.

> Within yourself, no fixed positions:
> Things as they take shape disclose themselves.
> Moving, be like water,
> Still, be like a mirror,
> Respond like an echo.
> Blank! as though absent:
> Quiescent! as though transparent.
> Be assimilated to them and you harmonize,
> Take hold of any of them and you lose.[279]

For all three traditions—Confucianism, Daoism, and Chinese Buddhism—proper self-cultivation can help develop the full potential of one's individual *t'i*.

In place of performing traditional religious rites in the correct way, which Confucianism still emphasized, Daoism encouraged meditation, which Daoists called "mind fasting" (*wang xin*) and used to harmonize one's *t'i* with the Dao. Instead of cultivating virtues, the Daoist goal is to decondition the mind so that we return to our natural state, recovering the gentleness and pliancy of a newborn infant or the limitless potential of an "uncarved block" before it is sculpted into a fixed self. According to the *Daodejing*:

> The reason there is great affliction is that I have a self.
> If I had no self, what affliction would I have?
> Therefore to one who honors the world as his self
> The world may be entrusted,
> And to one who loves the world as one's self
> The world may be consigned.[280]

Once again, the way to transcend our usual way of experiencing this world is to "forget" our usual sense of a separate self, in which case the world *becomes* our self—and thereafter to honor and love it as one's self. To realize that is to become so empty of any particular form that one can become anything according to the situation.

In the Diamond Sutra the Buddha says that he has no fixed form by which he can be identified. Those who attempt to see him by sight or sound cannot see him, for he is not to be recognized by any physical characteristics.[281] Those who realize they are no-thing remain no-thing even as they playfully assume some temporary role or unfixed form. And when there is no self exerting itself to do something or get somewhere, spontaneous actions are experienced as effortless nonaction, "doing without doing" (*wei wu wei*).

To forget oneself is not to transcend this world but to *fall into* it, no longer experienced as a collection of objective things but as a confluence of "empty" events and processes. We become one with its impermanent manifold of interdependent phenomena transforming into each other.

## Waking Up to the Dream

> Once Zhuangzi dreamt he was a butterfly, a butterfly flitting and fluttering around, happy with himself and doing as he pleased. He didn't know he was Zhuangzi. Suddenly he woke up and there he was, solid and unmistakable Zhuangzi. But he didn't know if he was Zhuangzi who had dreamt he

was a butterfly, or a butterfly dreaming he was Zhuangzi. Between Zhuangzi and a butterfly there must be some distinction! This is called the Transformation of Things.

—**Zhuangzi**[282]

Everything in this world can be taken as real or not real; or both real and not real; or neither real nor not real. This is the Buddha's teaching.

—**Nagarjuna**[283]

In addition to Zhuangzi's famous butterfly there are two other reflections on dreaming in the *Zhuangzi*:

While we dream we do not know we are dreaming, and in the middle of a dream interpret a dream within it; not until we wake do we know that we were dreaming. Only at the ultimate awakening shall we know that this is the ultimate dream. Yet fools think they are awake, so confident that they know what they are, princes, herdsmen, incorrigible! You and Confucius are both dreams, and I who call you a dream am also a dream.[284]

This dreaming is less ambiguous than Zhuangzi's butterfly. We are all dreaming, something we will realize when we finally awaken. Just before this passage in the *Zhuangzi*, Zhuangzi wonders whether we are wrong to love life and fear death. Perhaps doing so makes us exiles who have forgotten the way home. Is life itself the ultimate dream, and death the ultimate homecoming?

There are also prominent passages in Mahayana Buddhist scriptures that unambiguously assert this world is unreal and dreamlike. The Ashtasahasrika Prajnaparamita Sutra declares that all beings, including the Buddha and even nirvana itself, are like an illusion and a dream. The Diamond Sutra concludes that we should view phenomena as like a bubble, a lightning flash, a phantom, or a dream.

There is one more important dream in the *Zhuangzi*:

> You dream that you are a bird and fly away into the sky, dream that you are a fish and plunge into the deep. There's no telling whether the man who speaks now is the waker or the dreamer. Rather than go toward what suits you, laugh: rather than acknowledge it with your laughter, shove it from you. Shove it from you and leave the transformations behind; then you will enter the oneness of the featureless sky.[285]

This dream is more like the butterfly dream. The speaker does not know whether he is awake or dreaming. But why is it so important for us to know that? Instead of dreaming about waking up, perhaps we should consider why we are so wary of dreams.

What makes a dream a dream? Things in a dream are unreal in the sense that they do not have any objective stability or self-existence. They are constantly appearing, disappearing, maybe transforming into something else. Yet that is also true for things in this world, according to Zhuangzi and Nagarjuna! But then the distinction between the two realms becomes blurred. To say it again, perhaps we do not need to awaken *from* this world—attaining salvation somewhere else—but instead awaken *into* it . . .

To dream of waking up from this world is to fantasize about attaining a transcendent reality that will save me from my empty, unfixed, ever-shifting nature, which makes me uncomfortable insofar as I want to remain self-identical as the rest of my world changes. But would "waking up" in that way be falling asleep into the ignorance that thinks "I" am this body, one separate, nonempty self among an assortment of other discrete things? And is dreaming that I am a butterfly and so on a way of experiencing my selfless, endlessly transforming nature?

The *Zhuangzi* passage tells us that the alternative to dreaming is not another reality but "the oneness of the featureless sky." This inscrutable, ungraspable oneness—indistinguishable from no-thing-ness—exceeds all names but nonetheless has many, as we have noticed: God, buddha nature, Brahman, the Dao. In forgetting oneself and becoming no-thing, the delusion of a separate self evaporates. It is just as important not to remain in that featureless oneness because, in Buddhist terms, that is "clinging to emptiness." In China, mystic absorption was considered inferior to the "marvelous functioning" of the true sage, who responds appropriately to any situation that arises. In the Chan tradition, the eighth Oxherding Picture[286] celebrates realizing the emptiness in which "both ox and self are forgotten," but the tenth and final Oxherding Picture depicts "returning to the marketplace with helping hands."[287]

Needless to say, lots of helping hands are needed today.

Does becoming a sage qualify as spiritual salvation? Well, what if there is really nothing to be saved from—for example, Satan, *maya, samsara*—and there is really nowhere else to go? And if there is no one, no separate self, who needs to be saved, is realizing all that as much salvation as we need?

And so long as you haven't experienced
This: to die and so to grow,
You are only a troubled guest
On the dark earth.

—**Johann Wolfgang von Goethe**


This reenchantment with the earth as a living reality is the condition
for our rescue of the earth from the impending destruction that we
are imposing upon it. To carry this out effectively, we must now, in
a sense, reinvent the human as species within the community of life
species.

—**Thomas Berry,** *The Dream of the Earth*


All civilizations, including those that might occur on other worlds,
are expressions of their planet's evolutionary history. From this
perspective, our project of civilization is just one consequence of the
Earth's history, not its future master. Every civilization must be seen
as a new form of biospheric activity arising within a planet's history
of transformation and evolutionary innovation.

Sustainable civilizations don't "rise above" the biosphere, but
must, in some way, enter into a long, cooperative relationship with
their coupled planetary systems. . . . Our project of civilization must
become a way for the planet to think, to decide, and to guide its own
future. Thus, we must become the agent by which the Earth wakes up
to itself.

—**Adam Frank,** *Light of the Stars: Alien Worlds and the Fate of
the Earth*

I'm now convinced that our times are indeed unique and critically important, perhaps determining everything to come. Of 117 billion people who've ever lived, we're part of the 1% who can make a difference this century. We're at a historic crossroads. The future hinges on what we do next.

—Rutger Bregman

You have the biggest opportunity in all of human history to live an incredibly meaningful life. The actions that you take because of the accident of the time of your birth are of an order of magnitude in importance compared to most people who've lived before, because you are going to affect the future of life on Earth in fifty, five hundred, and five hundred thousand years by what you do in the next couple of decades. So no one is asking for an easy life. Really deep down we're asking for a meaningful life.

—Tom Rivett-Carnac

# Conclusion

## *Globalizing the Spiritual Path*

THE TWENTIETH CENTURY was the era of globalization, in which humanity for the first time achieved a truly global civilization. Thanks to new communication and transportation technologies, we now live in a world not only interconnected but interdependent, for better (in lots of ways!) and worse (world wars, nuclear weapons, ecological crises).

Today we take international organizations such as the United Nations and multinational corporations for granted, but there is another dimension to this extraordinary development that is easy to overlook because it is just beginning: the globalization of our spiritual traditions. Although most of the world's religions have been ethnic, largely confined to a particular society—for example, Shintoism in Japan—the major religions became major because they were missionary and so successful at proselytizing. But today they find themselves in a new situation.

Until very recently religions have usually viewed other religions primarily as competitors—deluded and inferior, maybe even satanic—whose adherents need to be converted to the true faith, sometimes by force if necessary. That attitude has not disappeared today, of course, but deeper exposure to other traditions has also led to greater curiosity about their teachings, and sometimes openness to alternative perspectives. Religious institutions are perhaps the most conservative of all human organizations, and their reluctance to change, whether doctrinal or administrative, tends to be instinctive and formidable. One example among many: religious hierarchies remain, with few exceptions, the last and strongest bastions of patriarchy.

Nonetheless, something fresh has begun, an alternative perspective is burgeoning, and if our now-global civilization manages to avoid self-destructing, I suspect it will sooner or later lead to a spiritual revolution. The world's religious traditions arose and developed as the products of particular times and places, and despite resistance they cannot avoid indefinitely the challenges provided by new, radically different times and places—including each other. The introduction mentioned Paul Tillich's theology of correlation: the answers that a religion has to offer should correspond to the questions that a society is asking. If it fails at doing this, then that religion becomes irrelevant.

Our spiritual traditions are still struggling to cope with modern and postmodern worldviews more compatible with the physical sciences, but now their predicament is compounded by the unprecedented dangers recently highlighted by Noam Chomsky (also mentioned in the introduction): the ecological crisis, the very real possibility of nuclear war, and the rise of authoritarian regimes replacing democratic governments.

Perhaps the most important claim in this book is that our spiritual traditions will be unable to respond appropriately to these challenges without examining and questioning premodern transcendentalist assumptions that view this world as a means to another end—that treat *here and now* as the place where we can qualify for *somewhere better later*.

Insofar as they have focused our attention on salvation in some postmortem reality, the major religions have contributed to the devaluation and degradation of this reality. Does that mean we need a new kind of religion? Should we yield to the Four Horsemen of the New Atheism[288] and outgrow religion altogether? Or do we need a new way of appreciating our imperfect but nonetheless insightful spiritual traditions?

The attraction of atheism or agnosticism is understandable, especially since the warmed-over orthodoxies still taught today fail to correlate with the urgent questions that our dangerous situation impels us to ask. Nonetheless, we do well to remember that each tradition is (whether or not it recognizes it) an impermanent, historically conditioned, and ever-evolving product of complex individual contributions and social influences, experiential and institutional, and often political as well—from Ashoka to Constantine to the caliphs who succeeded Muhammad. The last chapter highlighted the mystics in each tradition, who offer alternatives to the dualistic dogmas that divert our attention from this world by offering an escape from it. Rediscovered and recuperated, those alternatives can help us realize something usually overlooked about the nature of our lives here.

It is also important to avoid reductionism on either side—both the fundamentalism that believes the teachings of one's particular religious denomination are superior to all others, and the mirror-image fundamentalism of atheistic convictions that believe much the same thing. We have noticed that contemporary conceptions of secularity are as much historically conditioned as our religions. Atheistic worldviews often base themselves on the principles of modern science, but scientists are well aware that their paradigms are subject to sometimes radical revision. Whether religious or materialistic, our understanding of the cosmos is far from complete, and it would be foolish to assume that the future holds no big surprises for either inquiry.

When I reflect on what globalization means for our spiritual traditions, the metaphor that comes to mind is a rotary tumbler—the type of jar used to polish stones. As it rotates, the stones rub against and burnish each other, usually with the help of some abrasive grit. After some weeks the surfaces become smooth and the grain of the stones is revealed.

Rocks have no defensive ego, individual or institutional, so the parallel may be limited. We may nonetheless wonder: Can dialogue with other religions not only challenge each tradition but also help it clarify what is truly essential in its own teachings? Given that the future is open-ended, I also wonder if that possibility is inevitable in the long run. The last chapter highlighted some profound parallels among the mystics of different faiths. Perhaps the most important similarity among them is the common emphasis that what we seek has always been here, right in front of us but usually unnoticed.

If there is actually nothing to gain, what the Axial Age traditions call salvation is simply becoming able to see what has always been revealing itself. According to the indigenous Nasa elder Alcibiades, we are the land made human; the thoughts of the earth are our own thoughts, the voice of the earth is our voice. As the *Zohar* tells us, "God fills all the worlds and surrounds all the worlds." I become a vessel for this presence when I become nothing. Paul said that Jesus "emptied himself," and if we do the same then "everything becomes new." The way that Thomas Merton expressed this is worth repeating:

> Life is this simple: we are living in a world that is absolutely transparent, and God is shining through it all the time. . . . If we abandon ourselves to God and forget ourselves, we see it sometimes, and we see it maybe frequently. God shows himself everywhere, in everything—in people and in things and in nature and in events.[289]

The Qur'an also declares that God is everywhere: "Wherever you turn, there is the face of God" (2.115). If we practice *dhikr* (devotional exercises) we can experience that for ourselves when our hearts are "annihilated in unity."

For Zen Master Dogen, to study the self is to forget the self and realize our nonduality with all (the ten thousand) things. As Hakuin said, nirvana is right here, before our eyes, and our own bodies are the body of the Buddha. According to Ramanuja, this world is the body of Brahman. And for Daoists the Dao is "an empty vessel that yet may be drawn from without ever needing to be filled," which we can realize when we "mind fast" to become no-thing and let go of the great affliction: our (sense of) self.

In each case, the spiritual path is not about transcending this world, except in a metaphorical sense. Instead, we can transcend our usual dualistic ways of experiencing and realize that we *are* it, in which case the world is not an "it" but something much more.

But wait a minute—not so fast! What about death? So much of the attraction of conventional religion is the reassurance that we don't really die, because one's soul (or something like that) lives on. Although becoming one with God or Brahman, or waking up to one's buddha nature, may be blissful, what does realizing one's nonduality with God and so forth mean when it's time to die?

Confucius said that if we don't understand life in this world, how can we expect to understand what happens afterward? But then what about those who evidently have awakened to the true nature of this world: the Christian mystics, Hasidic and Sufi sages, Buddhist and Daoist masters, and so on? What do they say about our postmortem destiny?

Remarkably little, usually. They describe how this world is transformed, while seeming relatively indifferent to "the next"—as if taking care of business here is also doing what we need to do for whatever may follow. Nonetheless, it is hard to avoid speculation about something so consequential. We can't help wondering about what happens after we die. If we return to the source—that is, God and so on—what might that experience be like?

There may be little if anything we can know for sure about postmortem experience, but perhaps we know enough to speculate about something it would *not* be. We fear extinction, becoming nothing, but the annihilation of self here and now that mystical traditions encourage is not nihilism as usually understood—that is, it's not *the end*, full stop. Sufis say, die before you die, so that when it is time to die you are already dead. And Buddhism emphasizes that the self cannot be extinguished because it has never existed. For Ibn 'Arabi and many others, the so-called separate self is an appearance (*ayat*) of God, an attribute of Brahman, part of a dream that we do not know we are dreaming until the moment of awakening.

Does that give us insight into *postmortem* experience? Not much. Most Indian traditions including Hinduism and Buddhism teach that we reincarnate (Buddhists prefer the term *rebirth*), according to the karma that we have created. Far from being confined to India, however, this belief is widespread, even in the Abrahamic religions. Reincarnation has been a common folk belief in Judaism, and at times even a mainstream doctrine for some Kabbalists. It was also accepted by many of the early Gnostic sects of Christianity, although later declared heretical by Church authorities. It still survives in the esoteric doctrines of Abrahamic splinter sects such as the Alawites, Druze, Manichaeans, and Rosicrucians, as well as in many other past and present religious movements.

Today there is intriguing anecdotal evidence to support it, especially the apparent past-life memories of some young children studied by Ian Richardson and others at the University of Virginia.[290] Needless to say, those studies are controversial. In any case, the more extraordinary the claim, the stronger the empirical evidence needed to corroborate it, especially when there is no scientific support—when reincarnation seems incompatible with what modern science has otherwise discovered (so far!) about the universe.

That does not refute the possibility, but what I have read (so far!) leaves me agnostic: what happens after physical death, if anything, remains the great mystery. Yes, I know the Buddha claimed to have remembered his past lives, and what he said may well be true, but do we know for sure that assertion wasn't added later? The good news is that, sooner or later, all of us will have the opportunity to solve that mystery, if only for ourselves.

That brings us back to this life and this world.

If what we have been seeking all along is nothing other than the true nature of this world, which also happens to be our own true nature, shouldn't we be doing a better job taking care of the earth—especially since it is also the best way to take care of ourselves?

We return to the fundamental question, What does it mean to be human? Up to now, our species might be fairly described as the narcissistic collective ego of the biosphere, but it has become clear that our own well-being is not separate from others' well-being, or from the biosphere's. As the *Daodejing* says, the world may be entrusted to those who love it as their own body.

Not that loving it automatically solves its problems, but if we truly love the world then we will do whatever we can to heal it. That's especially true if we can no longer evade the problems with our own lives in this world by qualifying for something better elsewhere. Love by itself doesn't directly address the challenges cited by Chomsky, nor does awakening to our true nature spontaneously eliminate the greed, ill will, and delusion at the root of our predicament today. This applies both to the personal version of those three poisons bequeathed to us by our evolutionary psychology, as well as their collective counterparts (institutionalized greed and so on) that so often frustrate our best efforts today. But if salvation is not to be found elsewhere, well, we have no more excuses.


## Touching the Earth

To end, let me offer not a final philosophical reflection but an image that symbolizes much of what this book has been trying to say. It depicts Gautama, the historical Buddha, yet it can be appreciated in a nonsectarian way, and I believe that now is the time for other spiritual traditions to share it.

A popular representation of the Buddha shows him seated cross-legged, with his left hand in his lap, palm up. The right hand overhangs his right knee and touches the ground. This posture, known as the *bhumisparsha mudra*, the "earth witness" pose, commemorates the Buddha's victory over a challenge by the demon king Mara. According to the usual account, Mara wanted to distract him from his deep meditation. He tried to intimidate Gautama with armies of demons and monsters, then sent his daughters to seduce him from his meditation seat. When neither ploy worked, Mara claimed that he himself was the one who deserved to sit in the seat of enlightenment.

In response, the Buddha touched the earth, and when the earth roared "I bear you witness," Mara and his hosts vanished, vanquished.

It is a curious story, obviously a myth rather than an historical event. But what does it mean?

This *bhumisparsha* incident is not found in the earliest Buddhist texts, although it was soon added to the traditional narrative of the Buddha's quest. The issue is whether Gautama was indeed entitled to sit on the same spot where (according to the story) all previous buddhas had attained their enlightenment.

From our perspective, however, another aspect of the myth becomes important. Notice, here too, that the story makes no reference to any "higher" reality that transcends this world. Instead, touching the earth implies awakening to a different relationship with the earth. In place of the usual trope—"rising above" the natural world—this suggests another, opposite metaphor: descending back into the earth, returning to the generative Mother of all life, which is also to settle back into one's physical body, to become fully embodied. This includes getting in touch with and working through repressed emotions and traumas, thus avoiding what John Welwood calls *spiritual bypassing*: the "widespread tendency to use spiritual ideas and practices to sidestep or avoid facing unresolved emotional issues, psychological wounds, and unfinished developmental tasks . . . trying to rise above the raw and messy side of our humanness before we have fully faced and made peace with it."[291]

But can we push the *bhumisparsha* story a little further? To be more speculative—and perhaps that is exactly what's needed today— can we say that it is the earth itself that wakes up when someone becomes enlightened? Is that why it roared when Gautama appealed to it? This would answer the old question that the *anatta*, or "no-self," teaching of Buddhism raises: If there is no self, then who or what becomes enlightened? As Sufism emphasizes, none knows God but God: we are the mirror by which God contemplates himself and becomes self-aware. Given what is now known about biology, DNA, and the evolution of all life from a single-celled universal ancestor, it doesn't seem that far-fetched to propose such an answer—in which case touching the earth becomes an evocative symbol for realizing one's nonduality with the earth. As Joseph Campbell says, "If you will think of ourselves as coming out of the earth, rather than having been thrown in here from somewhere else, you see that we are the earth, we are the consciousness of the earth. These are the eyes of the earth. And this is the voice of the earth."[292]

According to Ervin Laszlo, this nondual perspective is consistent with an emerging postmaterialist paradigm that also happens to be the traditional premodern paradigm:

> At the cutting edge of contemporary science a remarkable insight is surfacing: the universe, with all things in it, is a quasi-living, coherent whole. All things in it are connected. . . . A cosmos that is connected, coherent and whole recalls an ancient notion that was present in the tradition of every civilization: it is an enchanted cosmos. . . . We are part of each other and of nature. We are a conscious part of the world, a being through which the cosmos comes to know itself. . . . We are at home in the universe.[293]

To be *at home in the universe*—how wonderful! Is that what the mystics are talking about?

This new paradigm also raises the fascinating possibility of understanding evolution in the broadest possible sense as the creative groping of a self-organizing cosmos. In *The Universe Story*, Thomas Berry and Brian Swimme make the point more poetically: "The eye that searches the Milky Way Galaxy is itself an eye shaped by the Milky Way. The mind that searches for contact with the Milky Way is the very mind of the Milky Way Galaxy in search of its inner depths."[294]

Shouldn't that become the role of religion today: not encouraging us to transcend this world, but inspiring us to awaken to our true body? Berry concludes that humans "are the self-consciousness of the universe."

By bringing forth the planet Earth, its living forms, and its human intelligence, the universe has found, so far as we know, its most elaborate expression and manifestation of its deepest mystery. Here, in its human mode, the universe reflects on and celebrates itself in a unique mode of conscious self-awareness.[295]

To become self-aware, then, is to realize that each of us is what the whole universe—our true body—is doing, right here and now. Could there be a better homecoming?

Finally, one important implication of this needs to be emphasized. For archaic civilizations, humans had an essential role to play in the cosmos. Our sacrifices and other ritual activity kept it from collapsing back into chaos. In the modern era, of course, we no longer have any such function, which raises basic questions about the meaning (or meaninglessness) of our lives, both individually and collectively. All we can do, apparently, is enjoy ourselves while we can . . . until the inevitable happens. But if we are not separate from the rest of the biosphere—if humans are, in fact, one way that it becomes self-aware—that implies a meaning and a role for us.

Loving the world as our own body means that the culmination of the spiritual path is not to achieve some blissed-out state but to become fully engaged, with each other and with the earth: contributing to what Judaism describes as *tikkun olam*, "repair of the world," or following what Mahayana Buddhism calls the bodhisattva path, vowing to help relieve the suffering of all sentient beings (and now their deteriorating ecosystems).

Are we here to cherish and take care of the biosphere, our larger body? To help it heal? Will that also be our own healing?

# Notes

1  George Eaton, "Noam Chomsky: The World Is at the Most Dangerous Moment in Human History," *The New Statesman*, September 17, 2020, https://www.newstatesman.com/world/2020/09/noam-chomsky-world -most-dangerous-moment-human-history.

2  Olivia Rosane, "Humans and Big Ag Livestock Now Account for 96 Percent of Mammal Biomass," *EcoWatch*, May 23, 2018, https://www.ecowatch .com/biomass-humans-animals-2571413930.html.

3  Matt Wilce, "How Many Trees Are Lost to Deforestation Every Year?," *Tree-Nation*, October 13, 2020, https://tree-nation.com/projects/inside-tree -nation/article/9739.

4  Vaclav Smil, "Harvesting the Biosphere: The Human Impact" in *Population and Development Review* 37, no. 4 (Dec. 2011): 613–36; Ceballos, Ehrlich, and Dirzo, "Biological Annihilation via the Ongoing Sixth Mass Extinction Signaled by Vertebrate Population Losses and Declines," *Proceedings of the National Academy of Sciences*, July 2017. For more on the ecological crisis, see chapter 1 in David Loy, *Ecodharma: Buddhist Teachings for the Ecological Crisis* (Wisdom Publications, 2019). Of course, some of that information is already outdated.

5  John Harris, "From Trump's Victory, a Simple, Inescapable Message: Many People Despise the Left," *The Guardian*, November 10, 2024, https:// www.theguardian.com/commentisfree/2024/nov/10/donald-trump-the-left -social-media-rightwing-propaganda-progressives-woke.

6  Thomas Berry, "The Dream of the Earth: Our Way into the Future," *CrossCurrents* 37, no. 2/3 (Summer/Fall 1987): 200–215.

7  John Gray, *Straw Dogs: Thoughts on Humans and Other Animals* (Granta, 2002), 7.

8   "An Intellectual Entente," *Harvard Magazine*, September 10, 2009, https://harvardmagazine.com/breaking-news/james-watson-edward-o-wilson-intellectual-entente.

9   Matt Ridley, *The Origins of Virtue: Human Instincts and the Evolution of Cooperation* (Penguin, 1996), 38.

10   Ridley, *Origins of Virtue*, 193.

11   Karl Jaspers, *The Way to Wisdom: An Introduction to Philosophy* (Yale University Press, 1954), 98.

12   Loyal D. Rue, *Everybody's Story: Wising Up to the Story of Evolution* (State University of New York Press, 1999), 37.

13   Lynn White Jr., "The Historical Roots of Our Ecologic Crisis," in Ian G. Barbour, ed., *Western Man and Environmental Ethics* (Addison-Wesley, 1973), 28.

14   Arnold Toynbee, *Change and Habit: The Challenge of Our Time* (Oxford University Press, 1966), 112.

15   Anna Franklin, "The Shamanic Crisis," *Hearth Witchery*, April 18, 2023, https://annafranklinhearthwitch.wordpress.com/2023/04/18/the-shamanic-crisis-2/.

16   Kazuaki Tanahashi, ed., *Treasury of the True Dharma Eye: Zen Master Dogen's Shobo Genzo* (Shambhala Publications, 2010), 30.

17   Brian Swimme and Thomas Berry, *The Universe Story* (HarperCollins, 1992), 45.

18   Gaia Vince, *Transcendence* (Basic Books, 2020), 247.

19   Matt Ridley, *Nature Via Nurture* (HarperCollins, 2003), 194.

20   As quoted in Ridley, *Origins of Virtue*, 18.

21   E. O. Wilson, *Consilience: The Unity of Knowledge* (Vintage, 1999), 61.

22   As quoted in Donald Hoffman, *The Case Against Reality: Why Evolution Hid the Truth from Our Eyes* (Norton, 2019), 104.

23   Hoffman, *Case Against Reality*, 50.

24   Wes Nisker, *You Are Not Your Fault and Other Revelations* (Soft Skull Press, 2016), 253.

25   Hugo Mercier and Dan Sperber, *The Enigma of Reason* (Harvard University Press, 2017), 330.

26   Robert Wright, *The Evolution of God* (Little, Brown, 2010), 464.

27   Todd Rose, *Collective Illusions: Conformity, Complicity, and the Science of Why We Make Bad Decisions* (Hachette, 2022), 54.

28   One in four Republicans (25 percent) are QAnon believers, compared to 14 percent of independents and 9 percent of Democrats. The share of Americans who completely reject QAnon conspiracy theories dipped slightly in 2021, from 40 percent in March to 34 percent in October. Public Religion Research Institute, "New PRRI Report Reveals Nearly One in Five Americans and One in Four Republicans Still Believe in QAnon Conspiracy Theories," PRRI, February 24, 2022, https://www.prri.org/press-release/new-prri-report-reveals-nearly-one-in-five-americans-and-one-in-four-republicans-still-believe-in-qanon-conspiracy-theories/.

29   E. O. Wilson, *The Social Conquest of Earth* (Liveright, 2012), 13.

30   Joshua Greene, quoted in Robert M. Sapolsky, *Behave: The Biology of Humans at Our Best and Worst* (Penguin, 2018), 505.

31   Robert Wright, *The Moral Animal: Why We Are the Way We Are: The New Science of Evolutionary Psychology* (Pantheon, 1994), 9–10.

32   Gregory Cochran and Henry Harpending, *The 10,000 Year Explosion: How Civilization Accelerated Human Evolution* (Basic Books, 2009), 22–23.

33   Leda Cosmides and John Tooby, *Evolutionary Psychology: A Primer* (University of California–Santa Barbara, 1997), 11–12, https://www.scribd.com/document/613017397/Cosmides-Leda-Tooby-John-Evolutionary-Psychology-A-Primer.

34   Gary Marcus, as quoted in Jonathan Haidt, *The Righteous Mind: Why Good People are Divided by Politics and Religion* (Vintage, 2013), 153.

35   Kevin J. Mitchell, *Innate: How the Wiring of Our Brains Shapes Who We Are* (Princeton University Press, 2018), 78; Juan Enriquez and Steve Gullans, *Evolving Ourselves* (Portfolio, 2016), 200.

36   Steven Pinker, *The Blank Slate: The Modern Denial of Human Nature* (Viking, 2002), 316.

37   William von Hippel, *The Social Leap: The New Evolutionary Science of Who We Are, Where We Come From, and What Makes Us Happy* (Harper, 2018), 239.

38   Ila Lottes, Martin Weinberg, and Inge Weller, "Reactions to Pornography on a College Campus: For or Against?" *Sex Roles* 29 (1993): 69–89.

39   Nicholas A. Christakis, *Blueprint: The Evolutionary Origins of a Good Society* (Little, Brown Spark, 2019), 134. For an alternative view of hunting-gathering sexuality, see Christopher Ryan and Cacilda Jetha, *Sex at Dawn: The Prehistoric Origins of Modern Sexuality* (HarperCollins, 2010).

40 Dacher Keltner, *Born to Be Good: The Science of a Meaningful Life* (Norton, 2009), 172–73.

41 Pinker, *Blank Slate*, 50, 260.

42 Mitchell, *Innate*, 238, 221. Jerome Kagan's groundbreaking studies into the temperament of newborns established that shy infants tend to become anxious adults, regardless of how they are nurtured.

43 Mitchell, *Innate*, 240.

44 Lawrence Wright, "Double Mystery," *New Yorker*, July 30, 1995, https://www.newyorker.com/magazine/1995/08/07/double-mystery.

45 Nancy L. Segal, *Born Together—Reared Apart* (Harvard University Press, 2012), 151–52.

46 Seth Stephens-Davidowitz, "The One Parenting Decision That Really Matters," *The Atlantic*, May 7, 2022, https://www.theatlantic.com/ideas/archive/2022/05/parenting-decisions-dont-trust-your-gut-book-excerpt/629734/.

47 Edwin Chen, "Twins Reared Apart: A Living Lab," *New York Times*, December 9, 1979, https://www.nytimes.com/1979/12/09/archives/twins-reared-apart-a-living-lab.html. See also Katie Serena, "Twins Separated at Birth Reunited to Find They'd Led the Same Life," *All That's Interesting*, September 26, 2017, https://allthatsinteresting.com/jim-twins.

48 Segal, *Born Together*, chap. 1.

49 Pinker, *Blank Slate*, 38.

50 Kathryn Paige Harden, *The Genetic Lottery: Why DNA Matters for Social Equality* (Princeton University Press, 2021), 234.

51 As quoted in Haidt, *Righteous Mind*, 130.

52 Rue, *Everybody's Story*, 91.

53 Carl Sagan and Ann Druyan, *Shadows of Forgotten Ancestors: A Search for Who We Are* (Random House, 1992), 38–39. Humans have the most expressive face, with forty-four muscles, about twice that of chimpanzees.

54 Frans de Waal, *Our Inner Ape: A Leading Primatologist Explains Why We Are Who We Are* (Penguin, 2006), 179, 184–85.

55 de Waal, *Our Inner Ape*, 205–21.

56 Sagan and Druyan, *Shadows of Forgotten Ancestors*, 35.

57 Frans de Waal, *Mama's Last Hug: Animal Emotions and What They Tell Us about Ourselves* (Norton, 2020), 22.

58  de Waal, *Mama's Last Hug*, 24.

59  Ridley, *Origins of Virtue*, 249.

60  Kwame Anthony Appiah, "Digging for Utopia," *New York Review of Books*, December 16, 2021, https://www.nybooks.com/articles/2021/12/16/david -graeber-digging-for-utopia.

61  Michael Ghiselin, *The Economy of Nature and the Evolution of Sex* (University of California Press, 1974), 247.

62  Michael Tomasello, in Steve Stewart-Williams, *The Ape that Understood the Universe: How Mind and Culture Evolve* (Cambridge University Press, 2019), 96.

63  Richard Wrangham, *The Goodness Paradox: The Strange Relationship Between Virtue and Violence in Human Evolution* (Pantheon, 2019), 235.

64  Charles Darwin, *The Descent of Man* (Appleton, 1875), 132.

65  Jonathan Rauch, "Rethinking Polarization," *National Affairs* 61 (Fall 2024), https://www.nationalaffairs.com/publications/detail/rethinking-polarization.

66  Rutger Bregman, *Humankind: A Hopeful History* (Little, Brown, 2021), 19.

67  Ridley, *Origins of Virtue*, 147.

68  Liz Mineo, "Good Genes Are Nice, but Joy Is Better," *The Harvard Gazette*, April 11, 2017, https://news.harvard.edu/gazette/story/2017/04 /over-nearly-80-years-harvard-study-has-been-showing-how-to-live-a -healthy-and-happy-life.

69  Piotr Radkiewicz and Krystyna Skarżyńska, "Who Are the 'Social Darwinists'? On Dispositional Determinants of Perceiving the Social World as Competitive Jungle, *PLoS ONE* 16, no. 8 (2021), https://doi.org/10.1371 /journal.pone.0254434. More generally, people who vote conservatively tend to have a larger amygdala, which is the brain's fear center.

70  Edward O. Wilson, *The Meaning of Human Existence* (Liveright, 2015), 178–79.

71  Wilson, *Social Conquest of Earth*, 57.

72  Wilson, *Social Conquest of Earth*, 17.

73  Adam Smith, *The Wealth of Nations* (Collier and Son, 1902), 56–57.

74  Adam Smith, *The Theory of Moral Sentiments* (Murray & Son, 1869), 1.

75   Lewis Dartnell, "Out of Our Minds: Opium's Part in Imperial History," *The Guardian*, May 23, 2023, https://www.theguardian.com/society/2023/may/23/out-of-our-minds-opium-imperial-history-opium-wars-china-britain. According to Jonathan Haidt, we are *Homo duplex*: 90 percent chimp and 10 percent bee (*The Righteous Mind*, 312).

76   Edward O. Wilson, as quoted in David Sloan Wilson, *Does Altruism Exist? Culture, Genes, and the Welfare of Others* (Yale University Press, 2015), 71.

77   George Williams, as quoted in Wilson, *Does Altruism Exist?* 165, 193.

78   Ezra Klein, *Why We're Polarized* (Simon & Schuster, 2021), 404.

79   Joseph Henrich, *The Secret of Our Success* (Princeton University Press, 2016), 170.

80   Quoted in Andrew Bacevich, "Freedom without Constraints: How the US Squandered Its Cold War Victory," *The Guardian*, January 7, 2020, https://www.theguardian.com/news/2020/jan/07/freedom-without-constraints-how-the-us-squandered-its-cold-war-victory.

81   McKay Coppins, "The Man Who Broke Politics," *The Atlantic*, November 2018, https://www.theatlantic.com/magazine/archive/2018/11/newt-gingrich-says-youre-welcome/570832/.

82   Louis Bolk, as quoted in Chip Walter, *Thumbs, Toes, and Tears: And Other Traits That Make Us Human* (University of California Press, 2006), 33.

83   Robert Wright, *Why Buddhism Is True: The Science and Philosophy of Meditation and Enlightenment* (Simon & Schuster, 2018), 237.

84   Charles Duhigg, "The Real Roots of American Rage," *The Atlantic*, January/February 2019, 70.

85   See Robert L. Trivers, "The Evolution of Reciprocal Altruism," *The Quarterly Review of Biology* 46, no. 1 (1971).

86   Paul R. Lawrence and Nitin Nohria hypothesize in their book *Driven: How Human Nature Shapes Our Choices* (Josse-Bass, 2001) that the imperative of having to choose between multiple independent drives is what gives birth to free will.

87   Samuel Butler, *The Note-Books of Samuel Butler* (London: A. C. Fifield, 1912), https://gutenberg.org/cache/epub/6173/pg6173-images.html.

88   See Robin Dunbar, *Grooming, Gossip, and the Evolution of Language* (Harvard University Press, 1997).

89   James V. Neel, as quoted in Paul Shepard, *Coming Home to the Pleistocene* (Island Press, 2004), 99.

90   Paul Shepard, *The Only World We've Got: A Paul Shepard Reader* (Sierra Club Books, 1996), 206.

91   Graeme Barker, as quoted in Jeremy Lent, *The Patterning Instinct: A Cultural History of Man's Search for Meaning* (Prometheus Books, 2017), 111.

92   Paul Shepard, *The Other: How Animals Made Us Human* (Island Press, 2004), 163.

93   Shepard, *Coming Home to the Pleistocene*, 111.

94   Jeremy Rifkin, *The Empathic Civilization: The Race to Global Consciousness in a World in Crisis* (Tarcher/Penguin, 2009), 24. Emphasis mine.

95   Charles Darwin, *The Descent of Man and Selection in Relation to Sex* (1874), https://charles-darwin.classic-literature.co.uk/the-descent-of-man /ebook-page-83.asp.

96   Carlo Levi, as quoted in Morris Berman, *Wandering God: A Study in Nomadic Spirituality* (State University of New York Press, 2000), 79.

97   Paul R. Ehrlich, *Human Natures: Genes, Cultures, and the Human Prospect* (Island Press, 2000), 256.

98   Robert Bellah, *Religion in Human Evolution: From the Paleolithic to the Axial Age* (Harvard University Press, 2017), 232.

99   Thorkild Jacobsen, as quoted in Bellah, *Religion in Human Evolution*, 262.

100   Quoted in Daniel C. Maguire, *Ethics for a Small Planet* (State of New York Press, 1998), 154.

101   Christakis, *Blueprint*, 388.

102   David Sloan Wilson, *This View of Life: Completing the Darwinian Revolution* (Pantheon, 2020), 78.

103   Wright, *Why Buddhism Is True*, 230.

104   See Martin Gilens and Benjamin I. Page, "Testing Theories of American Politics: Elites, Interest Groups, and Average Citizens," *Perspectives on Politics* 12, no. 3 (September 2014), 564–81: "Multivariate analysis indicates that economic elites and organized groups representing business interests have substantial independent impacts on U.S. government policy, while average citizens and mass-based interest groups have little or no independent influence."

105   Naomi Klein, *This Changes Everything: Capitalism vs. The Climate* (Simon & Schuster, 2014), 21.

106   This quotation is widely attributed to Keynes, but I have been unable to find its source.

107   Amitav Ghosh, *The Nutmeg's Curse: Parables for a Planet in Crisis* (University of Chicago Press, 2022), 122–23.

108   "Smedley Butler on Interventionism," Federation of American Scientists, https://man.fas.org/smedley.htm.

109   Wikiquote, "Douglas   MacArthur,   https://en.wikiquote.org/wiki/Douglas_MacArthur.

110   Alex Carey et al., *Taking the Risk Out of Democracy: Corporate Propaganda versus Freedom and Liberty* (University of Illinois Press, 1995), 18.

111   Karl Jaspers, *The Origin and Goal of History*, trans. Michael Bullock (Routledge and Kegan, 1949), 1, 7.

112   Bellah, *Religion in Human Evolution*, 207–8.

113   Bruce G. Trigger, *Understanding Early Civilizations: A Comparative Study* (Cambridge University Press, 2014), 409.

114   Trigger, *Understanding Early Civilizations*, 453.

115   Brian K. Smith, *Reflections on Resemblance, Ritual, and Religion* (Oxford University Press, 1988), 50–51. Smith is referring specifically to Vedic priests and metaphysicians, but his point is more generally valid.

116   Gregory J. Riley, *The River of God: A New History of Christian Origins* (Harper San Francisco, 2001), 172.

117   The medieval Church in Europe replicated this by selling indulgences that could reduce the time one's ancestors suffered in Purgatory.

118   Vince, *Transcendence*, 100.

119   Stephen K. Sanderson, *Religious Evolution and the Axial Age: From Shamans to Priests to Prophets* (Bloomsbury, 2018), 219.

120   Rifkin, *Empathic Civilization*, 213.

121   S.N. Eisenstadt, *Japanese Civilization: A Comparative View* (University of Chicago Press, 1997), 13.

122   Jan Assmann, *Of God and Gods: Egypt, Israel, and the Rise of Monotheism* (University of Wisconsin Press, 2008), 75.

123   Jan Assmann, *The Mind of Egypt: History and Meaning in the Time of the Pharaohs* (Metropolitan Books, 2002), 193. See also Hugh Brody, *The Other Side of Eden: Hunters, Farmers, and the Shaping of the World* (Faber and Faber, 2000).

124   Karen Armstrong, *The Great Transformation: The Beginning of Our Religious Traditions* (Anchor, 2007), 391.

125   Sanderson, *Religious Evolution and the Axial Age*, 182.

126   Erik Davis, *TechGnosis: Myth, Magic, and Mysticism in the Age of Information* (North Atlantic Books, 2015), 25.

127   Jan Assmann, *From Akhenaten to Moses: Ancient Egypt and Religious Change* (The American University in Cairo Press, 2014), 13.

128   David Abram, *The Spell of the Sensuous: Perception and Language in a More-Than-Human World* (Vintage, 1997), 116–17.

129   Abram, *Spell of the Sensuous*, 131.

130   Quoted in Abram, *Spell of the Sensuous*, 180.

131   Thomas H. Eriksen, *Tyranny of the Moment: Fast and Slow Time in the Information Age* (Pluto Press, 2001), 36.

132   Assmann, *From Akhenaten to Moses*, 12.

133   Ivan Illich, quoted in David Cayley, *Ivan Illich in Conversation* (House of Anansi Press, 1992), 254.

134   Chapter 12 in Spinoza's *Theological-Political Treatise*, quoted in https://plato.stanford.edu/entries/spinoza/.

135   Henri-Jean Martin, *The History and Power of Writing*, trans. Lydia G. Cochrane (University of Chicago Press, 1994), 37.

136   Thomas Hylland Ericksen, *Globalization: The Key Concepts*, 3rd ed. (London: Bloomsbury, 2020), 38.

137   Martin, *History and Power of Writing*, 33.

138   Abram, *Spell of the Sensuous*, 267.

139   Carl B. Becker, "Hermeneutics and Buddhist Myths," *Soundings* 67, no. 3 (Fall 1984), 332.

140   David Porush, "Hacking the Brainstem," in Robert Markley, ed., *Virtual Realities and their Discontents* (Johns Hopkins University Press, 1996), 124.

141   Davis, *TechGnosis*, 13.

142   Abram, *Spell of the Sensuous*, 56.

143   Davis, *TechGnosis*, 19.

144   Davis, *TechGnosis*, 20.

145   George Bernard Shaw, "Maxims: Religion," in his play *Man and Superman: A Comedy and a Philosophy*, published in 1903.

146   Maguire, *Ethics for a Small Planet*, 37.

147   This quotation and its attribution to Renan is found many places, but I have not been able to locate the original source.

148   S. C. Humphreys, "Transcendence and Intellectual Roles: The Ancient Greek Case" *Daedalus* (Spring 1975), 92.

149   See, for example, *Lack and Transcendence: The Problem of Death and Life in Psychotherapy, Existentialism, and Buddhism* (Wisdom Publications, 2018).

150   Rifkin, *Empathic Civilization*, 211.

151   David Sloan Wilson, *Darwin's Cathedral: Evolution, Religion, and the Nature of Society* (University of Chicago Press, 2002), 159.

152   One could argue that an earlier Axial figure was the fourteenth-century BCE pharaoh Akhenaten, who tried to revolutionize Egyptian religion by downgrading polytheism in favor of a state cult devoted to a supreme god, the solar deity Aten. But Atenism did not long survive the pharoah's death, as successors soon reverted to the older tradition.

153   Richard C. Foltz, *Spirituality in the Land of the Noble: How Iran Shaped the World's Religions* (Oneworld, 2004), 40–41.

154   Isaiah 44:6. All Biblical quotations are from the New International Version.

155   Peter L. Berger, *The Heretical Imperative: Contemporary Possibilities of Religious Affiliation* (New York: Anchor, 1979), 146.

156   Daniel 7:27.

157   Daniel 12:2.

158   Isaiah 49:22–23.

159   Armstrong, *Great Transformation*, 44, quoting Isaiah 1:15–17.

160   Wikipedia, "Hillel the Elder," https://en.wikipedia.org/wiki/Hillel_the_Elder.

161   Lent, *Patterning Instinct*, 222.

162   John 10:30.

163   Matthew 5:43–45.

164   Luke 10:25–37.

165 Galatians 3:28.

166 Matthew 25:35–46.

167 Kucchivikara-vatthu, Mahavagga 8.26.1–8.

168 John 17:16.

169 John 2:16–17.

170 Genesis 2:7.

171 Rosemary Reuther, *Gaia and God: An Ecofeminist Theology of Earth Healing* (HarperOne, 1994), 29–30.

172 *Laws* 12.959 in Lane Cooper, trans., *Plato: The Collected Dialogues* (Princeton University Press, 2005).

173 Philippians 3:21.

174 *Metaphysics* 1–5 in W. D. Ross, trans., *The Basic Works of Aristotle* (Modern Library, 2001).

175 *Nicomachean Ethics* 1178a in Ross, *Basic Works of Aristotle.*

176 Armstrong, *Great Transformation*, 327.

177 Wendy Doniger, *Hindus: An Alternative History* (Penguin, 2009), 109.

178 See, e.g., Samyutta Nikaya 38.1; 45.6; 47.7, in Bhikkhu Bodhi, trans., *The Connected Discourses of the Buddha* (Wisdom Publications, 2000).

179 "Vatthūpama Sutta: The Simile of the Cloth" (Majjhima Nikaya 7) in Bhikkhu Bodhi, trans., *The Middle Length Discourses of the Buddha* (Wisdom Publications, 1995), 120–21.

180 Mark 7:15.

181 Gil Fronsdal, trans., *Dhammapada* (Shambhala Publications, 2008), verses 393–94.

182 Sutta Nipata 1.8.

183 Digha Nikaya 13. The four immeasurables were not unique to Buddhism. See, for example, Patanjali's Yoga Sutras I.33 and the early Jain Tattvartha Sutra 7.11.

184 The subtitle of Herbert Fingarette's book, *Confucius.*

185 As quoted in Bellah, *Religion in Human Evolution*, 422.

186 Pitirim Sorokin, *The Ways and Powers of Love: Techniques of Moral Transformation* (Henry Regnery, 1954), 71.

187    Robert Jensen, "A Practical Radical Politics," *CounterPunch*, February 4, 2022, https://www.counterpunchorg/2022/02/04/a-practical-radical-politics/.

188    See notes in main text.

189    Isaiah 10:2.

190    Matthew 5:43–44.

191    Sigmund Freud, *Moses and Monotheism* (Vintage, 1955), 144.

192    Jaspers, *Origin and Goal of History*, 194.

193    Jaspers, *Origin and Goal of History*, 51.

194    Raymond B. Williams, "So, What Are We Professing Here?" in *The Council of Societies for the Study of Religion Bulletin* 29 no. 3 (September 2000).

195    Sanderson, *Religious Evolution and the Axial Age*, 227.

196    Peter L. Berger, *The Sacred Canopy* (Doubleday Anchor, 1969) 90, 95. Italics in original.

197    From Le Guin's speech at the National Book Awards, November 19, 2014.

198    Berger, *Sacred Canopy*, 39.

199    See Bart D. Ehrman, *Lost Christianities* (Oxford University Press, 2003), especially chapters 5–8.

200    Randel Helms, *Gospel Fictions* (Prometheus Books, 1998), 9.

201    Helms, *Gospel Fictions*, 50, 133–34.

202    See https://en.wikipedia.org/wiki/Catholic_Mariology#Dogmatic_teachings.

203    "Alagaddupama Sutta: The Simile of the Snake" (Majjhima Nikaya 22).

204    Bhikkhu Anālayo, *Early Oral Buddhist Tradition: Textual Formation and Transmission* (Wisdom Publications, 2022), 197.

205    See Grace Burford, *Desire, Death and Goodness: The Conflict of Ultimate Values in Theravada Buddhism* (Peter Lang, 1991) and Gil Fronsdal, *The Buddha before Buddhism: Wisdom from the Early Teachings* (Shambhala Publications, 2016).

206    Marcus J. Borg, *The Heart of Christianity: Rediscovering a Life of Faith* (HarperOne, 2003), 69.

207    Quoted in Brian C. Muraresku, *The Immortality Key: The Secret History of the Religion with No Name* (St. Martin's Press, 2020), 10–11.

208  Galatians 2:20.

209  Sermon 17 in Maurice O'C Walshe, trans., *The Complete Mystical Works of Meister Eckhart* (Herder & Herder, 2010). All sermons cited by Meister Eckhart are from this translation.

210  C. S. Nott, trans., "Full Text of 'The Conference of the Birds by Attar," https://archive.org/stream/AttarTheConferenceOfTheBirdstr.C.S.Nott/Attar%20%20The%20Conference%20of%20the%20Birds%20(tr.%20C.S.Nott)_djvu.txt. The famous Rumi quote is found many places on the internet.

211  Franklin, "The Shamanic Crisis."

212  Davi Kopenawa, *The Falling Sky: Words of a Yanomani Shaman* (Harvard University Press, 2013), 93. My italics.

213  Alcibiades, Nasa indigenous elder in Colombia, quoted in Helena ter Ellen, "Seeding the Work That Reconnects in Colombia in Times of War and Peace," *Deep Times Journal*, April 16, 2017, https://journal.workthatreconnects.org/2017/04/16/seeding-the-work-that-reconnects-in-colombia-in-times-of-war-and-peace.

214  Ancient Navaho song, as quoted by Lisa Nakamura in "Indigenous Circuits: Navajo Women and the Radicalization of Early Electronic Manufacture," *American Quarterly* 66, no. 4 (December 2014): 919–41.

215  Rodger Kamenetz, *The Jew in the Lotus: A Poet's Rediscovery of Jewish Identity in Buddhist India* (HarperCollins, 2007), 86.

216  Keith Thomas, *Religion and the Decline of Magic: Studies in Popular Beliefs in Sixteenth and Seventeenth-Century England* (Penguin, 1973), 320–21.

217  Menahem Nahum, quoted in Arthur Green, *Tormented Master: The Life and Spiritual Quest of Rabbi Nahman of Bratslav* (Jewish Lights, 1992), 109, 115.

218  Nahman of Bratslav, quoted in Arthur Green, *Tormented Master: A Life of Rabbi Nahman of Bratslav* (New York: Schocken Books, 1981), 319.

219  Moshe Idel, *Hasidism: Between Ecstasy and Magic* (State University of New York Press, 1995), 107.

220  Elaine Pagels, *Beyond Belief: The Secret Gospel of Thomas* (Random House, 2003), 10.

221  Matthew 24:30–31.

222  Luke 17:20–21.

223  Thomas 51, 113.

224    John 8:12,14:6–7.

225    Thomas 3.

226    John Dominic Crossan, *God and Empire: Jesus Against Rome, Then and Now* (HarperOne, 2008), 28.

227    Philippians 2:6.

228    Galatians 2:20.

229    Acts 17:28.

230    2 Corinthians 5:17–18.

231    1 Corinthians 13:13.

232    Marcus J. Borg and John Dominic Crossan, *The First Paul: Reclaiming the Radical Visionary Behind the Church's Conservative Icon* (HarperOne, 2009), 204.

233    Sermon 68 in Walshe, trans., *Complete Mystical Works of Meister Eckhart*.

234    Sermon 4.

235    Pagels, *Beyond Belief*, 193. See also my article comparing *The Cloud of Unknowing* (fourteenth century) with Zen *koan* practice: "Dying to the Self That Never Was" in *Awareness Bound and Unbound* (State University of New York Press, 2009).

236    Jakob Boehme, "The Supersensual Life," trans. William Law, http://www.gnosis.org/library/super.htm.

237    Rita Nakashima Brock and Rebecca Ann Parker, *Saving Paradise: Recovering Christianity's Forgotten Love for This Earth* (Beacon Press, 2008), 155.

238    Thomas Merton, recorded lectures, tape 8, side B, 1962.

239    Strictly speaking, God [Allah] in Islam is not gendered, which is important for challenging patriarchal perspectives. Nonetheless, many translators have found it difficult to avoid the usual pronouns.

240    Qur'an 57:1, 17:44, 80: 32–34; see also *sura* 16, "The Bee."

241    William C. Chittick, *The Sufi Path of Knowledge: Ibn al-Arabi's Metaphysics of Imagination* (State University of New York Press, 1989), 425.

242    Paul Smith, trans., *Diwan of Ibn 'Arabi* (New Humanity Books, 2018).

243    Chittick, *Sufi Path of Knowledge*, 250–51.

244    Chittick, *Sufi Path of Knowledge*, 260.

245    William C. Chittick, *The Sufi Path of Love* (State University of New York Press, 1984), 210.

246    Compare the Chinese Chan master Linchi, who spoke of "the man of no rank" as the highest stage of enlightenment.

247    Ibn 'Arabi, *Fusus al-Hikam* (*The Bezels of Wisdom*), 2, 133.19, in William Chittick, "Ibn 'Arabî," *The Stanford Encyclopedia of Philosophy* (Spring 2020 Edition), https://plato.stanford.edu/archives/spr2020/entries/ibn-arabi/.

248    Chittick, *Sufi Path of Knowledge*, 327.

249    Chittick, *Sufi Path of Knowledge*, 151.

250    "A Hidden Treasure," Wikipedia, https://en.wikipedia.org/wiki/A _Hidden_Treasure.

251    Qur'an 16:40.

252    *Fusus al-Hikam* I, 143, 83, as quoted in Henry Corbin, *Creative Imagination in the Sufism of Ibn 'Arabi* (Princeton, 1969), 124.

253    Maria Shrady, trans., *Angelus Silesius: The Cherubinic Wanderer* (Paulist Press, 1986), 64, 87.

254    *Fusus al-Hikam* I, 178, in Corbin, *Creative Imagination*, 117.

255    Chittick, "Ibn 'Arabî," *The Stanford Encyclopedia of Philosophy*.

256    Heinrich Zimmer, *Myths and Symbols in Indian Art and Civilization* (Princeton University Press, 1972), 131.

257    *Gaudapada Karika*, 3.46–48, https://en.wikipedia.org/wiki/Ajativada.

258    "Channovada Sutta: Advice to Channa" (Majjhima Nikaya 144), in Bodhi, trans. *Middle Length Discourses*, 1136. The Buddha is speaking.

259    Reginald A. Ray, *Buddhist Saints in India: A Study in Buddhist Values and Orientations* (Oxford University Press, 1994), 88.

260    Fronsdal, *Buddha before Buddhism*, vii and 3. See also Burford, *Desire, Death and Goodness.*

261    Fronsdal, *Buddha before Buddhism*, 10, 17, 19.

262    Salayatanasamyutta 23.1, in Bodhi, trans., *Connected Discourses*, 1140.

263    "Dhatuvibhanga Sutta: The Exposition of the Elements" (Majjhima Nikaya 140), 1092–93.

264    Philip B. Yampolsky, trans., *The Platform Sutra of the Sixth Patriarch* (Columbia University Press, 2012), 133n41.

265    Nagarjuna's *Mulamadhyamakakarika*, in Mervyn Sprung, trans., *Lucid Exposition of the Middle Way: The Essential Chapters From The Prasannapada of Candrakirti* (Prajna Press, 1979), 259, 255, 162.

266    Tanahashi, ed., *Treasury of the True Dharma Eye*, 30.

267    For a fuller explication of this process, see David Loy, "Dying to the Self That Never Was," in *Awareness Bound and Unbound*, 89–106.

268    Quoted in Philip Kapleau, *The Three Pillars of Zen: Teaching, Practice, and Enlightenment* (Weatherhill, 1965), 205. Kapleau capitalizes *Mind* but the original term *shin/kokoro* is better translated as "heart/mind." This assertion was not original to Dogen; he was quoting an early Chan text.

269    Yasutani Hakuun in Kapleau, *Three Pillars of Zen*, 107, 137.

270    Norman Waddell, trans., "Hakuin's Song of Zazen," *The Zen Site*, https://www.thezensite.com/ZenTeachings/Translations/Song_of_Zazen. htm.

271    Mary Evelyn Tucker and Duncan Ryuken Williams, eds., *Buddhism and Ecology: The Interconnection of Dharma and Deeds* (Harvard University Press, 1998), 338.

272    *Lunyu* 11:11, trans. A. C. Muller, http://www.acmuller.net/con-dao /analects.html#div-13.

273    "The Brahmin," chapter 26, verse 407 in Fronsdal, *Dhammapada*. The rest of the chapter elaborates on the various traits of a true Brahmin.

274    *Lunyu* 12:1, 6:30. Muller translation.

275    A. Charles Muller, "East Asia's Unexplored Pivot of Metaphysics and Hermeneutics: Essence-Function/Interpenetration," http://www.acmuller .net/articles/indigenoushermeneutics.htm.

276    *Daodejing*, chapter 14.

277    *Daodejing*, chapter 4.

278    A. C. Graham, trans., *Chuang-Tzu: The Inner Chapters* (Hackett Classics, 2001), 103.

279    Graham, trans., *Chuang-Tzu*, 281.

280    *Daodejing*, chapter 13.

281    Wong Mou-lam and A. F. Price, trans., *The Diamond Sutra and The Sutra of Hui-Neng* (Shambhala, 2005), 21.

282    Burton Watson, trans., *The Complete Works of Zhuangzi* (Columbia University Press, 2012), 18.

283 Nagarjuna's *Mulamadhyamakakarika* 18:8, in Sprung, trans., *Lucid Exposition of the Middle Way*, 247–64.

284 Graham, trans., *Chuang-Tzu: The Inner Chapters*, 59–60.

285 Graham, trans., *Chuang-Tzu: The Inner Chapters*, 91.

286 The ten Oxherding Pictures, designed by a Chinese Buddhist master in the twelfth century, are a series of illustrations with commentary depicting the progressive stages of enlightenment.

287 See, for example, Kapleau, *The Three Pillars of Zen*, 301–31.

288 The four horsemen are Richard Dawkins (*The God Delusion*), Daniel Dennett (*Breaking the Spell*), Sam Harris (*The End of Faith*), and Christopher Hitchens (*God Is Not Great*).

289 Thomas Merton, recorded lectures, tape 8, side B, 1962.

290 "Ian Stevenson," Wikipedia, https://en.wikipedia.org/wiki/Ian_Stevenson.

291 See John Welwood, "Human Nature, Buddha Nature: On Spiritual Bypassing, Relationship, and the Dharma," interview by Tina Fossella, https://www.johnwelwood.com/articles/TRIC_interview_uncut.pdf.

292 "Joseph Campbell and the Power of Myth," interview with Bill Moyers, https://billmoyers.com/content/ep-1-joseph-campbell-and-the-power-of-myth-the-hero%E2%80%99s-adventure-audio/.

293 Ervin Laszlo, *Science and the Reenchantment of the Cosmos: The Rise of the Integral Vision of Reality* (Inner Traditions, 2006), 1.

294 Thomas Berry and Brian Swimme, *The Universe Story: From the Primordial Flaring Forth to the Ecozoic Era—A Celebration of the Unfolding of the Cosmos* (HarperOne, 1994), 45.

295 Thomas Berry, "The Viable Human," in *The Great Work: Our Way into the Future* (Crown, 2000), 56.

# Index

# About the Author

David R. Loy began Zen practice in Hawaii in 1971 with Yamada Koun and Robert Aitken, and continued with Koun Roshi in Japan, where he lived for almost twenty years. He was authorized to teach in 1988 and has led retreats and workshops at Mountain Cloud Zen Center, Barre Center for Buddhist Studies, Omega Institute, Spirit Rock Meditation Center, Centro Kushi Ling in Italy, Ecodharma Centre in Spain, Terre d'Eveil in Paris, Gaia House Retreat Center in the UK, Dharma Gate Buddhist College in Budapest, and various Centro de Estudos Budistas Bodisatva Centers in Brazil, among others.

In 2014 David received an honorary PhD from his alma mater, Carleton College, for his years of work on socially engaged Buddhism. In 2016 he returned the degree, to protest the decision of the board of trustees not to divest from fossil fuel companies.

David's books and articles have been translated into many languages. Recent books include *A New Buddhist Path* and *Ecodharma: Buddhist Teachings for the Ecological Crisis*. He is one of the founders of the Rocky Mountain Ecodharma Retreat Center in Colorado. David's writings, podcasts, and videos are available at www.davidloy.org.

# What to Read Next
# by David Loy
# from Wisdom Publications

**Ecodharma**
*Buddhist Teachings for the Ecological Crisis*

How can we respond urgently and effectively to the ecological crisis—and stay sane doing it?

**Money, Sex, War, Karma**
*Notes for a Buddhist Revolution*

"A flashy title, but a serious and substantial book."—*Buddhadharma*

**Nonduality**
*In Buddhism and Beyond*

"Scholarly but leisurely and very readable."—*Spectrum Review*

**The World Is Made of Stories**

"Loy's book is like the self: layer after layer peels away, and the center is empty. But the pleasure is exactly in the exploration. At once Loy's most accessible and most philosophical work."—Alan Senauke for *Buddhadharma*

**The Great Awakening**
*A Buddhist Social Theory*

"A groundbreaking book from an original thinker."—Melvin McLeod, editor of *The Best Buddhist Writing* series and *Mindful Politics*

**The Dharma of Dragons and Daemons**
*Buddhist Themes in Modern Fantasy*

"Eloquent. Loy and Goodhew find Buddhist truths in contemporary non-Buddhist stories. Pullman's dead are released to become images of interpermeation reminiscent of Thich Nhat Hanh's teachings. Frodo's quest is not to find a treasure or slay a dragon, but to let go. Thus, aspects of Buddhist teachings come alive for children of the West."—*Inquiring Mind*

**A New Buddhist Path**
*Enlightenment, Evolution, and Ethics in the Modern World*

"This gripping, important, and ultimately heartening book by David Loy is a wake-up call for Buddhists and everyone else on how to respond to the current multiple crises."—Lila Kate Wheeler, author of *When Mountains Walked*

**Lack and Transcendence**
*The Problem of Death and Life in Psychotherapy, Existentialism, and Buddhism*

Whatever the differences in their methods and goals, psychotherapy, existentialism, and Buddhism are all concerned with the same fundamental issues of life and death—and death-in-life.

# About Wisdom Publications

Wisdom Publications is the leading publisher of classic and contemporary Buddhist books and practical works on mindfulness. To learn more about us or to explore our other books, please visit our website at wisdom.org or contact us at the address below.

Wisdom Publications
132 Perry Street
New York, NY 10014 USA

We are a 501(c)(3) organization, and donations in support of our mission are tax deductible.

Wisdom Publications is affiliated with the Foundation for the Preservation of the Mahayana Tradition (FPMT).